Biological Studies of Mental Processes

Edited by
David Caplan

The MIT Press
Cambridge, Massachusetts,
and London, England

First MIT Press paperback edition, 1982

This book was set in Paladium
by A & B Typesetters, Inc.,
and printed and bound by
Halliday Lithograph Corporation
in the United States of America.

Library of Congress Cataloging in Publication Data

Main entry under title:

Biological studies of mental processes.

"This volume derives from a conference . . . held June 8-11, 1978, under the auspices of the MIT Workgroup on Cognitive Science."
Includes bibliographies and index.
1. Languages—Physiological aspects—Congresses. 2. Higher nervous activity—Congresses. 3. Developmental neurology—Congresses. I. Caplan, David, 1947- II. MIT Workgroup on Cognitive Science.
[DNLM: 1. Cognition—Congresses. 2. Language development—Congresses. 3. Mental processes—Congresses. 4. Psycholinguistics—Congresses. WS105.5.C8 B615 1978]
QP399.B56   153.6   80-243
ISBN 0-262-03061-6 (hard)
ISBN 0-262-53041-4 (paperback)

Contents

III

**Studies of Neural Mechanisms
Underlying Language in the
Adult**

Contents

14

Jason W. Brown

Brain Structure and Language
Production: A Dynamic
View   287

15

Norman Geschwind

Some Comments on the
Neurology of Language   301

Preface
David Caplan

This volume derives from a conference on Maturational Factors in Cognitive Development and the Biology of Language held June 8–11, 1978, under the auspices of the MIT Workgroup on Cognitive Science. Participants included linguists, psychologists, neurologists, and representatives of various subsections and cross sections of these disciplines. The conference was designed as a workshop in which discussion and informal presentations would play as important a role as prepared talks. This book includes revisions of the delivered papers and comments and interchanges in the form of discussions and perspectives prepared by the participants after the conference.

The title of this book reflects both a common interest of the contributors and an emergent common approach. In this symposium cognitive systems are considered biological entities and studied along lines appropriate to such entities. This perspective was nicely stated by George Zipf when he wrote in the introduction to his *Psycho-biology of Language*, "It occurred to me that it might be fruitful to investigate speech as a natural phenomenon, much as a physiologist may study the beating of the heart, or an entomologist the tropisms of an insect, or an ornithologist the nesting-habits of a bird." Speech as an object of study has been replaced by other systems, many more abstract, but the biological perspective is retained in this volume.

The study of cognitive systems in the setting of biology requires a model of biological processes as a framework for thought. This model uses three levels of description. The level of *phenomena* includes a representation of a domain of knowledge and a theory of utilization of this knowledge. It allows for partially overlapping representations of knowledge and its utilization, each of which may re-

flect different neural or genetic devices. The *neural* level is characterized by anatomical, biochemical, physiological, and other organic
information regarding the organic system whose operations correspond to and produce the phenomena. The *genetic* level describes
the hereditarily transmitted material in which is encoded the information determining the structure of the neural level, its maturational
sequences, certain of its operations, and the limits of its response to
environmental influences. Ontogenetic and phylogenetic progressions can be studied at each level.

Environmental influences affect all levels. Genetic and neural
structures and functions are influenced primarily by organic factors;
phenomena, by exposure to other phenomena. In simple cases it is
clear that genetic structures are altered by viral invasion, exposure
to irradiation; neural structures are damaged by circulatory insuf-
ficiency, neoplasia; and humans learn the language of their surroundings, acquire the culture in which they are raised.

Interactions between environmental influences and the unfolding
of the genetic plan or the functioning of the neural apparatus can be
quite complex. For instance, sexual function at both the behavioral
and endocrine levels is a result of genetic sex modified by the level
of sex hormones in the perinatal period, the latter produced by
genetically determined endocrine function, and exogenous delivery
of hormones, toxins, and drugs. The combination of hormonal and
genetic influences induce neural structures responsible for regulating
sex hormones in the adult. The intriguing effects of environmental
phenomena on neural structures are being investigated in studies of
active versus passive exposure to visual displays, deprivation of
visual stereopsis, monocular visual acuity impairments, and similar
systems, as well as in a host of experiments on the chemical and
molecular changes seen in neural tissue following certain types of
learning in simple organisms. This type of effect raises the possibility
that abstract variables in environmental phenomena, such as those
that characterize the differences between languages, may induce
neural structural changes. Another category of interaction is the
effect of phenomena on genetic structures. Post-Darwinian evolutionary theory deals with the consequences of behavioral reper-
toires—seen here as phenomenological entities—on genetic load, a
process mediated through natural selection over several generations
of organisms.

The work reported and discussed in this volume seeks to clarify descriptions of the three levels of biological concern and explore the mechanisms relating one to another in the area of human cognitive functioning. This is the area of common interest.

The common approach that I believe is crystallizing begins with the recognition that all three levels and their interaction constitute an interrelated field of study. Detailed, abstract characterizations of knowledge and its use, such as are available in contemporary linguistics, psychology, artificial intelligence, and other disciplines, are not ignored in favor of more concrete schemata; nor are they created by scientists in these fields as purely abstract, formal systems. It is the task of the "organic biologists" to find mechanisms that are suggested by and underlie these systems, as gene structure was suggested by the laws of inheritance of phenotypes. It is the hope of the "mental biologists" that studies incorporating organic features will help constrain the formal systems and decide between competing descriptions. On the other hand, scarcely a discovery about structure or physiology of the nervous system is not greeted today by inquiries about its functional or dynamic significance, and this attitude applies to cognitive as well as perceptual, emotional, and other systems.

A second concept that interested many contributors is that of "mental organ." Spearheaded by the linguists' observation that the formal and functional properties of language, at the phenomeno-logical level, are not found in other cognitive systems in humans or animals, the hypothesis arose that in the domain of language there exists a unique biological mechanism that includes a genetic endow-ment, a neural mechanism, and a phenomenological result, all of which are species- and domain-specific. This strong claim, generated by studies of phenomena alone, has served to stimulate and organize research in the field, and parallel models are being developed in other areas of cognition. Whether or not the hypothesis proves cor-rect, it highlights the effort to find unified theories of a cognitive function across the three levels of biological reality. I believe it would be legitimate to speak of a mental organ when such a unified system has been demarcated, whether or not its mechanistic des-cription at each of the three levels is unique with respect to domain and species.

A third theme is maturation. Intrinsic biological development of the organism creates new neural systems, which allow the child to formulate new classes of hypotheses about the structure of the phenomenological world and utilize these hypotheses in new ways. Studies in maturation attempt to characterize these neural changes, identify the factors that trigger them, and explore their consequences for phenomenological capacities. A concomitant task is to distinguish this class of neural changes—those produced by intrinsic maturational sequences—from the class resulting from exposure to and mastery of particular phenomenological systems.

The last major concept is that of parallel or partially overlapping mechanisms. The description of phenomena and utilization procedures is now largely developed in formal, often computational, terms. Alternative descriptions of a single phenomenological domain are available. Many studies have suggested that different neural structures use these different phenomenological analyses. This observation does not solve the problem of choosing between competing phenomenological descriptions on formal grounds, but it suggests that biology need not fear this application of Occham's razor. On the contrary, this realization opens new approaches to the understanding of neural function and the effects of brain lesions on behavioral strategies and capacities, and it may have practical applications in retraining.

Certain traditional questions did not emerge directly in this symposium. The question of innateness, for instance, was not debated per se. I believe that this concept is being redefined and becoming better understood in terms of genetic load and internal organic environmental effects on neural function (maturation), which result in changes in computational capacities. On the other hand, the traditional psychological and philosophical term *acquired* is being restricted to the results of exogenous organic factors and the computational consequences of exposure to particular phenomena (as, for instance, occurs in learning the language of the environment). Detailed hypotheses are available concerning both these areas, and discussion is focused on specific hypotheses more than on the status of the distinction that spawned them. Thus new concepts and themes are partially replacing our former ideas about the biology of cognition. It is the hope and expectation of the investigators at this symposium that many of the concepts and ideas raised here will in turn be spelled out in increasingly precise terms and this will provide a deeper understanding of this aspect of human, and nonhuman, biology.

I

Studies of the
Maturational Component
of Cognitive
Development

1   Maturational Factors in Human Development

Susan Carey

The rationalist-empiricist argument with respect to the human capacity for language has been extensively debated in recent years (Chomsky, 1975; Fodor, Bever, and Garrett, 1974; Lenneberg, 1967). What in human language is due to genetic endowment, and what is due to interactions with the linguistic community? Rationalists and empiricists agree that there are contributions from each; they differ in their specifications of how much is innate, what kinds of things can be innate, and what kinds of interactions with the environment affect acquisition.

Related to nativism is the explanation of developmental change. It is natural though not logically compulsory for the extreme rationalist to expect major maturational contributions to development. Similarly, it is natural for the extreme expiricist to expect that most development is due to learning. Thus Eric Lenneberg, who was committed to the rationalist position, wrote, "It can scarcely be doubted that the development of language capability is somehow related to the maturation of the nervous system" (Lenneberg, 1974). He went on to bewail the lack of hypotheses about what changes in the brain might be relevant to the acquisition of the language. Nothing has changed, of course, since Lenneberg wrote those words. Whatever is known about maturational changes of the nervous system has not yet been made to yield specific hypotheses about the course of language development. These observations also apply to perceptual and cognitive development more generally.

Perhaps it is premature to attack the issue of a maturational component to behavioral change from this direction. Lenneberg might also have gone on to bewail the small number of hypotheses based on behavioral studies about which aspects of language development might be affected by maturation of the central nervous system. The papers in part 1 suggest that for human development the issue can fruitfully be addressed from the direction of behavioral studies alone, perhaps more fruitfully at this time than from studies of development of the human nervous system.

What is meant by a maturational component to linguistic, perceptual, or conceptual development? No genetic program is carried out in the absence of environmental input, including genetic programs for development. All behavioral development results from a series of interactions between neural substrate and feedback from the world. By the maturational component to conceptual development we mean the developmental changes resulting from the aspects of growth or reorganization of neural substrate that are determined by the genetic program.

A hypothetical example might clarify what is meant by a maturational component. Suppose that all genetically programmed developments in the nervous system are completed by the second decade of life. Suppose then that a blind man regains his sight and learns to discriminate faces. We could describe his acquisition of face-recognition skills in terms of changes in his representations of faces and in the processes by which he recognizes familiar faces and encodes previously unfamiliar faces. By hypothesis there would be no maturational component to this development, since all maturational changes in the state of his nervous system are complete. We must also describe a child's acquisition of face-recognition skills in these same terms. But in the child's case it is possible (but only possible) that some maturational changes affect this developmental course. The challenge, of course, is to specify reasonable hypotheses about the maturational factors that might contribute to development and then to bring relevant evidence to bear on those hypotheses.

Waber comments that in an earlier era of psychological inquiry, assessing the maturational component to development was considered a legitimate and exciting topic for research. In light of the progress made in developmental neurobiology since then, some of the work from that era seems naive and was certainly inconclusive but, I would argue, not fundamentally misconceived. Most of the work of that earlier period concerned motor development (Carmichael, 1926; McGraw, 1935, 1943; Gesell and Thompson, 1943). The starting point was Carmichael's classic demonstration that the emergence and organization of swimming in infant frogs and salamanders is under maturational control. He showed that young animals paralyzed for the five-day period during which normal controls begin to swim, swam identically to the controls when the paralyzing drug wore off.

In the case of development in human infants, three kinds of evidence were taken to support the hypothesis of similar maturational control of the emergence of motor skills. First, descriptive work established detailed invariance in the sequential steps of motor development across children. This invariance holds at fine levels of detail and sometimes appears arbitrary with regard to imaginable experiential sources. In many cases these sequences were strictly contemporaneous in freely developing identical twins (Gesell and Thompson, 1943). Second, deprivation studies were devised to directly mimic the logic of Carmichael's experiments. Dennis (1940) compared the onset of walking in Hopi infants strapped to cradle boards for nine months with Hopi infants allowed to move freely, creep, crawl, and stand like American children. The age of onset of walking was identical (fifteen months) in the two groups. In another study (that makes one grateful for current HEW guides on use of human subjects) a mother lent her newborn twins to two experimenters for nine months. During this period the twins were kept lying on their backs all day, sometimes with their hands bound or secured under sheets, with no toys and no opportunities to interact with each other. Caretakers did not smile at or vocalize to the babies. Nonetheless, the emergence of all the major infant milestones (smiling, cooing, sitting, grasping) in the first nine months was within the normal range for both twins (Dennis and Dennis, 1935). Finally, Gesell and his co-workers developed the method of co-twin control, in which one member of a pair of identical twins was given practice and exercise in some emerging skill while the control was denied it. For example, at forty-six weeks one twin was given six weeks of practice, ten minutes a day, at climbing stairs. The other twin was denied access to stairs. After this period the practiced twin performed the skill better than the control, but the control climbed the stairs spontaneously, and training was markedly more efficacious for the control twin when begun at this time. Two weeks of training for the control twin were equal to the six weeks for the experimental twin, and after three weeks the control twin had completely caught up (Gesell and Thompson, 1943).

As is typical of American developmental psychology of the time, there was little theoretical work on alternative models of how maturation might contribute to development. The basic concept was maturational readiness; the child cannot benefit from relevent experience until his nervous system has matured in some relevant respects. In the case of motor development two candidate sites had their partisans: the cerbral cortex (McGraw, 1943) and the cerebellum (Shirley, 1933). Arguments in favor of each were indirect; each was known to play a role in the control of motor activity in adults, and each was known to develop markedly during infancy.

Although this evidence is suggestive, it is certainly not conclusive. No maturational argument follows directly from invariant sequences. Further, Dennis's deprivation studies and Gesell's method of co-twin control depend crucially on the successful identification of the experience relevant to the acquisition of a particular skill. In the absence of more detailed hypotheses about mechanisms of development, we should be skeptical about the ease with which this can be done. Finally, although these studies demonstrate the theoretical need for a concept of readiness in explanations of development, they do not succeed in demonstrating that readiness emerges as the result of maturation of the nervous system. A concrete example is the method of co-twin control used in a study of vocabulary acquisition (Strayer, 1930). At nineteen months a pair of twins was separated for five weeks. During this period the experimental twin was given two hours of vocabulary drill daily and was otherwise provided with her normal environment. The control was cared for by loving caretakers who hummed to her, played games with her, gestured to her, but did not speak. The control twin apparently remained cheerful through all this and gestured and pantomimed a great deal by the end of the period. Not surprisingly, the experimental twin's vocabulary was much greater. The twins were reunited, and the control twin was given training treatment that had been given the experimental twin. Day for day, the control twin learned faster, and Strayer concluded this was due to maturational readiness. But the control twin's conceptual development had not been impeded; her daily activities, including play with toys, had been normal. It is equally possible that the readiness that allowed her to make better use of the same vocabulary training was conceptual (see Brown, 1958; Bowerman, 1977; Leehey and Carey, 1978; Carey and Bartlett, 1978, for discussions of the conceptual component to vocabulary acquisition). It is possible that maturational factors played no role whatsoever.

I am not denying that motor development is largely under maturational control or even that vocabulary development may have a maturational component. My point is simply that the available evidence relevant to these hypotheses is inconclusive with regard to vocabulary development and merely highly suggestive with regard to motor development.

The work reported in the four papers in part 1 differs from the early work in several respects. First, its domain is not motor development but perceptual and conceptual change. Second, it concerns not infancy but development in childhood through adolescence. Most important, this work attempts to make very clear the kinds of maturational influences on development that are supported by the behavioral data. This is a necessary step in constraining hypotheses about an actual maturational mechanism.

Recent advances in developmental neurobiology have provided animal models of maturational mechanisms of various kinds. There are three familiar examples.

• The genetic program specifies critical periods during which the conditions of input determine permanent characteristics of the nervous system (Hubel and Wiesel, 1970).
• Immaturity of the functional organization of particular areas of the brain places upper limits on the capacities that can be achieved at that point in development (Goldman, 1972).
• Species-specific behavior patterns emerge at a predetermined time, and some features of their organization are relatively uninfluenced by environmental variables (Nottebohn, 1970).

In all these cases, as in the case of motor development, the goal is to relate changes at the behavioral level to maturational events within an individual. Carey and Diamond entertain a fourth maturational hypothesis of this type—that maturationally induced changes in the nervous system cause a temporary disruption of behavior. Waber's research departs from the tradition that examines the maturational components in an individual's developmental history. She relates stable differences in cognitive profiles among different people to differences in their rates of maturation in childhood and, especially, adolescence.

The goal of the papers in this section is to reopen the issue of the maturational component to cognitive development as a legitimate, and empirically tractable, area of research. The approaches of Waber, Carey and Diamond, Rose, and Denckla, Rudel, and Broman differ in specifics but share common assumptions. First, they share the belief that psychological evidence for maturational factors in developmental change must precede and constrain specific hypotheses about neural mechanisms. Second, assuming that such behavioral evidence is forthcoming, they share the belief that specific hypotheses about mechanism can and must be formulated and tested. Finally, they look to the burgeoning field of developmental neurobiology as a source of animal models for maturational mechanisms. In Rose's case the role of the animal model is most transparent. Although a much wider net for relevant data (from normal development, brain-damaged adults, learning-disabled children, lesioned animals) is cast and much more theoretical latitude allowed, it should be obvious that the approach in these papers is continuous with that of the twenties and thirties.

In sum, like Lenneberg, we believe that genetically programmed changes in the nervous system must play a role in the explanation of human conceptual and linguistic development. Unlike Lenneberg, we do not start from what is known about maturation of the human nervous system. We propose to start from behavioral evidence for a maturational component to human development. We then use what is known about the development of nervous systems in general to generate more specific hypotheses about what maturational changes in the human nervous system might underlie these maturational influences that have been supported by behavioral evidence.

REFERENCES

Bowerman, M. 1977. The structure and origin of semantic categories in the language learning child. Paper presented at Burg Wartenstein Symposium No. 74, July.

Brown, R. 1958. How shall a thing be called? *Psych. Rev.* 65: 14–21.

Carey, S., and Bartlett, E. 1978. Acquiring a single new word. In *Proceedings of the Stanford Child Language Conference*. Stanford, CA: University of California.

Carmichael, L. 1926. The development of behavior in invertebrates experimentally removed from the influence of external stimulation. *Psych. Rev.* 33: 51–58.

Chomsky, N. 1975. *Reflections on language.* New York. Pantheon.

Dennis, W. 1940. The effect of cradling practices upon the onset of walking in Hopi children. *J. Genet. Psych.* 56: 77–86.

Dennis, W., and Dennis, M. 1935. The effect of restricted practice upon the reaching, sitting, and standing of two infants. *J. Genet. Psych.* 47: 17–32.

Fodor, J., Bever, T., and Garrett, M. 1974. *The Psychology of Language.* New York: McGraw-Hill.

Gesell, A., and Thompson, H. 1943. Learning and maturation in identical infant twins: An experimental analysis by the method of co-twin control. In *Child behavior and development,* ed. Barker, Kounir, and Wright, pp. 209–227. New York: McGraw-Hill.

Goldman, P. S. 1972. Developmental determinants of cortical plasticity. *Acta Neurobiologiae Experimentalis* 32: 495–511.

Hubel, D. H. and Wiesel, T. N. 1970. The period of susceptibility to the physiological effects of unilateral eye closure in kittens. *Journal of Physiology* 206: 419–436.

Leehey, S. and Carey, S. 1978. Up front: The acquisition of a concept and a word. In *Proceedings of the Stanford Child Language Conference.*

Lenneberg, E. H. 1967. *Biological foundations of language.* New York: John Wiley and Sons.

Lenneberg, E. H. 1974. Language and brain: Developmental aspects. *Neurosciences Research Program Bulletin,* 12.

McGraw, M. 1935. *Growth: A study of Johnny and Jimmy.* New York: Appleton-Century-Crofts.

McGraw, M. 1943. *The neuromuscular maturation of the human infant.* New York: Columbia University Press.

Nottebohm, F. 1970. Ontogeny of birdsong. *Science* 167: 950–956.

Shirley, M. M. 1933. Locomotor and visual-manual functions. In *A handbook of child psychology,* ed. C. Munchison, Worcester, MA: Clark University Press.

Strayer, H. 1930. Language and growth: The relative-efficacy of early and deferred vocabulary training studied by the method of co-twin control. *Genet. Psych. Monograph.*

2

Maturation:
Thoughts on Renewing
an Old Acquaintanceship

Deborah P. Waber

It is somewhat ironic that we now find ourselves struggling not only to understand maturation as a concept but to defend it as a respectable subject for scientific investigation. Child psychology in this country emerged as a discipline firmly rooted in a maturational theory of development. G. Stanley Hall, considered by many to be the first American child psychologist, believed that childhood was a natural progression through a series of stages whose basis lay in the biology of the species. Captivated by Darwin's ideas, he argued that the evolution of man was embodied in the development of the individual child.

Hall's work was soon eclipsed by that of other investigators. Yet his assumption about an intrinsic biological program for behavioral development clearly persisted in the minds of many of his successors, even though they themselves did not articulate a clear theoretical framework. Much of the child development literature of the 1930s and early 1940s focuses on descriptions of physical growth, the maturation of motor skills, and the development of intelligence. From the writings of these early researchers it appears that many of them viewed childhood as a process of unfolding according to some regular, biologically based scheme. They saw their task as the observation of the natural events of childhood, extracting regularities that characterized all children as well as the range and possibility of individual differences among them.

To observe the course of development and the interrelationships among its aspects, they initiated massive projects with the goal of collecting longitudinal data, birth to maturity, on cohorts of normal children. Among these projects were the Berkeley, Fels, and Harvard

growth studies, invaluable sources of data on human development
that scholars continue to mine.

From these studies it became clear that physical growth is an ex-
ceedingly lawful, regular process. It was therefore anticipated that
human mental development might show a characteristic pattern of
growth as well. Demonstrating this proved to be far more difficult.
Mental growth spurts were hard to document and, where they appeared, were much more variable than physical growth spurts. Of
course, measurement of mental abilities is far less precise than
measurement of height. Thus the failure to detect distinct spurts in
mental ability by no means ruled out their existence.

Another aspect of these studies was the effort to discover relationships between physical growth and mental development. Behind this
effort lay the hypothesis that there exists an underlying maturation
factor, that physical and mental growth should go hand in hand. In
1893 William Townsend Porter reported that in St. Louis pupils in
the higher grades were taller and heavier than pupils of the same
age in lower grades. The later growth studies of the 1930s yielded
similar findings, indicating a positive relationship between height
and mental abilities (Shuttleworth, 1939; Bayley, 1956) and between
menarcheal age and mental abilities (Abernethy, 1935; Stone and
Barker, 1937). The anthropologist Franz Boas determined that
skeletal age was also related to mental abilities (Boas, 1941). Yet in a
response to Porter written in 1895, Boas had already sensed the ambiguity inherent in all such data. "Dr. Porter has shown that mental
and physical growth are correlated, or depend upon common
causes; not that mental development depends on physical growth"
(Boas, 1895, p. 227). As social science research methods became
more sophisticated, social class, health, family size, and nutrition
were shown to be confounding factors that could account for much
of the relationship between physical and mental growth (Tanner,
1969). In short, the results of these studies did not support the existence of a unitary process of maturation that could account for intellectual development.

Arnold Gesell and his group, more than any others, rendered
maturation an unacceptable explanation for development among
American psychologists. Gesell made careful observations of infant
behaviors, describing the behaviors that emerged with lawful regu-
larity at each chronological age. According to him, events proceeded
along this rigid chronological timetable, and it was against chrono-

logical age that normality was measured. Maturation, as a unitary force, was viewed as an end in itself, a sufficient explanation for the elaboration of complex behaviors (Gesell and Amatruda, 1945). Thus if a three-year-old child acted like a two-year-old, his behavior was ascribed to immaturity. On the other hand, the three-year-old who managed to achieve some element of four-year-old behavior was hailed as precocious. Parents were advised to expect two-year-old children to do what Gesell had laid out in his books as two-year-old behavior, since this was the normal course of maturing. Not surprisingly, the Gesell movement, whose simplicity was so appealing to parents, led other child psychologists to reject maturation as a reasonable explanation for behavioral development. Another problem with the maturational position was that it was essentially atheoretical. The mainstream of psychology at that time was intensely theoretical. Placed in opposition to the intricate systems of learning theorists such as Clark Hull, the maturational position could not compete as a scientific psychology.

Since Gesell, maturation has been treated as little more than a dull background for other, more easily operationalized, aspects of child development. Most investigators have favored a more experimental approach in which the child's behavior can be manipulated by external contingencies. Psychological processes can thus be demonstrated in the context of situations in which hypotheses could be empirically verified or discarded in the service of building theory. That is not to say that the issue has lain dormant. Numerous studies have attempted to demonstrate relationships between physical growth and mental development as well as discontinuities in mental growth. However, none has yielded results so startling or compelling as to convince the mainstream of developmental psychologists that maturational processes are a necessary consideration for them.

Several new themes in American psychology may make the intellectual climate hospitable for maturation to make a respectable comeback. One is the notion brought to American psychology by Piaget's theory that the child is an active thinker who, through his constant interaction with the physical and social world, creates mental constructions of it. These constructions develop over time in such a way as to successively approximate or, in Piaget's terms, become adapted to, the physical reality of the world. This concept has been extended by theorists of social development, who give increased importance to the reciprocal influence that the developing child exerts on his social world (Bell, 1971). Thus the child is a major source of his own development and not simply a subject of manipulation.

A more important development is the growing appreciation of the relationship of brain to behavior, specifically the rejection of the principle of equipotentiality and the adoption of the notion of functional specialization. By now it is clear that the adult human brain is characterized by complex functional specialization whose structure is in some sense universal; man therefore does not simply accumulate experience in an undifferentiated substrate. In light of this fact the study of behavioral development must assume a different cast. How do these structures undergo transformation from the immature to the mature form? What is the relationship between the developing structures and behavioral functions? How can the regularities in development be described? Clearly, unless we posit that either the structures are fully present in miniature form at birth or some specific collection of experiences is required in order for differentiation to occur and in nearly all cases such experience is provided, we must conclude that some process most economically called maturation plays a central role in the development of brain-behavior relationships. We can therefore hypothesize that the structure of cognitive development reflects, in part, an intrinsic biological program. In addition, the study of brain-behavior relationships has produced new methodologies for investigating biologically based behaviors. These new behavioral methodologies, based on psychobiological principles, are far better suited to answering questions about the maturation of cognition than those based on psychometric principles. Using these new neuropsychological methods, we can increase the likelihood of detecting maturational processes and lawful relationships between somatic and behavioral development.

Even with the new methodologies, however, we still confront many of the same conceptual problems that our intellectual predecessors faced. Maturation is by its nature strongly correlated with physical time and experience and is therefore difficult to distinguish from them. This is the paradox; for while maturation is intuitively a very apparent aspect of behavioral development, it is methodologically elusive. Moreover, it is often so obvious an aspect of cognitive development that we may fail to appreciate its importance, attending rather to those developmental events that can be manipulated or tied to experience.

Inhelder et al. (1966), for example, conducted a study in which, through training, they were able to accelerate the achievement of concrete operational thought. They were successful, however, only among those subjects identified as transitional or, in Piaget's terms, in a state of disequilibrium. As Inhelder points out, this dependence on initial state is a characteristic of most training studies. She reports that the state of cognitive disequilibrium provides the optimal condition for cognitive change or reorganization. If experience were the critical factor, it should be possible through guided experience to move the preoperational child into a state of disequilibrium. Yet training studies have succeeded only in moving the child from an existing state of disequilibrium to equilibrium at a higher level and not from equilibrium at the lower level to the intervening state of disequilibrium. One can therefore entertain an alternative hypothesis, that some intrinsic (biologic) maturational process plays a critical role in permitting the child to benefit from experience.

In lower animals, for whom experience plays a much more circumscribed role in development than it does for us, these maturational processes stand out much more clearly. The developmental period is typically quite short, and discrete events occur according to a fairly rigid timetable. We can specify to the day when the laboratory rat will open its eyes and locomote; we can describe quite precisely the nature of the interaction between the mother and pups from birth and the date when weaning will occur. Moreover, by discrete experimental manipulations we can modify the course of development and in so doing define the mechanisms underlying these behaviors. This is very important, for we do not contend that rats are weaned at twenty-eight days because twenty-eight days of maturation have occurred. Rather, comparative psychologists have identified complex feedback loops by which physiological changes modify behavior and vice versa (Rosenblatt, 1969). It is these loops that are of greatest scientific interest. Viewed from this perspective, the term *maturation* is construed as a general one referring to these more specific processes. It is at this more specific, mechanistic level of analysis that the studies of humans must seek to focus if they are to be productive ultimately.

These mechanisms become far more difficult to detect as we ascend the phylogenetic scale. As the evolutionary biologists have pointed out, the period of immaturity becomes greatly extended in primates, especially in man, and with it the role of experience gains

much greater significance. The extended period of immaturity and
the expanded role of experience means that uncertainty, to borrow a
term from the information theorists, is greatly increased. Mechanisms of maturation specific to the human species are therefore likely
to assume as infinite a variety of forms as the number of available
experiential constellations. Moreover, individual differences, attributable to both biological and experiential factors, lead children
to extract different features from the environment as well as to react
differently to the same stimulus.

The challenge, then, is to develop methods to define the mechanisms of maturation and in so doing to make of this amorphous concept an acceptable object for study by a scientific psychology.
Specifically, we must be clever enough to decouple the maturational
process from its usual companions, time and experience, and to
describe its interaction with them. Unless we can generate specific
hypotheses that can be disproven, the newer maturational explanations may fare little better than those of Gesell.

Two broad concepts can form a basis for developing methodologies in this area. The first is prepared learning. The term
prepared learning refers to the phenomenon that organisms are
biologically prepared to be sensitive to specific kinds of stimuli and
accomplish particular kinds of learning with greater facility than
other kinds of learning (Seligman and Hagen, 1972). The classic experiment in this area was performed by Garcia and Koelling (1966).
Using a classical conditioning paradigm, they exposed rats to a taste
and an audiovisual stimulus, both paired with radiation sickness.
Only the taste became aversive and not the audiovisual stimulus.
Yet when the same two conditioned stimuli (CS) (taste and audiovisual stimulus) were paired with a different unconditioned stimulus,
(UCS) foot shock, it was the audiovisual stimulus and not the taste
that became aversive. They suggested that "natural selection may
have favored mechanisms which associate gustatory and olfactory
cues with internal discomfort since the chemical receptors sample the
materials soon to be incorporated into the internal environment"
(p. 124). This experiment constituted a Copernican revolution in
learning theory.

The concept of prepared learning has enormous applicability for
developmental research. For example, naive Peking ducklings, who
have had no previous exposure to the parent, will, in the vicinity of
several different birds, selectively follow the bird that is emitting the

call of its own species. At first glance this appears to be an example of "instinct" à la Lorenz. Gottlieb (1975a, b, c) showed experimentally, however, that in order for this following to occur, the duckling auditory system had to be primed by the sound of its own voice during hatching. Devocalized ducklings did not show the following response at twenty-four hours of age. Gottlieb was able to restore the following response in the devocalized duck by exposing it during hatching to a recording of a sibling call in the same auditory range as the call of the parent. In yet another experiment Gottlieb found that if he waited to test until the birds were forty-eight hours old, the unprimed devocalized ducklings showed the following response with the same strength as controls. Maturational processes appeared to compensate, but experience had accelerated the appearance of the response. By sixty-five hours, however, the unprimed devocalized ducks had begun to show deterioration of the response, suggesting that early experience during hatching is required to maintain the maturational effect that appears without experience forty-eight hours later. Not only is learning prepared here (the naive duckling selectively follows the call of its own species), but learning is intimately tied to the maturational state of the animal. Moreover, the maintenance of the mature response depends on an experiential event earlier in life.

Prepared learning probably operates in the human throughout development as well. In humans language may be the clearest example of prepared learning. Lenneberg discussed this issue in his paper "On Explaining Language," which appeared in *Science* in 1969.

The development of language in the child may be elucidated by applying to it the conceptual framework of developmental biology. Maturation may be characterized as a sequence of states. At each state, the growing organism is capable of accepting some specific input; this it breaks down and resynthesizes in such a way that it makes itself develop into a new state. This new state makes the organism sensitive to new and different types of input, whose acceptance transforms it to yet a further state which opens the way to still different input, and so on. This is called epigenesis. It is the story of embryological development observable in the formation of the body, as well as in certain aspects of behavior.

When language acquisition in the child is studied from the point of view of developmental biology, one makes an effort to describe developmental stages together with their tendencies for change and the conditions that bring about that change. I believe that the schema of physical maturation is applicable to the study of language development because children appear to be sensitive to successively different aspects of the language environment. The child first reacts only to intonation patterns. With continued exposure to these patterns as they occur in a given language mechanisms develop that allow him to process the patterns, and in most instances to reproduce them (although the latter is not a necessary condition for further development). This changes him so that he reaches a new state, a new potential for language development. . . . Furthermore, the correlation between language development and other maturational indices suggests that there are anatomical and physiological processes whose maturation sets the pace for both cognitive and language development; it is to these maturational processes that the concept differentiation refers. We often transfer the meaning of the word to the verbal behavior itself, which is not unreasonable, although, strictly speaking, it is the physical correlates only that differentiate.

Inhelder's conservation training experiments may in fact reflect prepared learning as a mechanism in the development of human cognition as well. These studies show that the preoperational child can be trained to demonstrate concrete operational thought only with great effort, and it is difficult to sustain the new level of thinking. A child of the same chronological age, who is already transitional, can be trained without heroic effort to show concrete operational thought and shows it in a variety of domains. The transitional child, through experience combined with some presumed new maturational event, has reached a state in which he is now prepared to master the regularities of the physical environment, the same regularities that have been present in his environment since birth. Inhelder (Inhelder and Sinclair, 1969) hints at this:

we conclude that the evolution of operativity is malleable only within certain limits imposed by the laws of development. No matter whether they are exposed to a confrontation with physical experience or to verbal training, children at the preoperational level do not acquire truly logical structures and, at best, reach an intermediate level. Although learning may accelerate development (within certain limits), such acceleration apparently obeys limitative conditions of assimilation which, in turn, are subject to temporal regulations reminiscent of the "chronological succession of competences" in embryology, as Waddington calls them. . . .
To summarize, learning is subordinate to the laws of development, and development does not consist in a mere successive accumulation of bits of learning, since development follows structuration laws that are both logical and biological.

The challenging task is to discover independent indicators of the maturational process and show empirically that maturational state provides a necessary but not sufficient condition for cognitive development. Preparedness for specific kinds of experience, as well as the sequential waxing and waning of sensitivities throughout development, surely constitutes a good deal of what we mean by maturation.

A second approach that can be applied in developing method-ologies is to exploit the enormous range of normal variation between individuals in human development. One use of this approach is to correlate advancement in one system with advancement in another. Another is to study the ways in which different patterns of matura-tion are associated with different outcomes. It is this area that I have pursued in my own research.

I have examined the relationship between the differing rates of physical development in males and females and patterns of cognitive abilities at adolescence. Differences between adult males and females on specific cognitive abilities are most frequently reported for verbal abilities, at which females excel, and spatial abilities, at which males excel. While these differences sometimes appear during childhood, they emerge most clearly at adolescence. The question was whether the emergence of differential ability patterns at adolescence results from the individual's recognition of physiological differentiation with puberty and consequent adherence to a sex role or whether it reflects a more direct effect of the physiological aspects of puberty on the brain.

It is commonly recognized that males and females differ in their rate of physical maturation; that is, females mature earlier than males; and I wondered whether this difference in rate of maturation was somehow related to a differentiation of the central nervous system that became apparent at puberty. In this study females were conceptualized as a population of early maturing individuals and males as late maturing individuals (Waber, 1976, 1977). Instead of comparing behavior across sexes, I looked at early and late maturers within each sex in order to discover the effect of variation in maturational rate and the implication this might have for findings of sex differences in mental abilities. Thus early and late maturing females were compared, as were early and late maturing males, in order to see whether the effect of rate of maturation was greater than the effect of sex. According to the hypothesis, early maturers ought to show the more femalelike pattern (verbal better than spatial) independent of sex; and late maturers ought to show the more malelike pattern (spatial better than verbal) independent of sex.

A sample of Caucasian middle-class children was selected using

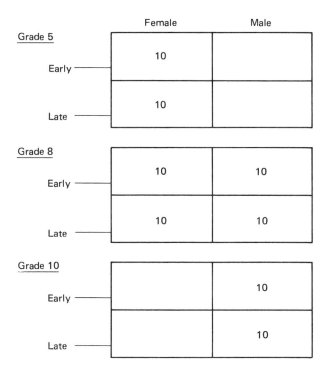

2.1
Experimental design

the design shown in figure 2.1; there were twenty fifth-grade girls,
half early and half late maturers; twenty eighth-grade girls, half
early and half late maturers; twenty eighth-grade boys, half early
and half late maturers; and twenty tenth-grade boys, half early and
half late maturers. The staggered design with missing cells reflects
the sex difference in maturational rate. To be included in the study,
the child had to be at an age when rate of physical maturation could
be observed. For example, in fifth-grade boys, variability in physical
maturation is not apparent, so they cannot be classified as early or
late maturers. The same is true for tenth-grade girls, most of whom
would be expected to have already matured. Each child was given a
physical examination that included Tanner staging for secondary
sexual characteristics (Tanner, 1962). From this sample I selected
children who were at least one standard deviation from the mean for
their age on the basis of the Tanner norms.

Each child who had been classified as an early or a late maturer
was given a battery of mental ability tests chosen because adults had

shown sex difference on them in earlier studies. The linguistic tests were the following: (1) the Stroop color-naming test (the child is asked to name a series of repeated colors as quickly as possible, and articulation speed is measured); (2) the coding subtest of the Wechsler Intelligence Scale for Children (WISC) (the digits 1–9 are each paired with a nonsense symbol and a field of random digits is presented below; the child is asked to draw the appropriate nonsense symbol under the number for each random digit as quickly as possible. This is considered to test visuomotor speed); and (3) the verbal fluency subtest of the Primary Mental Abilities (PMA) (the child is asked to name in five minutes as many words as he can think of that begin with the letter s). Among adults, females show an advantage on all these tests. The spatial tests were the following: (1) the embedded figures test (the child is shown a simple line drawing which is then taken away, and he is then shown a more complex colored drawing that has the simple line drawing embedded in it; the child's task is to find the line drawing); (2) the block design subtest of the WISC (the child is given a set of colored blocks and asked to copy designs of increasing complexity using the blocks); and (3) the spatial ability subtest of the PMA (the child is asked to perform mental rotations on nonsense shapes). Previous studies indicate that males excel on these three tests.

As predicted, within each sex late maturers at every age scored better than early maturers on each of the spatial ability tests; however, contrary to prediction, none of the groups scored differently on any of the linguistic or perceptual-motor sequencing tasks. Table 2.1 shows the means for each of the scores for both spatial (mean of the normalized scores for three spatial measures) and verbal (mean of normalized scores for the three verbal measures). The last two columns show the mean difference scores, that is, the verbal score minus the spatial score computed for each child. A positive difference score means that the verbal performance is better than the spatial performance, and a negative difference means that spatial is better than verbal. As the means indicate, although there was no difference for any of the groups on the verbal tests, the late maturers scored better than the early maturers at every age on the spatial tests. On the difference scores the late maturers scored higher on spatial tests than verbal, and the early maturers scored higher on verbal than spatial. Thus, at least for spatial ability, the hypothesis was borne out.

Table 2.1
Means and standard deviations of ability scores (expressed in standard scores)

Group	Verbal score		Spatial score		Difference score	
	Mean	S.D.	Mean	S.D.	Mean	S.D.
Females, younger						
Early maturers	-0.076	0.616	-0.378	0.628	0.302	0.749
Late maturers	0.076	0.737	0.378	0.803	-0.302	0.740
Females, older						
Early maturers	0.502	0.612	-0.204	0.793	0.706	0.732
Late maturers	-0.151	0.981	0.189	0.776	-0.340	1.267
Males, younger						
Early maturers	-0.350	0.795	-0.359	0.920	0.009	0.926
Late maturers	-0.002	0.451	0.374	0.694	-0.376	0.700
Males, older						
Early maturers	-0.019	0.935	-0.424	0.800	0.405	0.615
Late maturers	-0.027	0.681	0.390	0.741	-0.417	0.685

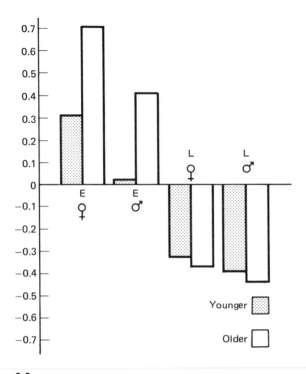

2.2
Mean values of difference scores grouped by sex, age level, and maturation

Figure 2.2 shows the difference scores for each age and maturation group. The white bars show the younger group for each sex and the black bars show the older group for each sex. They are arrayed by early and late maturing groups. All the early maturing groups show verbal better than spatial, and all the late maturing groups show spatial better than verbal. Although the sex differences were in the predicted direction, they were not statistically significant.

The second part of the study addressed the issue of brain mechanisms more directly by examining cerebral lateralization of function. In normal right-handed individuals the left hemisphere of the cerebral cortex is thought to subserve linguistic functions and the right hemisphere to subserve spatial configurational functions. While this statement is obviously an oversimplification, it is sufficient for heuristic purposes. Levy (1969) has hypothesized that verbal and spatial functions are inherently incompatible processes and that hemispheric specialization of function evolved in order to keep them separate. Thus an individual in whom language is less well lateralized would be expected to have more difficulty performing spatial tasks than someone in whom language was more completely lateralized. It was therefore predicted that late maturers, who scored better at spatial tasks, would also show more lateralization of linguistic function than early maturers.

This hypothesis was tested by administering a dichotic listening test for phonemic perception to the same subjects. This test consists of the six phonemic stimuli /ba/, /da/, /ga/, /pa/, /ta/, and /ka/, presented in randomly ordered pairs so that different stimuli are presented simultaneously to each ear. For example, the subject might hear /ba/ in the left ear and /ta/ in the right ear. The children are asked to report what they heard and scored for whichever ear was correctly reported. If the subject reported hearing /ba/, the left ear was scored correct, and if he reported hearing /ta/, the right ear was scored correct. To control for channel and order effects 240 trials were administered. Scores were computed using laterality coefficients, which yield an ear advantage; they give the percentage of time that stimuli presented to one ear are reported more correctly than those presented to the other. A positive value conventionally indicates a right-ear advantage and a negative value a left-ear advantage. The magnitude of the coefficient reflects the magnitude of the ear advantage. Since pathways from the right ear project primarily to the left cerebral hemisphere, the normal pattern is to show a right-ear advantage for linguistic stimuli, such as the phonemes used in this test.

There was an interaction of maturational rate with age for these dichotic listening scores (table 2.2). In the younger groups there is no systematic effect of maturational rate or sex on ear advantage; but in the older group the late maturers consistently showed a strong right-ear advantage while the early maturers showed a very small right-ear advantage and sometimes a left-ear advantage. These data were also analyzed using absolute value scores that were independent of left or right ear but showed merely the magnitude of the ear advantage, indicating the magnitude of the functional separation between the hemispheres (figure 2.3). Here again there was no effect for the younger group, the ten-year-old girls and the thirteen-year-old boys; but the older group showed a large effect such that late maturers were much more strongly lateralized than early maturers.

Thus in both sexes the rate of physical maturation is system-

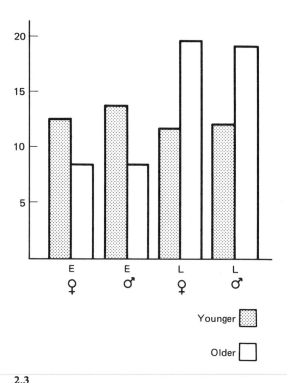

2.3
Mean values of absolute mean ear-advantage scores grouped by sex, age level, and maturation

atically related to spatial ability as well as to the lateralization of linguistic perception. The fact that there were behavioral differences on these two types of measures suggests that rate of maturation is associated with differences in the organization of function in the central nervous system.

It is not sufficient, however, simply to show a relationship between maturational rates and behavior. It is important to determine what specific mechanisms might underlie this relationship. That is, what is it about maturational rate that yields this particular behavioral pattern?

First, individuals who differ in maturational rate differ along other physiological dimensions as well. For example, early maturers are fatter, that is, a higher proportion of their body weight is fat than is that of late maturers, even at the same stage of sexual maturity. Fat has been associated with variations in sex hormones levels (Brown and Strong, 1965). It is possible, therefore, that the

Table 2.2
Means and standard deviations of ear-advantage variables

Group	Mean of the ear advantages (A) for tape 1 and tape 2		Mean of the absolute value of the ear advantages ($|A|$) for tape 1 and tape 2	
	Mean	S.D.	Mean	S.D.
Females	4.3	16.2	13.7	11.6
Younger	4.9	14.4	12.1	7.9
Early (N=9)	10.6	9.8	12.5	7.3
Late (N=10)	−0.4	14.5	11.8	8.5
Older	3.6	19.1	13.9	12.8
Early (N=9)	−3.5	11.8	8.3	9.2
Late (N=9)	10.8	20.9	19.6	13.1
Males	5.3	16.8	13.3	10.8
Younger	4.1	16.1	13.0	10.1
Early (N=9)	2.9	17.0	13.9	10.3
Late (N=10)	5.1	13.8	12.1	8.3
Older	6.6	18.3	13.8	13.2
Early (N=8)	−1.1	10.5	8.7	6.0
Late (N=8)	14.3	19.4	19.0	14.9

observed effect has more to do with fatness and sex hormones than time to reach maturity.

Second, in other mammalian species, when sex hormones have been shown to influence behavior at puberty, the mechanism is developmentally biphasic (Harris, 1964). High levels of sex hormones postnatally serve to organize brain structures early in life. These are activated behaviorally by the second rise in hormone production at puberty. If the observed behavioral pattern is indeed related to sex hormone levels, the behavior might reflect not only the current physiological state of the individual but also exposure earlier in life (as in the case of the Peking ducklings). Humans show the same pattern of hormone secretion as other mammals. That is, levels are quite high in the first year of life and drop during childhood, rising again at puberty (Forest and Cathiard, 1975, 1978). If these hormones affect hemispheric organization of function, for example, the effect could depend on an early influence as well as the effect of the hormones present at puberty.

Finally, there are data suggesting that stable individual differences in body composition emerge early in life. Longitudinal data from the Fels sample show a significant correlation between fatness at one and eleven years in boys and at one, nine, and eleven years in girls (Falkner, 1975). Therefore, it may be that patterns of neuropsychological functioning related to hormonal status are laid down in the central nervous system early in life, but it is only at puberty that they can be clearly observed.

These speculations are set forth, not in an attempt to offer a definitive explanation of the findings, but rather to illustrate that maturation in itself ought not be considered an acceptable explanation for behavioral development. The concept of maturation, however, can serve as an enormously useful tool for understanding more specifically the mechanisms that link physiology and behavior in the developmental process.

REFERENCES

Abernethy, E. M. 1935. Relationships between mental and physical growth. *Monographs SRCD* 1, no. 7.

Bayley, N. 1956. Individual patterns of development. *Child Development* 27: 45–74.

Bell, R. G. 1971. Stimulus control of parent or caretaker behavior by off-spring. *Developmental Psychology* 4: 63–72.

Boas, F. 1895. On Dr. William Townsend Porter's investigation of the growth of school children of St. Louis. *Science, New Series* 1: 225–230.

Boas, F. 1941. The relation between physical and mental development. *Science* 93L 339–:342.

Brown, J.B., and Strong, J. A. 1965. Affect of nutritional status and thyroid function on the metabolism of oestradiol. *J. Endocrinology.* 32: 107–115.

Falkner, F. 1975. Body composition. In *Puberty*, ed. S. R. Berenberg. Leiden: H. H. Stenfert Kroese.

Forest, M. G., and Cathiard, A. M. 1975. Pattern of plasma testosterone and Δ^+-androstenedione in normal newborns: Evidence for testicular activity at birth. *Journal of Clinical Endocrinology and Metabolism* 41: 977–980.

Forest, M. G., and Cathiard, A. M. 1978. Ontogenetic study of plasma 17 α-hydroxyprogesterone in one human. I. Postnatal period: Evidence for a transient ovarian activity in infancy. *Pediatric Research* 12: 6–11.

Garcia, J., and Koelling, R. A. 1966. Relation of cue to consequence in avoidance learning. *Psychonomic Science* 4: 123–124.

Gesell, A. L., and Amatruda, C. S. 1945. *The embryology of behavior: The beginnings of the human mind.* New York: Harper.

Gottlieb, G. 1975a. Development of species identification in ducklings. I: Nature of perceptual deficit caused by embryonic auditory deprivation. *J. Comp. Physiol. Psych.* 89: 387–399.

———. 1975b. Development of species identification in ducklings. II: Experiential prevention of perceptual deficit caused by embryonic auditory deprivation. *J. Comp. Physiol. Psych.* 89: 675–684.

———. 1975c. Development of species identification in ducklings. III: Maturational rectification of perceptual deficit caused by auditory deprivation. *J. Comp. Physiol. Psych.* 89: 899–912.

Harris, G. W. 1964. Sex hormones, brain development, and brain function. *Endocrinology* 75: 627–648.

Inhelder, B., Bovet, M., Sinclair, H., and Smock, C. D. 1966. On cognitive development. *American Psychologist* 21: 160–164.

Inhelder, B., and Sinclair, H. 1969. Learning cognitive structures. In *Trends and issues in developmental psychology*, ed. P. H. Mussen, V. Langer, and M. Covington. New York: Holt, Rinehart and Winston.

Lenneberg, E. H. 1969. On explaining language. *Science* 164: 635–643.

Levy, J. 1969. Possible basis for the evolution of lateral specialization of the human brain. *Nature* 224: 614–615.

Porter, W. T. 1893. The physical basis of precocity and dullness. *Transactions Academy of Science, St. Louis* 6: 161–181.

Rosenblatt, J. 1969. The development of maternal responsiveness in the rat. *Am. J. Orthopsychiatry* 39: 36–56.

Seligman, M., and Hagen, J. 1972. *Biological boundaries of learning.* Englewood Cliffs, N.J.: Prentice-Hall.

Shuttleworth, F. K. 1939. The physical and mental growth of girls age six to nineteen in relation to age at maximum growth. *Monographs SRCD* 4, no. 3.

Stone, C. P., and Barker, R. G. 1937. Aspects of personality and intelligence in post-menarcheal girls and pre-menarcheal girls of the same chronological ages. *J. Comp. Physiol. Psych.* 23: 439–455.

Tanner, J. M. 1962. *Growth at adolescence.* London: Blackwell.

———.1969. Relation of body size, intelligence test scores, and social circumstances. In *Trends and issues in developmental psychology*, ed. P. H. Mussen, J. Langer, and M. Covington. New York: Holt, Rinehart and Winston.

Waber, D. P. 1976. Sex differences in cognition: A function of maturation rate? *Science* 192: 572–574.

———.1979. Sex differences in mental abilities, hemispheric lateralization, and rate of physical growth at adolescence. *Developmental Psychology* 13: 29–38.

3

Some Functional Correlates of the Maturation of Neural Systems

David Rose

The search for a maturational basis for cognitive development seems likely to have very much the same plot line as the television show "Columbo." The basic structure of the show is always the same. From virtually the first scene, Columbo (a rumpled detective played by Peter Falk) and everyone in the viewing audience know who the murderer is. The dramatic tension, if it can be called that, arises from the fact that the crime has been so artfully orchestrated and embedded that there will never be a smoking gun, a last-minute eye-witness—never the direct and shocking proof one expects to find in Perry Mason. Instead, the case is solved in just about two hours by Columbo's truly dogged pursuit of the clearly circumstantial. The only reason the circumstantial evidence works is that it turns out to form a consistent pattern of evidence—consistent with only one theory of the crime.

Similarly, I think that most psychologists believe maturation to be guilty of something in the development of cognition, at the very least of being an accomplice. Proving it in any useful way, however, turns out to provide sufficient dramatic tension to have convened this symposium. Moreover, most of the methods we use seem much like Columbo's. It is unlikely that we will catch maturation red-handed—no eyewitness accounts in the cerebellum or forced confessions in the medulla oblongata. Instead, we are likely to look for the kinds of footprints and dips that Susan Carey has discussed, hoping that a pattern may be convincing where individual items are not.

The pattern that would be most convincing to developmental psychologists involves predictions. Maturation is often used—too often in fact—as an explanation of developmental changes in behavior;

but it is usually a default explanation, employed only in the most
generalized sense whenever no other obvious explanation suffices.
At such a general level it is empirically meaningless, of course, and
is adopted only post hoc. It is perhaps true that only when maturational arguments can lead to predictions about development will
they become attractive suspects.

This paper looks at brain structure as a potential source of predictions. The central question is whether our present knowledge about
neural structure and its development allows predictions about behavioral development.

As in everything, the matter of units is an important preliminary.
To neuropsychologists, the units of functional interest are each of
the several hundred structural assemblages of which the brain is
composed. Most structural types have several kinds of neurons in-
terconnected in a highly stereotyped fashion. Several of the more
prominent structures are illustrated schematically in figure 3.1.
These structures are stable, even across species; the hippocampus in
the rat is composed of cell types virtually identical to those in the
human hippocampus, and they both share the pattern of intercon-
nectivity illustrated in figure 3.1.

For the purposes of this discussion I want to take these structures
as units. Each of them reaches maturity in the same fashion: precur-
sors of neurons are generated in germinal sites; they migrate to terminal locations where they differentiate into appropriate neuron
types, are myelinated, form synapses with other neurons, and
undergo some selective attrition.

From a behavioral point of view the interesting question is
whether the structures develop at the same rate. Does the brain get
bigger and better in some general fashion, or do differential rates of
development in various structures result in a brain that reaches
maturity through the successive addition of separable components?
The answer appears to be, as Himwich (1976) has put it recently,
that the brain matures as a collection of organs, each of which
matures at its own rate. Consequently, at any point during the
development of the whole brain, individual components or organs
may be at quite different stages of development with respect to one
another, and some components obviously reach maturity before
others.

Moreover, the relative maturity of structures during development
is not random. Several broad generalizations can be made about the

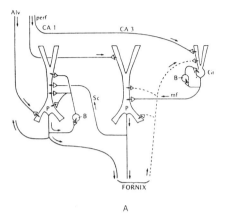

A

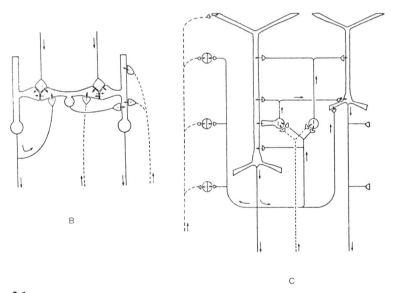

C

3.1
Basic circuit diagram. (A) The hippocampus and dentate gyrus. (B)
Thalamus. (C) Neocortex. (From *The Synaptic Organization of the Brain*,
Gordon M. Shepherd. Copyright © 1974 by Oxford University Press, Inc.
Reprinted by permission)

pattern observed. One of these generalizations, the much maligned "ontogeny recapitulates phylogeny," is actually very helpful as a rough approximation. It is clear that in general the phylogenetically more recent structures mature later than older ones.

None of this would be particularly interesting to behavioral scientists were it not that in most species birth occurs before the brain has completed its structural development. The point during the developmental sequence at which birth actually occurs turns out to vary dramatically between species. For some, birth comes very late with respect to the structural maturation of the brain, and there is actually very little structural difference between the neonatal brain and the adult brain. Species at this extreme are called precocial, the guinea pig being one common example. The altricial rat, on the other hand, is born at a much earlier point in the sequence, and a significant number of structures must undergo prolonged postnatal maturation. Humans are an altricial species, more like the rat than the guinea pig. They are born with substantial structural development yet to be completed. Compared with the guinea pig, at least, we are born as embryos (Gould, 1978).

Of what behavioral significance is it to have been born as a member of an altricial species rather than a precocial one? At even a superficial level the differences are obvious; compare, for instance, the behavior of a newly born horse (a relatively precocial species) with that of the human, or even rat, infant. Note, for that matter, how awkward it would be to use the term *infant* to describe a neonatal horse, while such a term is easily used with altricial rats.

At a less superficial level the anatomy suggests that the brain in altricial species may actually undergo postnatal changes in the type of organ it is through the sequential addition of functional subcomponents. Such a developmental pattern seems to imply that some components should contribute significantly to behavior only in the later stages of ontogeny or adulthood. That such is the case has been given strong preliminary support by the exciting work of Pat Goldman. She has employed lesion techniques at various stages of ontogeny to investigate the functional contribution of a number of brain structures. She has shown, for instance, that lesions in the prefrontal cortical regions of the infant and juvenile monkey have little or no effect on behavior when compared with the same lesions at adulthood. Moreover, she has shown that early lesioned monkeys eventually show deficits as adults, presumably because they had no prefrontal cortex to eventually mature (Goldman, 1972, 1974). Not surprisingly, prefrontal cortex is among the latest phylogenetic additions to the brain and among the latest to reach maturity.

Pat Goldman's work indicates that anatomical differences in maturity can be related to functional differences. If the brain as a whole matures through the sequential addition of later structures, then it seems reasonable to expect changes in behavioral capabilities as new structures emerge. Can any of the many "qualitative" changes in behavior described by developmental psychologists actually be predicted from an anatomical basis?

In the remaining sections of this paper I would like to explore one maturational hypothesis recently presented in the literature. Its foundation comes from the work of Altman and his colleagues (Altman and Das, 1965; Altman, 1967; Bayer and Altman, 1975), who found that in one specific structure of the rat brain—the dentate gyrus of the hippocampus—85 percent of one type of constituent neuron was generated postnatally. That is, most of these neurons are not even present when the animal is born. The functional consequence of this state of affairs was the central concern of a recent paper by Altman, Brunner, and Bayer (1973). They reasoned on the basis of the observed timing of neuron generation that the hippocampus could not function normally until about thirty days of age. They then predicted an observable transition in the behavioral capabilities of normal rats at around thirty days of age—a change from an organism that behaved as if it did not have a functional hippocampus to one that behaved as if it did. The substance of what constituted "as if" behavior came from lesion studies. The surprising fact is that for the most part the predictions were upheld.

By reviewing behavior in many tasks Altman, Brunner, and Bayer (1973) have shown that young rats (under about thirty days) do behave like hippocampectomized rats. None of the individual correspondences is convincing, but the overall pattern of correspondences makes the case compelling—particularly the fact that behavioral transitions seem to occur at about thirty days, as predicted.

Altman's work is entirely with rats. Humans, and primates generally, take longer to reach maturity than the rat, but the essential adult structures, like the hippocampus, are the same. In an intriguing set of papers Douglas (Douglas, Packouz, and Douglas, 1972; Douglas, 1975) has proposed that the anatomical and behavioral transitions seen in the rat at thirty days of age are seen in the human at about 4½ to 5 years. At the neural level the evidence to support Douglas's hypothesis is meager. Altman's work on the ontogeny of the dentate gyrus granule cells in rats required sacrificing the animals, and no acceptable alternative procedure is available for work with humans. Without that critical anatomical data Douglas's hypothesis about human development cannot be fully evaluated. No smoking gun or eyewitnesses yet.

Some interesting "circumstantial" evidence is available, however. If Douglas is right, there should be a predictable pattern of transitions in behavior at about five years of age. And there is, at least to a remarkable degree.

Again, as in the animal literature, predictions come from lesion literature (admittedly a troublesome source). Douglas himself has already shown that there are several interesting correspondences between the behavior of preschool children and that of lesioned animals. I extended his work by examining nearly all the behavioral tests found to be sensitive to hippocampal lesion and by seeking out, mostly in the available developmental literature, identical or analogous behavioral tests in young children. A few examples of what I found will help to clarify the nature of the argument.

Spontaneous Alternation   When faced with two alternatives, neither of which leads to reinforcement, normal animals tend to choose one and then the other. There is a stable bias toward not repeating unrewarded responses, which results over a series of trials in spontaneous alternation. Hippocampectomized animals, in contrast, show a striking tendency to choose the same alternative on successive trials. This lack of spontaneous alternation (often called perseveration) is one of the most striking findings of the hippocampal literature (Altman, Brunner, and Bayer, 1973; Douglas, 1975).

It is also a striking finding of the early childhood literature. Douglas, Packouz,, and Douglas (1972) found that all children over 4½ were reliably above-chance alternators while only one of twelve below that age was. Many other experiments with procedures closely analogous to the hippocampal studies are consistent with the observation that children older than 4½ to 5 tend to alternate choices while those below that age do not (Gratch, 1964; Jeffrey and Cohen, 1965; Manley and Miller, 1968; Pate and Bell, 1971).

Conditional Discrimination   In conditional discrimination no invariant relationship exists between some specific cue and the correct or rewarded choice. The correct choice over a number of trials depends instead on taking some contextual factor into account. For example, choosing a red box may be rewarded when a tone is on, a blue box when the tone is off. Only on the basis of the contextual information in the tones can a correct choice be made consistently.

Hippocampectomized animals have consistently been shown to be impaired in conditional discriminations (Hirsch, 1974). Moreover, as in many other tasks, hippocampals show a predictable pattern of behavior. When individual records were analyzed, Isaacson and Kimble (1972) showed that hippocampectomized animals responded nearly perfectly in one context while responding at chance or worse in the other. This disparity continued for many trials and was unlike the performance of normals.

A number of studies on conditional discrimination in young children have been completed. Those that have looked at children within the appropriate age range strongly suggest that children under five are sharply inferior in acquisition to those over five. Moreover, preliminary work suggests that the pattern of errors of young children is like that of the hippocampals, that is, high performance in one context sustained with very poor performance in the other (Doan and Cooper, 1971; Gollin and Liss, 1962; Gollin, 1965; Heidbreder, 1928).

Mazes   Another characteristic and consistently reported finding in the hippocampal literature is impaired performance in complex mazes (Nadel and O'Keefe, 1974). It is not surprising that preschool children are poorer solvers of mazes than are older children—almost any theoretical position would predict that finding.

Again it is the type of error that is interesting. Hippocampals tend to repeat errors, to be perseverative, rather than to commit random errors. One of my students investigated children's performance in full-scale body mazes. He found that, like hippocampal animals, the youngest children proved to be highly perseverative in their errors; that is, they tended to repeat entries into the same blind alleys. When the proportion of perseverative errors to total errors is plotted at each age, the following picture shown in figure 3.2 emerges. Note that there is a particularly sharp drop in perseverative errors for the five-year-olds, as predicted.

Classical and Operant Conditioning   There are many tasks in which deficits do not occur after hippocampal lesions. A large number of experiments, for example, have demonstrated that hippocampals condition at least as rapidly as normals on a large variety of classical and operant schedules (Haddad and Rabe, 1969; Jarrard, 1965; Schmaltz and Isaacson, 1966; Schmaltz, Wolf, and Trejo, 1973).

Similarly, there has been a large body of evidence for many years of both classical and operant conditioning in very young children, probably even neonates (for reviews see Munn, 1954; Reese and Lipsitt, 1970; Stevenson, 1970). The theoretical orientation of researchers in this area is not such that developmental differences over age are of critical interest, since it is generally assumed that the learning processes remain constant; consequently, few studies have directly tested age differences. Summaries of the literature as a whole, however, have concluded either that young children are as easily conditionable as the older children and adults, or, interestingly, that ease of conditionability decreases somewhat after age four or five (Goldman and Denny, 1963; Munn, 1954; Razran, 1933; White, 1965).

Probability Learning   On several tasks, the performance of animals with hippocampal lesions is actually facilitated. Probability learning appears to be one of these (Stevens, 1973). In probability learning tasks, rewards are given for several alternative choices but at differing probabilities. For example, choosing one alternative will

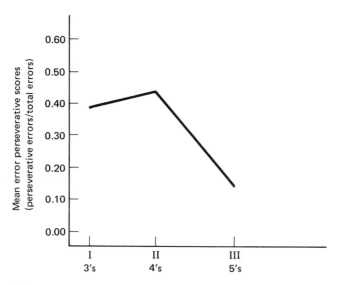

3.2
Proportion of perseverative errors by age. (From Wertlieb, 1975)

result in rewards 70 percent of the time, the other only 30 percent. Hippocampectomized rats learn to maximize faster than normals (or alternatively, one might say that hippocampals do not try new hypotheses to get 100 percent reward).

Similar experiments with children have shown that preschool children maximize earlier and to a greater extent than older children (Odom, 1967; Stevenson and Hoving, 1964; Stevenson and Weir, 1959; Weir, 1964). This is one of the more interesting results in the developmental literature, and its potential fit with hippocampal predictions is provocative.

These few examples of correspondences can hardly be convincing; they are intended to be merely representative of a longer list of changes in children at about five years that correspond well to Douglas's predictions (for a detailed analysis of these correspondences see Rose, in press). That there is a particularly significant change in children at about this age has been observed by developmental psychologists of widely varying theoretical backgrounds. Sheldon White (1970) has drawn much of this literature together and noted the unusually significant behavioral changes in five- to seven-year-old children. "One feels compelled to argue on the basis of the pattern of the literature that there must be—as one among several factors—a maturational substrate underlying the behavior changes between five and seven" (p. 8).

Is the hippocampus that maturational substrate found at last? While the behavioral data are consistent with such a position, some important cautions are necessary. To articulate them, I would like to look more closely at the dentate granule cells in context.

The axons of granule cells leave the dentate gyrus and synapse on the main output neurons (the pyramidal cells) of the hippocampus proper. From that perspective, they are clearly an integral part of the basic hippocampal circuitry (figure 3.1). Their input, however, is extrinsic to the hippocampus and comes from two major sources. One of them, entorhinal cortex, turns out to be anatomically linked to the highest neocortical association areas in the brain, notably the prefrontal association areas. This anatomical link between hippocampus (thought to be a phylogenetically older cortical structure) and prefrontal cortex (one of the most recent) has been fully described only recently (Leichnetz and Astruc, 1975a, b; Seltzer and Pandya, 1976; Van Hoesen and Pandya, 1975; Van Hoesen, Pandya, and Butters, 1975) but is consistent with an earlier observation that granule cells in hippocampus are closely associated with the evolution of neocortex (Angevine, 1975). The anatomical linkages suggest that whatever the dentate granule cells do, their function depends to some extent on the normal function of prefrontal association cortex and vice versa.

It is not surprising, therefore, to find that lesions in the hippocampus and prefrontal cortex (plus some related areas) lead to behavioral effects that are largely overlapping. So much so, in fact, that in the last few years many physiological psychologists have preferred to speak of the prefrontal system and to include the hippocampus in that designation (Iverson, 1976; Kolb, Nonneman, and Singh, 1974; Rosvold, 1972).

Thus the effects of hippocampectomy that Altman and Douglas describe are not unique. One might expect this, given the anatomy and the evolutionary relationship of granule cells to prefrontal cortex. Unfortunately, however, Altman's original argument now seems too narrow—young rats behave not only like adult rats with lesions in hippocampus but also like those with lesions elsewhere in the prefrontal system.

A second point concerns the onset of function. Here too it is important to view the dentate granule cells in context. On the one hand, their late postnatal genesis is a dramatic maturational change and clearly implies a late onset of function. On the other hand, the fact that neurogenesis occurs earlier in other structures does not necessarily imply an earlier onset of function in those structures. Neurogenesis is only the first of a sequence of morphological changes, and functional capacity clearly depends not just on the presence of neurons but on their state of differentiation, myelination, synaptic connectivity, and so on. On these other morphological criteria it is clear that other structures (including prefrontal cortex) in the rat brain are also immature postnatally and that the completion of neurogenesis in dentate gyrus at around thirty days is not the only maturational event at that time that is of potential significance to behavior (Berry, 1976).

In summary, a direct and isolable relationship between hippocampal maturity and behavioral changes in the rat at thirty days is probably unjustified. Instead, it will be necessary to move from a limited concentration on the granule cells as part of the hippocampus to a more careful look at the ontogeny and function of related structures, particularly those comprising the prefrontal system. That a similar approach is warranted at the level of child development can be easily illustrated. Pat Goldman's work on prefrontal cortex in primates suggests a late maturation of function one or two years postnatally. Luria, probably the most authoritative scholar and clinician of human prefrontal cortex, has asserted (1973) that prefrontal cortex in humans begins to mature at five to seven years of age, certainly an interesting figure in terms of this discussion. On other morphological criteria, an extended postnatal maturation of prefrontal cortical association area is apparent (Conel, 1939–1968; Yakovlev and Lecours, 1967).

Do young children behave like adult patients with prefrontal lesions? Actually, the correspondence is usually stated in the reverse. Adult prefrontal patients are almost universally described as childlike. The list of clinical descriptors for prefrontal patients sounds very much like the descriptors we use to describe young children. Both, for instance, are described as impulsive, unable to inhibit first available responses; stereotyped, perseverative; distractible, with short attention spans; concrete versus abstract; dominated by salient cues rather than rules or contexts. Moreover, on many tasks that have been implemented with both young children and adult prefrontal patients, the correspondences in behavior are evident (Rose, in press). But the adult patients are also clearly different from children, and a careful delineation of the specific ways in which they are alike and different is made difficult by the lack of control in human lesion studies.

The animal literature is again an important source of predictions. For the most part the prefrontal lesion literature overlaps with the hippocampal lesion literature and the same predictions would obtain. Because much of the lesioning of prefrontal association cortex has been done in primates rather than rats, however, a greater emphasis on more complex tasks has occurred, leading to a wider range of tasks. Again, it is impossible for me to review extensively the correspondences between the performance of prefrontals and preschool children, but it seems worth mentioning one of the tasks thought to be most representative of prefrontal functioning: delayed alternation.

The delayed alternation problem consists of a series of trials; in each trial two alternatives are presented, one of which contains a reward. After each trial there is a delay; then the same two alternatives are presented but with the reward switched to the formerly unrewarded alternative. Correct responding thus requires alternating choices and remembering the previous choice as a context. Most normal adults take only a few trials to learn the alternation strategy, and it is a very easy task.

Since there was no literature on children's performance, one of my students, Penny Cram, investigated preschool children's performance on this task. She found that even with thirty trials, only 15 percent of three-year-olds were able to alternate successfully, compared with 75 percent of five-year-olds (Cram, 1977).

Other tasks that show deficits after prefrontal lesions can similarly be shown to be impaired in preschool children (Rose, in press). In summary, young children behave not only like hippocampals but like prefrontals and perhaps others as well. And it is certainly true that much of human neocortex requires extended postnatal maturation. Is there anything left of Douglas-Altman? Yes, I think so. While an expansion to the prefrontal system rather than hippocampus alone certainly loses much of the tightness of their original argument, it loses little of the fabric itself. Whereas they concentrated on the granule cells as part of hippocampus, it will be necessary to look somewhat more carefully at the ontogeny and function of those structures afferent to the granule cells as well.

The expansion to a prefrontal system highlights the central weakness of Altman's original hypothesis, or any like it for that matter. At present there is simply no morphological marker or feature cluster that would by itself indicate *functional* maturity. Myelination enjoyed a short history as a marker of maturity, but its inadequacy is now apparent (many neurons, for instance, are never myelinated). Recent work concentrates on physical and chemical features of the synapses themselves and has shown remarkable resolution (Purpura, 1975; Shimono, Nosaka, and Sasaki, 1978). Ultimately, however, it seems apparent that for units at the level we have been discussing, the most logical indicator of functional maturity is behavior itself. In any case, only through the careful correlation of behavioral and structural morphology will the anatomical markers of maturity become apparent (for single neurons, rather than larger structures, the same argument would be made about the essential pairing of anatomy and physiology; Purpura, 1973, 1975).

The inability to directly establish the onset of function independent of behavior itself is a serious drawback; to some extent, any hypothesis like Altman's is inevitably weakened. There is simply no eyewitness to the critical maturational event. No unambiguous fingerprints are available.

Thus evidence that some aspect of the prefrontal system matures at around five years of age must be entirely circumstantial. It can be a credible case, however, to the extent that a predictable pattern of developmental changes occurs. No individual behavioral change would amount to much, even as circumstantial evidence. Only the fact that predictions about clusters of behavioral changes can be sustained is interesting. Under that condition any other explanation of development must also explain the observed pattern of changes—in this case the emergence at around age five of spontaneous alternation, the ability to successfully learn conditional discriminations, to perform delayed alternation, go–no go discriminations, and so on.

Other explanations are clearly possible, but they must also explain the interesting fact that ontogeny fractionates behavior along the same lines that lesions in some regions of the brain (and not others) do. This is not a trivial result, nor is it equally well explained by varying developmental theories.

Any other explanation of the observed developmental changes in behavior must also explain why a similar transition occurs in other animals, only much earlier in their ontogeny. It seems difficult to think of an experiential argument for this.

Not enough evidence for a guilty verdict yet; but perhaps enough for a continuance of the case.

BIBLIOGRAPHY

Altman, J. 1967. Postnatal growth and differentiation of the mammalian brain, with implications for a morphological theory of memory. In *Neurosciences: A study program*, ed. G. Quarton, T. Melnechuk, and F. O. Schmitt. New York: Rockefeller University Press.

Altman, J., Brunner, R. L., and Bayer, S. A. 1973. The hippocampus and behavioral maturation. *Behavioral Biology* 8: 557–596.

Altman, J., and Das, G. D. 1965. Autoradiographic and histological evidence of postnatal hippocampal neurogenesis in rats. *Journal of Comparative Neurology* 124: 319–336.

Angevine, J. B. 1975. Development of the hippocampal region. In *The hippocampus*, (vol. 1), ed. R. L. Isaacson and K. H. Pribram. New York: Plenum.

Bayer, S. A., and Altman, J. 1975. Radiation-induced interference with postnatal hippocampal cytogenesis in rats and its long-term effects on the acquisition of neurons and glia. *Journal of Comparative Neurology* 163: 1–20.

Berry, M. 1976. Development of the cerebral neocortex of the rat. In *Studies on the development of behavior and the nervous system*, ed. G. Gottlieb. New York: Academic Press.

Conel, J. R. 1959–1968. *The postnatal development of the human cerebral cortex*. 8 vols. Cambridge, Mass.: Harvard University Press.

Cram, J. P. 1977. "A comparison of the performance of three-year-olds and five-year-olds on two standard prefrontal tasks." Master's thesis, Tufts University.

Doan, H. M., and Cooper, D. L. 1976. Conditional discrimination learning in children: Two relevant factors. *Child Development* 42: 209–220.

Douglas, R. J. 1967. The hippocampus and behavior. *Psychological Bulletin* 67: 416–442.

Douglas, R. J. 1975. The development of hippocampal function: Implications for theory and for therapy. In *The hippocampus*, Vol. 2, ed. R. L. Isaacson and K. H. Pribram. New York: Plenum Press.

Douglas, R. J., Packouz, K., and Douglas, D. 1972. Development of inhibition in man. *Proceedings of the American Psychological Association* 7: 121–122.

Goldman, A. E., and Denny, J. 1963. The ontogenesis of choice behavior in probability and sequential programs. *Journal of Genetic Psychology* 102: 5–18.

Goldman, P. S. 1972. Developmental determinants of cortical plasticity. *Acta Neurobiologiae Experimentalis* 32: 495–511.

Goldman, P. S. 1974. An alternative to developmental plasticity: Heterology of CNS structures in infants and adults. In *Plasticity and recovery of function in the central nervous system*, ed. D. G. Stein, J. J. Rosen, and N. Butters. New York: Academic Press.

Gollin, E. S. 1965. Factors affecting conditional discrimination in children. *Journal of Comparative and Physiological Psychology* 60: 422–427.

Gollin, E. S., and Liss, P. 1962. Conditional discrimination in children. *Journal of Comparative and Physiological Psychology* 55: 850–855.

Gould, S. J. 1978. *Ever since Darwin*. Cambridge, Mass.: Harvard University Press.

Gratch, G. 1964. Response alternation in children: A developmental study of orientations to uncertainty. *Vita Humana* 7: 49–60.

Haddad, R. K., and Rabe, A. 1969. Modified temporal behavior in rats after large hippocampal lesions. *Experimental Neurology* 23: 310–317.

Heidbreder, E. F. 1928. Problem solving in children and adults. *Journal of Genetic Psychology*, 35: 522–545.

Himwich, W. A. 1976. Developmental neurobiology. In *Biological foundations of psychiatry*, ed. R. G. Grenell and S. Galay. New York: Raven.

Hirsh, R. 1974. The hippocampus and contextual retrieval of information from memory: A theory. *Behavioral Biology* 12: 421–444.

Isaacson, R. L., and Kimble, D. P. 1972. Lesions of the limbic system: Their effects upon hypotheses and frustrations. *Behavioral Biology* 7: 767–793.

Iverson, S. D. 1976. Do hippocampal lesions produce amnesia in animals? *International Review of Neurobiology* 19: 1–50.

Jarrard, L. E. 1965. Hippocampal ablation and operant behavior in the rat. *Psychonomic Science.* 2: 115–116.

Jeffrey, W. E., and Cohen, L. B. 1965. Response tendencies of children in a two-choice situation. *Journal of Experimental Child Psychology* 2: 248–254.

Kolb, B., Nonneman, A. J., and Singh, R. K. 1974. Double dissociation of spatial impairments and perseveration following selective prefrontal lesions in rats. *Journal of Comparative and Physiological Psychology* 87: 772–780.

Leichnetz, G. R., and Astruc, J. 1975a. Efferent connections of the orbito-frontal cortex in the marmoset (Sanguinus oedipus). *Brain Research* 84: 169–180.

Leichnetz, G. R., and Astruc, J. 1975b. Preliminary evidence for a direct projection of the prefrontal cortex to the hippocampus in the squirrel monkey. *Brain, Behavior and Evolution* 11: 335–364.

Lund, R. D. 1978. *Development and plasticity of the brain*. New York: Oxford University Press.

Luria, A. R. 1973. *The working brain: An introduction to neuropsychology*. New York: Basic Books.

Manley, S., and Miller, F. D. 1968. Factors affecting children's alternation and choice behaviors. *Psychonomic Science* 13: 65–66.

Munn, N. L. 1954. Learning in children. In *Manual of child psychology*, ed. L. Carmichael. New York: Wiley.

Nadel, L., and O'Keefe, J. 1974. The hippocampus in pieces and patches. In *Essays on the nervous system*, ed. R. Bellairs and E. G. Gray. Oxford: Clarendon Press.

Odom, R. D. 1967. Problem-solving strategies as a function of age and socio-economic level. *Child Development* 38: 747–752.

Pate, J. L., and Bell, G. L. 1971. Alternation behavior of children in a cross-maze. *Psychonomic Science* 23: 431–432.

Purpura, D. P. 1973. Analysis of morphophysiological developmental processes in mammalian brain. *Research Publications of the Association for Research in Nervous and Mental Disease* 51: 79–112.

Purpura, D. P. 1975. Dendritic differentiation in human cerebral cortex: Normal and aberrant developmental patterns. *Advances in Neurology* 12: 91–100.

Razran, G. H. S. 1933. Conditioned responses in children: A behavioral and quantitative critical review of experimental studies. *Archives of Psychology* 48: 1–192.

Reese, H. W., and Lipsitt, L. P. 1970. *Experimental child psychology.* New York: Academic Press.

Rose, D. Forthcoming. *Neural maturation and cognitive development.* New York: Columbia University Press.

Rosvold, H. E. 1972. The frontal lobe system: Cortical-subcortical interrelationships. *Acta Neurobiologiae Experimentalis* 32: 439–460.

Schmaltz, L. W., and Isaacson, R. L. 1966. The effects of preliminary training conditions upon DRL performance in the hippocampectomized rat. *Physiology and Behavior* 1: 175–182.

Schmaltz, L. W., Wolf, B. P., and Trejo, W. R. 1973. FR, DRL, and discrimination learning in rats following aspiration lesions and penicillin injection into hippocampus. *Physiology and Behavior* 11: 17–22.

Seltzer, B., and Pandya, D. N. 1976. Some cortical projections to the parahippocampal area in the Rhesus monkey. *Experimental Neurology* 50: 146–160.

Shepherd, G. M. 1974. *The Synaptic organization of the brain.* London: Oxford University Press.

Shimono, T., Nosaka, S., and Sasaki, K. 1978. Electrophysiological study of the postnatal development of neuronal mechanisms in the rat cerebellar cortex. *Brain Research* 100: 279–294.

Stevens, R. 1973. Effects of amount of training on reversal learning in hippocampectomized rats. *Physiological Psychology* 1: 377–379.

Stevenson, H. W. 1970. Learning in children. In *Carmichael's manual of child development* (3rd ed., vol. 1), ed. P. H. Mussen. New York: Willey.

Stevenson, H. W., and Hoving, K. L. 1964. Probability learning as a function of age and incentive. *Journal of Experimental Child Psychology* 1: 64–70.

Stevenson, H. W., and Weir, M. W. 1959. Variable affecting children's performance in a probability learning task. *Journal of Experimental Psychology* 57: 403–412.

Van Hoesen, G. W., and Pandya, D. N. 1975. Some connections of the entorhinal (area 28) and perirhinal (area 35) cortices of the Rhesus monkey. I. Temporal lobe afferents. *Brain Research* 95: 1–24.

Van Hoesen, G. W. Pandya, D. N., and Butters, N. 1975. Some connections of the entorhinal (area 28) and perirhinal (area 35) cortices of the Rhesus monkey. II. Frontal lobe afferents. *Brain Research* 95: 25–38.

Weir, M. W. 1964. Developmental changes in problem-solving strategies. *Psychological Review* 71: 473–490.

Wertlieb, D. 1975. "A developmental study of maze behavior in young children." Master's thesis, Tufts University.

White, S. H. 1965. Evidence for a hierarchical arrangement of learning processes. In *Advances in child behavior and development*, vol. 2, ed. L. P. Lipsitt and C. C. Spiker. New York: Academic Press.

White, S. H. 1970. Some general outlines of the matrix of developmental changes between five and seven years. *Bulletin of the Orton Society* 20: 41–57.

Yakovlev, P. I., and Lecours, A. R. 1967. The myelogenetic cycles of regional maturation of the brain. In *Regional development of the brain in early life*, ed. A. Minkowski. Oxford: Blackwell Scientific Publications.

4

The Development of a Spatial Orientation Skill in Normal, Learning-Disabled, and Neurologically Impaired Children

Martha Bridge Denckla, Rita G. Rudel, and Melinda Broman

Spatial disorders acquired in adult life are more likely to arise from damage to the right cerebral hemisphere, particularly if posteriorly placed (Critchley, 1953; McFie, 1969; Hecaen, 1969). Removal of half of the cortex in the first six months of life results in a more severely truncated ultimate level of spatial performance in the case of right-hemidecortication (Kohn and Dennis, 1974). Even when brain damage is more subtle, inferred from signs, and presumably congenital, right-hemisphere deficit contributes more heavily to impaired spatial performance in children than does left (Rudel and Teuber, 1971). The level of adult spatial performance supported by an isolated right brain (Kohn and Dennis, 1974) or an intact right brain (Critchley, 1953; McFie, 1969; Hecaen, 1969; Rudel and Teuber, 1971) coupled with an impaired left brain is thus demonstrably better (closer to normal) than when the reverse situation obtains.

The group of children called dyslexic have long been viewed as specifically developmentally deviant in the constitutional timing of language acquisition. Developmental dyslexia has recently been studied from a psychological perspective that emphasizes relative cognitive strengths rather than innate deficits or lags; Symmes and Rappaport (1972) reported above-average spatial ability in well-adjusted, intelligent, healthy children who presented at school-age with unexpected reading failure. These authors raised the issue of brain differences, or specialized brain organization, in dyslexic children and adults as opposed to brain damage. Neuropsychological studies have confirmed Symmes and Rappaport's finding of dyslexic children's strong spatial skill and added evidence that there is also a preponderance of right-hemisphere processing (reflected in "abnormal" specialization) in dyslexic children (Witelson,

1976). Other neuropsychologists have strengthened the case for
relative left-hemisphere deficiency in dyslexic children (Satz, 1973;
Rourke, 1975; Rourke, 1976; Denckla, 1977). Rourke has even noted
that "those abilities [of dyslexic children] that 'catch up' are not
subserved primarily by the left cerebral hemisphere and those that
either emerge . . . or continue to be significant differentiating
variables are those that are" (Rourke, 1976).

In normal development the performance of certain tasks that in
adults depend on posterior right-hemisphere systems shows curves
with two marked upward slopes, one in early childhood and the
second occurring at some period in the second decade of life (high
"ceiling" compared to verbal proficiency). Between these upward
curves occur plateaus or dips at or about the time of transition to
adolescence (Carey and Diamond, chapter 5, this volume).

We decided to study a task that had been used to test patients
with known acquired lesions and patients with presumed congenital
brain damage (adult and childhood) and to examine the performance
of this task in the contexts of developmental neuropsychology and
developmental dyslexia. We chose route walking, a spatial orientation task that is a simplified but active form of map skill. Our purpose was to study the populations of normal and dyslexic with a
task identifiably spatial in character (Thurstone's S2) and demonstrably associated with right-hemisphere dependency (Semmes et al.,
1955); (reproductions of the maps can be seen in Rudel and Teuber,
1971). Our hypothesis was that normal children would show a development curve with a plateau or dip and then a sharp upward
trend and that dyslexic children would show a steady increment
before the spurt but starting from a lower level than the normals in
early childhood. In short, we sought to demonstrate in dyslexic
children a relative imbalance consistent with previous evidence that
spatial ability may be seen with left-hemisphere deficiency, right-
hemisphere proficiency (Rudel and Teuber, 1971; Kohn and Dennis,
1974; Witelson, 1976).

Nondyslexic children who were otherwise learning disabled are included in the study as controls against the possibility of nonspecific
brain-based effects on task performance. Route drawing was included as a task controlling for visuospatial perception appreciation
of the connected dot-to-dot patterns of the maps but without the
body-movement-in-space requirements. Analysis of the association
of subtle, traditional lateralized neurological signs with route-

walking skills was undertaken in order to further test the hypothesis that inferred left-hemisphere deficit is compatible with better spatial performance than coexists with other neurological impairments.

SUBJECTS

Controls consisted of 152 children (76 boys, 76 girls) distributed thus: 20 in each of the age groups five through ten years and 16 in each of the age groups eleven and twelve years, with equal numbers of boys and girls at each level. They were tested in their own school library or nurse's office in Ft. Lee, New Jersey. Mean IQ was 106 ± 9 (Lorge-Thorndike group test). Teachers were asked to select only average children and to exclude the top 25 percent and the lowest 25 percent of each class or age level. All were observed to be right-handed.

Children with learning disabilities were selected from all those seen in a clinical practice between September 1975 and March 1976. The nature of this clinical practice was such that the physician (M. B. Denckla) accepted referrals only in the capacity of consultant to eleven school districts in a single suburban New Jersey county. All children referred to this practice were known to be of at least educable intelligence, neither legally blind nor hearing impaired, ambulatory, and nonpsychotic. All children came to the office with records documenting normal general physical, visual, and auditory examinations and results of tests (performed within the immediately preceding ten weeks) of intelligence, visual-motor copying skill, psycholinguistic level, reading, spelling, and arithmetic achievement. Also available were teachers' anecdotal descriptions and questionnaires reflecting classroom behavior and social workers' reports of home interviews of parents. Thirty percent of referred children had been interviewed by psychiatrists consulting to the school district of origin. Even these, most suspect of emotional disturbance, were declared "not primarily or significantly disturbed." Unfortunately lacking are more accumulated group data on IQ and achievement correlations for each grade level of the eleven sending districts; this data gap precluded construction and utilization of the multiple regression equation method (Rutter and Yule, 1975) of defining reading disabled, and so forth, later adopted and reported by us (Denckla, Rudel, and Broman, 1979). Fortunately, however, the sample of learning-disabled children selected in the present study of spatial orientation skill had IQ scores in the middle range (± 1 SD) of the normal IQ distribution. As discussed in Gaddes (1976) the expected relationship between reading (or other academic achievement) and IQ is not distorted within this middle range.

All children who were referred to the practice of Martha Bridge Denckla in the designated eighteen-month period were given the spatial tasks.

The criteria for selection of learning disabled children whose spatial scores were analyzed for this study, however, were derived from those of Myklebust and Boshes (cited in Gaddes, 1976), whereby a learning quotient, or LQ, below 90 on one or more of the tests of achievement in the presence of a verbal or performance IQ of 90 or above constitutes the operational definition of learning-disabled. If both verbal and performance IQ were below 90, the child could not be included in the study. If the reading quotient fell below 90, the child was designated dyslexic. If the spelling or arithmetic quotient fell below 90 but the reading quotient reached 90 or above, the child was designated nondyslexic but otherwise learning disabled and was subclassified by the algorithm of successive approximation (Gaddes, 1976; Denckla, 1977) starting with exclusion factors and task failures (not retarded, not psychotic, not paralytic, not sensory handicapped, not educationally deprived, demonstrably underachieving).

The algorithm proceeded by searching for physiological correlates as revealed by neurological examination and for marked intraindividual discrepancy as revealed by percentile rankings on two balanced multiple-choice tests of differing face validity, the Peabody picture vocabulary test, and the Raven's coloured progressive matrices, clinically presumed to be more polarized for verbal and spatial factors than are verbal and performance quotients (Mattis, French, and Rapin, 1975). Each child whose spatial scores were included in this study achieved fiftieth percentile or better on one but not both of these tests, but this was a de facto post hoc characteristic of the sample rather than a selection criterion by design.

The learning-disabled sample consisted of 153 children distributed thus: 25 six- and seven-year-olds (17 boys, 8 girls), 32 eight-year-olds (22 boys, 10 girls), 32 nine-year-olds (25 boys, 7 girls), 31 ten-year-olds (21 boys, 10 girls), 17 eleven-year-olds (14 boys, 3 girls), and 16 twelve-year-olds (12 boys, 4 girls).

Neurological examinations revealed that all but five of the

learning-disabled children had a minimum of four signs of either the traditional, classic type of the developmental, slow-for-age-type as summarized by Denckla (1978). Classical *neurological* signs (among which asymmetry of signs provide the most convincing evidence of abnormality, however subtle) include reflex hyper- or hypoactivity; pathological reflexes (Babinski sign); weakness; hyper- or hypotonia; pathological postures, arm movements, or gait patterns; involuntary movements; coordination deficits with qualitative characteristics of cerebellar impairment; fixed severe nonparalytic strabismus; abnormal extraocular movements; nystagmus; dysarthria qualitatively implicating corticobulbar, basal ganglia or cerebellar impairment; and deficits in sensation and discrimination (visual, auditory, haptic).

Signs that are developmental are not susceptible to interpretation as abnormal, although they may in some cases eventually implicate impairment, because descriptively these are appearances or performances normally seen in children of certain ages younger than the age of the patient. Examples are failure to reach a milestone such as walking or talking at an age within the normal range and persistence of unsolicited associated or overflow movements beyond the age at which these have normally disappeared. Only those with traditional signs (often subtle) were classified as neurologically impaired whether or not developmental signs coexisted. These were then further divided into those with right-sided signs only, left-sided signs only, or bilateral signs. All eight children found to have only right-sided neurological signs were also dyslexic.

A subcategory was pure familial developmental dyslexia, with at least one first-degree relative (mother, father, or sibling) having a history of dyslexia and with a neurological examination free of traditional neurological signs, that is, they had only developmental signs.

METHODS

We modified the route-finding task of Semmes et al. (1955) and Rudel and Teuber (1971) in two ways. Five of the ten maps were drawn by each child while five maps were walked, and time to complete each map was recorded, to evaluate strategies among children equally successful in route finding. Alternative subjects and controls received one set of five maps to draw and the other five maps to walk; order of walking and drawing was similarly alternated. Five-year-olds were given drawing only.

SCORING

Each map, whether walked or drawn, was scored for total number of correct moves. Minor deviations (slightly curved routes walked, line quality, and graphomotor control) were not considered incorrect so long as the point-to-point path was indicated. In addition, each map, walked or drawn, was also scored according to the method of Kohn and Dennis (1974). A score of 3 indicated a perfect performance; 2, correct localization of start and finish points with a maximum of two incorrect turns in the intervening moves; 1, incorrect localization of either start or end point; 0, complete inability to give a sense of the general configuration of the route. Failure to find the starting point on the third, fourth, and fifth maps led to a score of zero on all five maps. The scoring was done by two assistants who were blind to the children's diagnostic categories. Interrater reliability, tested by both assistants for the normal control eleven- and twelve-year-olds, was reflected in a correlation coefficient of 0.68.

ANALYSIS

Analysis of variance (ANOVA) was carried out on correct moves walked, correct moves drawn, Kohn-Dennis (1974) walking score, and Kohn-Dennis drawing score. These variables were analyzed for the normal sample by four separate two-way, age-by-sex, ANOVAs. Scores for normal, nondyslexic, and dyslexic children on the same variables were analyzed in the same way.

Retrospective comparisons of individual group means were made by the Newman-Keuls procedure. Such comparisons were carried out for normal-versus-nondyslexic, normal-versus-dyslexic, and nondyslexic-versus-dyslexic mean scores for each of the variables listed. Comparisons among age levels within groups of the same diagnostic category were also carried out.

Patients with classic neurological signs were divided into three groups, according to lateralization of signs or the presence of bilateral signs, and were compared with respect to rank scores on the spatial-orientation variables by Jonckheere's test and Dunn's multiple comparisons. Finally, Pearson product-moment correlations were computed between spatial orientation variables and several psychometric, academic, and neurological variables known for the learning-disabled population. (Statistical references are Bradley, 1968; Hollander and Wolfe, 1973; and Winer, 1971.)

RESULTS

Normal Children

Age was a significant factor. In both route walking and drawing, older children performed better (table 4.1). Walking and drawing scores computed by the Kohn-Dennis method showed similar age differences. Drawing of maps reached an asymptote earlier than walking.

Post hoc comparisons of differences between successive age levels revealed significantly better map drawing at six than at five years ($p < 0.01$) with little change in scores between age levels thereafter.

The mean number of correct moves walked (31.7) was still less than 75 percent of all possible correct moves at eleven years, with a relative plateau for ages eight through eleven.

Table 4.1
Mean scores of five- to twelve-year-old normal children of route-walking and route-drawing variables

		Drawing		Walking	
Age	Number	Correct moves[a]	Kohn-Dennis score[b]	Correct moves[c]	Kohn-Dennis score[d]
5	20	17.6	4.7	—	—
6	20	34.1	10.9	18.0	4.5
7	20	37.0	12.6	22.2	5.6
8	20	40.3	13.0	26.9	7.1
9	20	40.2	13.4	28.7	7.8
10	20	39.1	13.1	28.5	7.2
11	16	42.7	14.6	31.7	7.9
12	16	40.2	13.9	31.0	8.8

a. $F = 20.902$, $df = 7,136$, $p < 0.001$, for age.
b. $F = 21.169$, $df = 7,136$, $p < 0.001$, for age.
c. $F = 21.415$, $df = 6,118$. $p < 0.001$, for age.
d. $F = 3.473$, $df = 6,118$, $p < 0.001$, for age.

Sex was not a significant factor in any of the analyses of map drawing or walking, and age interacted significantly with sex for drawing only($F_{7,136} = = 2,130$, $p < 0.05$). On individual comparisons girls drew significantly fewer correct lines than boys at age five only ($p < 0.05$). At each age level; boys walked more correct paths, that is, means showed a consistent trend in favor of the boys, but the trend did not reach statistical significance.

Learning-Disabled Children

Diagnostic group was a major factor in all age-by-group analyses of route finding (table 4.2). Both dyslexic and nondyslexic children made fewer correct moves walking than normals (both p's < 0.01) and lower walking scores (both p's < 0.05). Dyslexic children did not differ from controls on any of the drawing tasks, whereas nondyslexic children (learning-disabled) were significantly worse than controls on drawing (all p's < 0.05; table 4.3).

Age was a significant factor in all analyses of variance (all p's < 0.05 or greater). For none of the variables did age interact significantly with group. For both walking variables, individual comparisons yielded significant differences between eleven- and twelve-year-old and among six-, seven-, and eight-year-old dyslexic children (all p's < 0.05). Again, a plateau is demonstrated, starting at eight and ending at eleven years, with an upward trend indicated.

Table 4.2
Mean scores of six- to twelve-year-old dyslexic and nondyslexic learning-disabled children on route-walking variables

Age	Number of dyslexics	Number of non-dyslexics	Correct moves[a]		Kohn-Dennis score[b]	
			Dyslexic	Nondyslexic	Dyslexic	Nondyslexic
6–7	10	13	16.1	10.1	3.8	3.1
8	17	22	14.2	11.9	3.4	3.6
9	15	17	17.0	28.0	4.3	7.7
10	14	17	23.6	21.7	5.5	5.3
11	10	9	29.6	23.7	8.1	6.3
12	9	7	34.0	30.3	8.9	8.7

a. $F = 6.569$, $df = 2,274$, $p < 0.01$ for group.
b. $F = 3.863$, $df = 2,272$, $p < 0.05$ for group.

Table 4.3
Mean scores of six- to twelve-year-old dyslexic and nondyslexic learning-disabled children on route-drawing variables

Age	Number of dyslexics	Number of non-dyslexics	Correct moves[a]		Kohn-Dennis score[b]	
			Dyslexic	Nondyslexic	Dyslexic	Nondyslexic
6–7	4	9	34.0	29.0	10.7	9.5
8	11	13	38.8	32.9	12.8	11.6
9	14	13	35.7	37.4	12.0	12.1
10	12	15	40.5	40.7	13.3	13.7
11	8	9	35.4	37.6	12.7	12.3
12	9	6	38.8	35.4	12.7	12.3

a. $F = 3.646$, $df = 2,237$, $p < 0.05$ for group.
b. $F = 3.403$, $df = 2,237$, $p < 0.05$ for group.

Table 4.4
Mean correct moves walked by familial dyslexics compared with normals at five age levels

Age	Dyslexic mean score (N)	Normal mean score (N)
8	19.5 (4)	26.9 (30)
9	35.3 (3)	28.7 (30)
10	31.5 (6)	28.5 (30)
11	39.7 (3)	31.7 (30)[a]
12	42.7 (3)	31.0 (30)[b]

a. $R_1 = 43.5$, $p < 0.10$.
b. $R_1 = 49.5$, $p < 0.025$.

The Kohn-Dennis scoring sharpened the age trend for dyslexic children and revealed a clear discontinuity; those over ten years made superior scores (figure 4.1).

Rank order of groups showed that at almost each age level (except age nine), where they merged, the controls were best and non-dyslexic subjects worse. However, in groups over ten years, the rank order of the groups changed; dyslexic children had the highest scores for walking (tables 4.2 and 4.3).

When route-walking scores were converted to ranks and compared (Wilcoxon rank sum) at each age level, the six familial dyslexic children aged eleven and twelve years scored significantly higher than same-age controls (table 4.4).

Classical neurological signs were negatively correlated with route-walking scores. The psychometric scores most positively correlated with route-walking scores were block design, object assembly, and Raven's progressive matrices scores (table 4.5).

Neurologically Impaired Children
The learning-disabled population consisted of some children with developmental signs only and some traditional neurological signs. In addition, some were dyslexic and some were not. Correlational analysis (table 4.5) revealed that traditional neurological signs in general were associated with impaired route-finding. The children were ranked as follows: those with right-sided signs did best; fol-

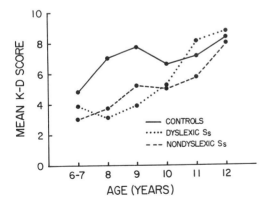

4.1
Relationship of age to Kohn-Dennis route-walking scores for learning-disabled subjects (dyslexic and nondyslexic) and controls

Table 4.5
Correlations of walking and drawing scores in learning-disabled subjects with IQ scores, academic test scores, and neurological status

Spatial orientation score	Nonsignificant correlation[a]	Moderately positive correlation[b] $r = +0.20$ to $+0.39$	Highly positive correlation[c] $r = +0.40$ to $+0.63$	Negative correlation[d] $r = -0.16$ to -0.39
Correct moves drawn	Verbal IQ Reading age Math age	Peabody	Full-scale IQ Performance IQ Block design Object assembly Ravens	Neurological signs
Correct moves walked	Reading age Math age	Verbal IQ Peabody	Full-scale IQ Performance IQ Block design Object assembly Ravens	Neurological signs

a. $p > 0.05$.
b. p between 0.05 and 0.001.
c. $p < 0.001$.
d. p between 0.05 and 0.001.

lowed by those with left-sided signs; those with bilateral signs were the worst group. For drawing, no subgroup differences were found (Jonckheere's test). With the route-walking variables, however, the ranking was confirmed as valid (table 4.6), again using Jonckheere's test.

Comparisons between individual groups (Dunn's multiple-comparison procedure with all reported p values for one-tailed tests) revealed more correct moves walked and higher Kohn-Dennis scores achieved by children with right-sided signs than by children in the other neurological groups. The mean scores of the children with right-sided signs (all were dyslexic) were consistently somewhat higher than those with left-sided signs, but the difference was not statistically significant (table 4.6).

DISCUSSION

Normal Development
The earlier ceiling of proficiency on route drawing suggests that despite common visuospatial perceptual demands, the movement of the whole body in space (route walking) requires a later developing aspect of neurological integration. The Kohn-Dennis route-finding score achieved by the average eight-year-old in our study was at the level of mature right-hemidecorticate subjects reported by Kohn and Dennis (1974). Concordant with this finding, eight years was the age level achieved by right-hemidecorticate subjects on other spatial tests (Kohn and Dennis, 1974).

Carey and Diamond (1977; chapter 5, this volume) have reported that for performances involving the encoding (for recognition) of unfamiliar faces and voices the normal developmental curve is one of steady improvement between ages six and ten years, then a plateau or dip between ages ten and fourteen before a spurt to adult

Table 4.6
Mean scores of neurologically impaired groups on walking variables

Group	N	Correct moves	Kohn-Dennis score
Right-sided signs	8	22.3[a]	5.6[b]
Left-sided signs	10	21.5	4.7
Bilateral signs	41	16.9	4.4

a. Better than all other groups, $p < 0.05$.
b. Better than all other groups, $p < 0.025$.

level of performance after age fourteen. These data suggest to Carey and Diamond that a major reorganization of task strategy, in turn based on a brain-maturational change, has taken place. Of neuropsychological interest is not only the relatively late blooming nature of the mature performance but the period of plateau or dip, which suggests a shift in the balance of contributing brain systems. Waber's data (chapter 2, this volume) correlating the timing of puberty to eventual mature level of performance suggests a further physical mechanism for the individual timing of brain-maturational change.

Learning-Disabled Children
Symmes and Rappaport (1972) and Witelson (1976) present evidence suggesting that the brains of children with pure developmental dyslexia are skewed (rather than defective) in specialization, with more proficiency in spatial than linguistic matters. In our studies learning-disabled children, whether dyslexic or not, did not equal controls in route-finding throughout the age range six through twelve years. Whatever differences there were, however, favored the dyslexic subgroup. (Nondyslexic children drew maps more poorly than normals, perhaps because of fine-motor incoordination or attentional impulsivity.) A trend toward spatial superiority among all dyslexic children, but particularly those pure familial cases, emerged only after age ten.

In addition, the developmental curve for dyslexic children (including the eight with right-sided-only classic neurological signs) is shaped differently from that of the controls or even the nondyslexic learning disabled, as seen in the figure 4.1. The dyslexic children, whom we strongly suspect are relatively left-hemisphere deficient, show no plateau but rather a steady upward growth curve in the performance of the route-walking spatial task. This suggests that the dyslexic group, unlike the other children, do not go through a transitional period of reorganization or shift in strategy. Their imbalance (Witelson, 1976) or bias toward a right-hemisphere-mediated strategy is bespoken by early poor and late good performance on this route-walking task.

Right-hemisphere-mediated skills spurt in performance about age thirteen for normal children on tasks as disparate as face recognition (Carey, chapter 1, this volume) or learning Braille letters by touch (Rudel, Denckla, and Spalten, 1974). Children with excellent right-hemisphere-mediated skills may appear to lag behind performance

of normal children, whose left-hemisphere-mediated processes uti-
lized for these tasks (walking or drawing a sequence of routes or
drawing Bender-Gestalt designs) develop earlier. Maturation of
callosal systems after age ten (Yakovlev, 1967) could connect a superior right hemisphere with an average left; even an impaired but
developing left hemisphere reaching a sufficient basal level could
underlie what appears to be a second-decade spurt. Another possible
underlying neural mechanism could be sufficient maturation of right
frontal system to allow output expression of right posterior brain
function. Spatial ability at the perceptual level, then, might actually
exceed the average but be effectively "mute," much like the language
comprehension capability of the right hemisphere. The hypothesis
that young dyslexic children already possess but cannot yet express
superior route-finding ability could be tested by a task of judging
the route-finding performance of another person. A study of judging
Bender-Gestalt productions found evidence of unexpressed excellent
spatial perception among young dyslexic children (Owen et al.,
1971). Although less proficient at Bender-Gestalt design copying,
these prepubescent dyslexic children surpassed age-matched peers
when judging the accuracy of others' copies.

Neurologically Impaired Children
Children with evidence of left-hemisphere damage (right-sided
neurological signs) only were the most spatially able of all neurologically impaired children. Kohn and Dennis (1974) found that even an
isolated right brain-half can support more spatial ability than an
isolated left brain-half. The isolated left brain-half "ceilings" at the
normal eight-year level. Integrity of the right hemisphere appears to
be necessary for later childhood development of spatial ability, even
though, when tested within the first decade, damage to either hemisphere impairs spatial performance. Aligned with data from studies
of facial and vocal recognition (Carey, chapter 1, this volume) our
study of route-walking ability seems consistent with the interpretation that there is a shift in strategy, left- to right-brain-preponder-
ant, on tasks that neuropsychologists categorize as visuospatial performances. It is suggested that callosal and/or frontal systems possess both functional capacities and timing of developmental anatomy appropriate to mediate this apparent shift.

ACKNOWLEDGMENTS

This work was supported by the Robinson Ophthalmic and Dyslexia Research Fund, Presbyterian Hospital, in the City of New York (Martha B. Denckla, chief investigator).

Grateful acknowledgments are due to Maureen Dennis and Judith Rappaport for helpful suggestions about data analyses and organization of the manuscript, to David Gilder for his editorial assistance, and to Donna Puccini for typing the manuscript.

REFERENCES

Bradley, J. V. 1968. *Distribution-free statistical tests.* Englewood Cliffs, N.J.: Prentice-Hall.

Carey, S., and Diamond, R. 1977. From piecemeal to configurational representation of faces. *Science* 195: 312–314.

Critchley, M. 1953. *The parietal lobes.* New York: Hafner Publishing Company.

Denckla, M. B. 1977. Minimal brain dysfunction and dyslexia: Beyond diagnosis by exclusion. In *Topics in child neurology,* ed. M. Blaw, I. Rapin, and M. Kinsbourne, pp. 243–262. New York: Spectrum Publications.

Denckla, M. B. 1978. Minimal brain dysfunction. In *Education and the brain,* ed. J. S. Chall and A. F. Mirsky, pp. 223–268. Chicago: University of Chicago Press.

Denckla, M. B., Rudel, R. G., and Broman, M. 1979. Tests which discriminate dyslexic boys from other non-dyslexic learning-disabled boys. Paper presented at the meeting of the International Neuropsychology Society, New York, February 3, 1979.

Gaddes, W. H. 1976. Prevalence estimates and the need for a definition of learning disabilities. In *The neuropsychology of learning disorders,* ed. R. M. Knights and D. J. Bakker, pp. 3–24. Baltimore, Md.: University Park Press.

Hecaen, H. 1969. Aphasic, apraxic, and agnosic syndromes in right and left hemisphere lesions. In *Handbook of clinical neurology.* Vol. 4: *Disorders of speech, perception, and symbolic behavior,* ed. P. J. Vinken and G. W. Bruyn. Amsterdam: North-Holland Publishing Company.

Hollander, M., and Wolfe, D. A. 1973. *Nonparametric statistical methods.* New York: Wiley.

Kohn, B., and Dennis, M. 1974. Selective impairments of visuospatial abilities in infantile hemiplegics after right cerebral hemidecortication. *Neuropsychologia* 12: 505–512.

Mattis, S., French, J. H., and Rapin, I. 1975. Dyslexia in children and adults: Three independent neurological syndromes. *Devel. Med. Child. Neurol.* 17: 150–163.

McFie, J. 1969. The diagnostic significance of disorders of higher nervous activity: Syndromes related to frontal, temporal, parietal, and occipital lesions. In *Handbook of clinical neurology.* vol 4: *Disorders of speech, perception, and symbolic behavior,* ed. P. J. Vinken and G. W. Bruyn, chap. 1. Amsterdam: North-Holland Publishing Company.

Owen, F. W., Adams, P. A., Forrest, T., Stolz, L. M., and Fisher, S. 1971. *Learning disorders in children: Sibling study.* Monograph of the Society for Research in Child Development 36, no. 4.

Rourke, B. P. 1975. Brain-behavior relationships in children with learning disabilities: A research program. *Am. Psychol.* 30: 911–920.

Rourke, B. P. 1976. Reading retardation in children: Developmental lag or deficit: In *The neuropsychology of learning disorders,* ed. R. M. Knights and D. J. Bakker, pp. 125–137. Baltimore, Md.: University Park Press.

Rudel, R. G., Denckla, M. B., and Spalten, E. 1974. The functional asymmetry of Braille letter learning in normal, sighted children. *Neurology* 24: 733–738.

Rudel, R. G., and Teuber, H.-L. 1971. Spatial orientation in normal children and in children with early brain injury. *Neuropsychologia* 9: 401–407.

Rutter, M., and Yule, W. 1975. The concept of specific reading retardation. *J. Child Psychol. Psychiatr.* 16: 181–197.

Satz, P., and Van Nostrand, G. K. 1973. Developmental dyslexia: An evaluation of a theory. In *The disabled learner: Early detection and intervention,* ed. P. Satz and J. J. Ross, pp. 121–148. Rotterdam: University of Rotterdam Press.

Semmes, J., Weinstein, S., Ghent, L., and Teuber, H.-L. 1955. Spatial orientation in man after cerebral injury. I: Analysis of locus of lesion. *J. Psychol.* 39: 226–244.

Symmes, J. S., and Rappaport, J. L. 1972. Unexpected reading failure. *Am. J. Orthopsychiat.* 42: 82–91.

Winer, B. J. 1971. *Statistical principles in experimental design.* New York: McGraw-Hill.

Witelson, S. F. 1976. Abnormal right hemnisphere specialization in developmental dyslexia. In *The Neuropsychology of learning disorders,* ed. R. M. Knights and D. J. Bakker, pp. 223–255. Baltimore, Md.: University Park Press.

Yakovlev, P. I., and Lecours, A. R. 1967. The myelogenetic cycles of regional maturation in the brain. In *Regional development of the brain in early life,* ed. A. Minkowski, pp. 3–70. Oxford: Blackwell.

5

Maturational Determination of the Developmental Course of Face Encoding

Susan Carey
and
Rhea Diamond

From measurements of head circumference, Epstein has shown that during childhood the brain grows in spurts and plateaus (Epstein, 1974a). He has also shown that growth spurts are correlated with periods of marked intellectual gain (ages five to seven) and that plateaus in growth are correlated with periods of relatively little intellectual gain (ages twelve to fourteen). These relationships certainly do not establish a maturational component to intellectual development. As Epstein (1974b) points out, periods of rapid brain growth might reflect intellectual activity caused by some third factor. Nonetheless, the correlations are suggestive. Of course, intellectual development is not all of a piece; not all cognitive skills spurt and plateau at the same time. Epstein's "whole-brain" approach can at most sketch the broadest lines of maturational constraints on intellectual development.

For a finer-grained attack on the possible contribution of maturational factors to cognitive development, a different approach is required. Relatively isolated cognitive systems must be identified, systems that might be expected to have distinctive developmental histories for which explanations can be sought. Language is widely held to be such a domain (Chomsky, 1974; Lenneberg, 1967, 1974); but language itself is a complex, multileveled capacity, and the relations of its components during development are not well understood. A preliminary hunch about a simpler, yet highly specialized, cognitive domain led us to examine face perception.

THE PSYCHOLOGY OF FACE ENCODING

Our capacity to recognize faces has two aspects: first, a productive ability to encode new faces, to form some representation in memory of a previously unfamiliar face and, second, the ability to recognize that face subsequently. Both are prodigious. Bahrick, Bahrick, and Wittlinger (1975) asked subjects to pick the familiar face from among five taken from high school yearbooks. Only one of the five came from the subject's own yearbook; the rest were from other yearbooks of the same period. Not only were recognition rates over 90 percent; they were independent of class size (from 90 to 800) and of time elapsed between graduation and test (from three months to thirty-five years). Thus in a three- or four-year period, and without conscious effort, high school students can make 800 faces familiar as easily as they can make 90 faces familiar. Even more astoundingly, they can recognize those faces years later as well as they can a few months later, indicating that learning new faces does not interfere with the representations of those already in memory. The limits of this enormous but everyday capacity, if any, have not been found.

Much more than a person's identity is read from a face; mood and momentary expression and a host of other properties such as age, health, and character are also read. The social functions served by face perception are considerable, and it is not surprising that adults have developed capacities for extracting from faces the information relevant to these functions.

Intuitively, then, people seem very good at exploiting the information contained in a human face. Faces seem to pose special problems to a pattern-recognition device. Large numbers of extremely similar stimuli must be discriminated, and mental representations must be formed adequate to support recognition when faces are transformed by age, fashion, or changes in weight or health.

Evidence from a number of sources supports the intuition that the encoding of faces (the making of a previously unfamiliar face familiar) has psychological properties not shared by the encoding of items from other perceptual classes. Encoding faces seems special in three ways: with respect to certain psychophysical effects, with respect to neural substrate, and with respect to developmental history.

The Psychophysical Effects

Hochberg and Galper (1967) showed that stimulus inversion dramatically interfered with success in encoding faces in a forced-choice recognition paradigm. This disadvantage was demonstrated in a situation in which faces were presented inverted during both inspection and subsequent recognition trials. Figure 5.1 presents sample items.

Inspection
(upright)

Recognition
(upright)

Inspection
(inverted)

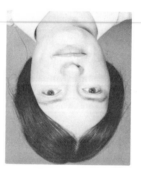

Recognition
(inverted)

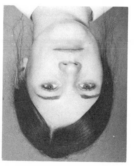 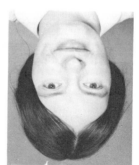

5.1
Sample of items used by Yin (1970a)

This effect differs then from Rock's demonstration (1974) that inversion affects recognition of a familiar face (figure 5.2). Hochberg and Galper's finding (1967) is that inversion affects the formation of an adequate representation of an unfamiliar face, even when there is no mismatch between the representation formed during inspection and the stimulus later presented for recognition.

Yin (1970a) extended the Hochberg and Galper findings by showing that the encoding of faces was more vulnerable to inversion than was the encoding of houses, stick figures of men, costumes, bridges, or airplanes. In these studies the effect of inversion on encoding faces was typically about 30 percent, while the effect on encoding of other stimuli was typically between 10 and 15 percent. Scapinello and Yarmey (1970) and Yarmey (1971) replicated Yin's findings for faces and buildings and extended the classes of stimuli that have been compared with human faces to include dogs' faces. Finally, Fish (1976) added landscapes to the classes of stimuli that are less vulnerable to inversion than are faces (the Yin effect). Thus the first way in which face encoding is special is that it is more impaired by stimulus inversion than is the encoding of members of any other stimulus class examined so far.

The Neural Substrate
Studies of the effects of brain lesions (Benton and Van Allen, 1968; De Renzi, Faglioni, and Spinnler, 1968; Milner, 1968; Warrington and James, 1967a), studies of commisurotomy patients (Levy, Trevarthen, and Sperry, 1972), and studies of visual field asymmetries in normal adults (Geffen, Bradshaw, and Wallace, 1971; Hilliard, 1973; Klein, Moscovitch, and Vigna, 1976; Rizzolatti, Umilta, and Berlucci, 1971) have demonstrated that the right hemisphere is critically involved in the encoding of unfamiliar faces. Of course, faces are not unique in this regard, since the right hemisphere is critically involved in the encoding of many aspects of spatial configuration (Fontenot, 1973; Gross, 1972; McKeever and Huling, 1970; Robertshaw and Sheldon, 1976). Yin (1970b) presented evidence that right-hemisphere specialization for encoding upright faces was a separable component of right-hemisphere specialization for encoding visual configurations. He showed that patients with right posterior lesions were impaired, relative to normals and patients with other lesions, on the encoding of upright faces but not on the encoding of inverted faces or on the encoding of upright

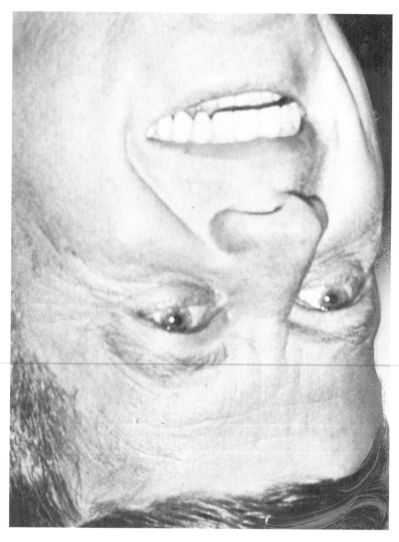

5.2
Example of Rock's demonstration (1974)

or inverted houses. The specificity of their deficit resulted in the absence of the normal materials-by-orientation interaction; inversion affected the encoding of faces no more than the encoding of houses.

The comparison of inverted faces and upright faces as stimuli becomes particularly relevant to the issue of neural specialization for faces. Right-hemisphere lesions have been shown to impair performance on a number of tasks involving visuospatial configurations such as nonsense figures (Kimura, 1963), overlapping figures (De Renzi, Scotti, and Spinnler, 1969), Raven's progressive matrices (Paterson and Zangwill, 1944), and irregular arrays of dots (Kimura, 1963; Warrington and James, 1967b). As visuospatial configurations, inverted faces do not differ from upright faces. Therefore something beyond the mere pattern properties of faces must account for the specific deficit of Yin's patients in encoding upright faces.

Suppose the view for which Yin presented evidence is correct, namely, that there is a component of right-hemisphere specialization for the encoding of visuospatial configurations that is specific to the encoding of upright faces. In this case a visual field study involving the encoding of unfamiliar faces should show that the left visual field advantage for upright faces is greater than the left visual field advantage for inverted faces. This result was obtained (Leehey et al., 1978). A previous study had failed to find this expected interaction (Ellis and Shepherd, 1975); the methodological problems with this earlier study are discussed by Leehey et al. (1978).

Leehey (personal communication) has repeated this study using a new set of faces as stimuli. She also examined lateral asymmetries for cars, houses, and chairs in both orientations. The pattern of results in Leehey et al. was replicated for faces but was not found for any of the other three materials.

Therefore the second way in which encoding of faces is special is that there is a component of right-hemisphere specialization for encoding upright instances. This is not the case for any of the other classes of stimuli so far examined.

The Developmental Curve
Several reports indicate that young children are worse at encoding unfamiliar faces than are older children (Goldstein and Chance, 1964, 1965; Kagan and Klein, 1973; Saltz and Sigel, 1967). Further, Goldstein showed that eight-year-olds were less affected by inversion of faces in a paired-associates learning task than were adults

(Goldstein, 1965). These results were from scattered age groups, on a variety of different tasks. In none of these studies were faces compared directly with other perceptual classes.

We have examined the development of face encoding in five separate studies. In all cases a characteristic course of development was discovered, a pattern not shared by performance on other stimuli, including inverted faces. First, we ran the Yin faces-and-houses task developmentally (Carey and Diamond, 1977; Carey, Diamond, and Woods, in press). We found that the performance of six- and eight-year-olds did not show the normal adult interaction between materials and orientation. That is, for the younger children the effect of inversion was no greater on faces than on houses (figure 5.3). Figure 5.4 shows that the emergence of a significant effect of orientation on faces at age ten is due entirely to the improvement between ages six and ten in the encoding of upright faces. There is no change in performance on inverted faces over the entire age range studied. These results were replicated in a second study with a new group of eight-, nine-, and ten-year-olds. Again there was no materials-by-orientation interaction at age eight, while the nine- and ten-year-olds showed the normal adult pattern. As figures 5.3 and 5.4 show, the Yin effect diminishes at ages twelve and fourteen, to reemerge at age sixteen. This is due to a decline in performance on upright faces at ages twelve and fourteen.

The third study involved upright faces alone, utilizing the depth-of-encoding paradigm of Bower and Karlin (1974). We found that young children, like adults, remembered faces better when they judged likability of the person during the inspection than when they assigned sex. There was no interaction between size of the depth-of-encoding effect and age, over the range seven to fourteen years (figure 5.5). Blaney and Winograd (1978) have recently reported similar results for six-, eight-, and ten-year-olds. For our present purpose, the importance of our depth-of-encoding study was that the course of development for encoding upright faces that had been obtained with the Yin materials was replicated with new subjects and new faces as stimuli. Again there was an increase until age ten or eleven, followed by a significant decline. Moreover, this basic developmental course did not change when more adequate encoding was induced at all ages by requiring subjects to make likability judgments during inspection (Carey, Diamond, and Woods, in press).

In the fourth study children's performance on a very different task

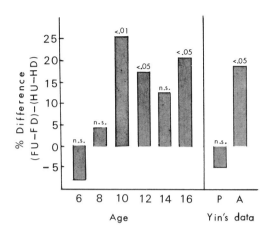

5.3
Effect of orientation on faces and houses. FU = faces upright; FD = faces
upside down; HU = houses upright; HD = houses upside down.

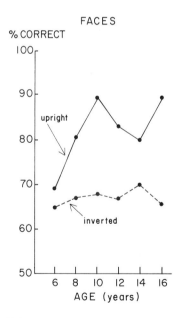

5.4
Performance on upright and inverted faces

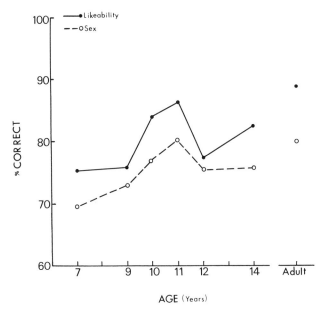

5.5
Recognition memory for upright faces

of face encoding was assessed and compared directly with published data on the performance of patients with right-hemisphere lesions. The task requires the subject to find three photographs of a target face among six comparison photographs. All stimuli are present simultaneously; the comparison photographs are either physical matches or differ from the target in lighting, expression, or angle of view. The results are shown in figure 5.6. There is a dramatic increase in performance until age nine or ten, no subsequent change through age fourteen, and then a significant increase to the adult level by age sixteen (Carey, Diamond, and Woods, in press). We believe that this curve is a variant of that in the Yin study and the depth-of-encoding study. The fact that ten-year-olds are not at the level of sixteen-year-olds (and adults) implies that some capacity tapped by this task increases during the years from ten to sixteen. We suggest that this advance is masked, in the years before sixteen, by another developmental process. This other developmental process, we propose, is the source of the decline in face encoding at ages twelve and fourteen seen in the two earlier experiments. The results of this study also confirm the finding that the performance of

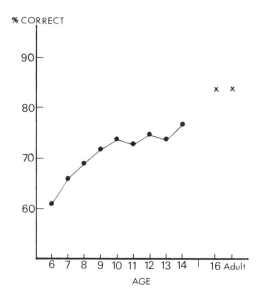

% CORRECT

5.6
Performance on upright faces (Benton and Van Allen's task)

children under nine resembles that of patients with right posterior lesions. The six- and seven-year-olds perform at the same level as
severely impaired patients with right-hemisphere damage, the eight-
and nine-year-olds perform like the possibly impaired, and the ten-
year-olds, while not at the normal adult level, are within the normal
adult range.

   Finally, the fifth study showed that children under ten rely on
more superficial, piecemeal cues in their encoding of unfamiliar faces
than do older children and adults (Diamond and Carey, 1977).
Young children were susceptible to confounding by hairstyle, hats,
glasses, and so on. If the recognition foil wore the same hat as the
target person, that recognition foil was frequently misidentified. Facial expression also played different roles in the encoding strategies
of younger and older children. Care was taken to ensure that the
children understood the task by providing practice on items in
which their classmates had been models. As long as the faces were
already familiar, the confounding cues had no effect on performance. From this result and others, (Carey, 1978), we hypothesized
that young children do not differ markedly from adults in the form

in which they ultimately represent a familiar face. That is, they do not represent their mother's face in terms of hairstyle or glasses. Rather, they differ in the efficiency with which they are able to encode new faces and are restricted to encoding new faces in terms of relatively piecemeal information. Much more input from a new face is required for a young child to form an adequate representation of that face.

To put our hypothesis concretely: six-year-olds may require several minutes of exposure to a moving, changing face to form as adequate a representation of that face as ten-year-olds form from a few seconds of exposure to a still photograph.

This statement of the hypothesis leaves open the nature of an adequate representation of a face and thus exactly what is developing during these years. A closer examination of the ways in which face encoding is psychologically different from the encoding of other stimuli (which do not show the same development) will constrain this description. The psychological results yield a series of questions. Why is there an inversion effect? What is different about faces, on the one hand, and houses, bridges, cars, landscapes, costumes, chairs, dogs' faces, stick figures of men, and buildings, on the other hand?

WHY IS FACE ENCODING SPECIAL?

A priori considerations of the problems solved by a device for encoding faces constrain any theory of how it works. When presented with a new face, a person must form a representation adequate not only to distinguish that face from all others already represented in memory but also to distinguish it from most other faces that might be encountered. If the input is a still photograph, the problems for the encoding device are compounded by the ambiguity of the stimulus. That is, those aspects of the stimulus contributed by permanent facial characteristics must be differentiated from those contributed by momentary expression—is that a wide mouth or a grin?

It is obvious that knowledge gained from experience with faces plays a role in the encoding of new faces. The range of structural differences among faces (constituted by differences in bone structure, muscle mass, and fat accumulation) and the way in which different faces are transformed by changes in expression would be aspects of the relevant experience. Knowledge of both would inform a guess about which properties of a new face are likely to be distinctive. And, of course, there is evidence that knowledge of faces plays a role in encoding. The most direct evidence comes from studies on encoding faces from racial groups unfamiliar to the subject (Shepard, Deregowski, and Ellis, 1974). It is likely that the accumulation of relevant knowledge is one source of the dramatic increase in face-encoding skills during the years prior to age ten.

We will say that a person has a "face-encoding schema" if knowledge of the range of variation among faces plays a part in encoding a new face. Face-encoding schema is shorthand for the general program that guides the processes of encoding any particular new face. By definition, we will not use the phrase x-encoding schema unless knowledge about the class of which x is a member guides encoding. That is, the child who has never seen a picture of a snowflake before may well be able to form a representation of that snowflake in memory and later recognize it. But no knowledge of snowflakes could have played a role. Successful encoding thus does not guarantee a "snowflake-encoding schema."

Our answer to the first question—why is there an inversion effect—is that the knowledge exploited by the encoding schema is represented spatially with respect to an internal frame of reference and that input from an inverted stimulus cannot be as efficiently compared with that stored knowledge as input from an upright stimulus. Thus two questions about encoding apply to any stimulus domain. The first is whether an encoding schema has been formed for that domain. In the encoding of photographs of houses, for example, knowledge of how houses vary probably plays a role in picking a row of columns or a large black drainpipe as potentially distinguishing features. The second question is whether the knowledge exploited by the encoding schema is spatially organized. Whether there is an orientation for, say, tablespoons, for which there is an encoding advantage, is not known. The stimuli that were examined in the experiments cited here are all customarily seen upright, and inversion effects were found in every case. Therefore we are taking an inversion effect as evidence for an encoding schema for that class of stimuli, an encoding schema that exploits knowledge organized with respect to an internal spatial frame of reference. There are, of course, other potential sources of inversion effects. For example, if stimuli are generally scanned from top to bottom, and if the important distinguishing features of a class of stimuli are at the top, then it is possible that members of that class would be better encoded upright than inverted (Ghent, Bernstein, and Goldweber, 1960). Effects of this sort may contribute in these studies but are unlikely to be a major source of these inversion effects.

Since all the classes just listed show a significant inversion effect, the presence of an inversion effect does not differentiate the encoding of faces from the encoding of these other classes. Therefore, to attempt to answer our second question, about the specialness of faces, we ask what encoding problems are posed by faces but not by other classes of stimuli. For one thing, faces all share a single basic configuration. Houses do not share a single basic configuration, certainly not the houses used in the experiments that we cited. Some were seventeenth-century frame houses, others nineteenth-century row houses.

The potential distinguishing properties that individuate members within a stimulus class can be arrayed on a continuum from piecemeal to relational (or configurational; here we will use relational). A distinguishing property is piecemeal if its mere presence or absence helps individuate a member of the class; examples for faces are mustache, mole, scar. If a distinguishing property's value can be assigned without reference to other parts of the object (bushy versus thin eyebrows), the property falls at the piecemeal end of the continuum. A relational distinguishing property involves spatial relations among several parts of the object (the highness of cheekbones, the width of eyes, or the length of a nose given the width of the face). The same parts of a face can be involved in both kinds of distinguishing properties. A scar can serve as a relational distinguishing property if its position is part of the description of a face.

The question whether the members of a class share a single basic configuration is independent of whether the distinguishing properties that individuate members of the class fall toward the piecemeal or relational end of the continuum. Even though faces share a single configuration, there are copious piecemeal as well as relational properties of faces relevant to their individuation. Landscapes do not share a single configuration, although copious relational as well as piecemeal properties distinguish them. Nonetheless, it seems likely that individuation of instances that share a configuration is likely to rely on subtle relational properties to a greater extent than do distinguishing stimuli that differ in basic configuration. Further, the necessity to encode members of classes that share a configuration in terms of relational distinguishing properties presumably becomes greater as the number of individuals to be distinguished increases.

We now have a framework within which to suggest why the encoding of faces has properties different from the encoding of the other classes of stimuli with which faces have been directly compared. We assume that faces are individuated largely in terms of relational distinguishing properties. Houses, bridges, buildings, and landscapes do not share single configurations and offer a great many piecemeal distinguishing properties. Stick figures of men differ only in the relation among their parts, but they do not share a single configuration. Costumes share a single configuration, but they are almost certainly distinguished mainly in terms of relatively piecemeal properties. Cars, chairs, and dogs' faces share a single configuration. It is possible that they are individuated mainly in terms of piecemeal properties. It is also possible that an encoding schema for individuating such items in terms of relational properties could be formed but that in general subjects have not had the relevant motivation or experience to form one.

In sum, we are suggesting that when a class of stimuli shares a single configuration for which there is an encoding schema that uses relational properties to individuate class members, the encoding of individuals of that class will share the psychological properties of face encoding. It is an open question whether there are stimulus domains, other than faces, that are so characterized.

These information-processing considerations permit a more specific statement of our current hypothesis about what develops between the ages of six and ten—namely, an increasingly powerful encoding schema for upright faces. The young child is limited to computing only relatively piecemeal distinguishing properties from a still photograph seen only briefly. With much more extended and varied input from a face, the young child succeeds in encoding the relational properties of that face; that is, children do not differ from adults in terms of the ultimate representations of faces they are capable of forming. But even a more precise description of the developmental changes in terms of information-processing considerations leaves completely open the significance, if any, of the behavioral parallels between children under nine and patients with right posterior lesions.

As part of her thesis concerning visual field effects on face recognition and encoding, Leehey found that eight-year-olds do not show a left visual field advantage for encoding unfamiliar faces. This result was obtained twice, with different subjects and different stimuli in the two cases. The normal right-hemisphere advantage was present at ages nine and ten and lost again at ages twelve and fourteen (Leehey, 1976). The emergence of the normal adult pattern at age nine was due entirely to improvement in the left visual field. Performance in the right visual field remained constant over the ages from eight to ten. Thus, at those ages when performance on upright faces is relatively poor (under nine and at ages twelve to fourteen), children also fail to show differential right-hemisphere involvement in face encoding.

Let us summarize the developmental results. We have identified a characteristic developmental history for face encoding. We will call this the target curve and note that it has two variants—one shown in figures 5.3 and 5.5 and the other shown in figure 5.6. Children under nine closely resemble patients with lesions in the right posterior cortex; further, at the ages when face encoding is poor, the normal adult right-hemisphere advantage is not obtained.

This pattern of results suggests that two maturational factors may contribute to the target curve. First, a limiting factor in the period before age ten may be immaturity of some aspect of the neural substrate for face-encoding skills. Second, events associated with the onset of puberty may temporarily disrupt face encoding between the ages twelve and fourteen.

None of the data we have presented thus far establishes that these (or other) maturational factors affect the developmental course of face encoding. The limiting factor before age nine or ten may simply be insufficient experience with enough faces for the child to have abstracted the knowledge needed to guide maximally efficient encoding of new faces. The dip at ages twelve to fourteen, like many well-documented cases of temporary declines in performance (Bower, 1976; Strauss, 1977) may reflect a reorganization of knowledge of faces at those ages. Even Leehey's lateralization results do not require a maturational explanation. The right hemisphere might be differentially involved in face encoding only to the extent that relational distinguishing properties are computed. If the child has not yet developed an encoding schema powerful enough to compute relational distinguishing properties of a face from a still photograph shown for 150 msec, then the right hemisphere will not be differentially involved. Thus the lack of a right-hemisphere advantage in encoding faces at ages eight, twelve, and fourteen, could simply reflect the strategy the child is using at those ages. The developmental changes in strategy could well be accounted for in information-processing terms without implicating any maturational factors.

EVIDENCE FOR A MATURATIONAL COMPONENT TO FACE ENCODING

The shape of the target curve suggests two maturational hypotheses. The first, hypothesis A, is that immaturity of some aspect of neural substrate limits the face-encoding skills that children under nine or ten can achieve. The second, hypothesis B, is that maturational events associated with the onset of puberty actually disrupt, temporarily, face encoding. The similarities in performance of young children and patients with right posterior lesions, along with evidence that the magnitude of a left visual field advantage in face encoding shows the same relation to age as does overall recognition performance, point to the right hemisphere as a prime candidate for the locus of both maturational effects. At this point, however, we are deliberately leaving the two hypotheses vague. In the course of searching for evidence that bears on them, we will attempt to constrain the two hypotheses with respect to the kind of maturational mechanisms involved and the sites of their influence.

The Search for the Target Curve

We have developed two approaches for bringing data to bear on hypotheses A and B. The first approach is relevant to the entire target curve, examining evidence for both hypotheses. The basic assumption of the first approach is that if there is a maturational component to the developmental history of face encoding, other capacities that share the neural substrate affected by the maturational factors may also show the target curve. Because the time course of experiential influences on such other capacities may differ from the time course of experiential influences on face encoding, it is not obvious that a developmental parallel will be observed. To give a trivial example: The maturational limit on the development of face-encoding skills might also limit the ability to read X rays, but since children do not, in general, learn to read X rays, the improvement from six to nine or ten characteristic of the target curve would not be observed on an X-ray reading task.

The logic of our first approach—the search for the target curve—demands that the development of a capacity sharing the relevant aspect of neural substrate *and* common environmental influences with face encoding also show the target curve. Finding the target curve in such a case is a prerequisite for proceeding. Of course, we do not yet know what the relevant aspect of neural substrate is, nor what environmental influences are pertinent. Voice encoding is known to be impaired in adult patients with right posterior damage (Assal et al., 1976), although the most sensitive sites differ from those that maximally impair face encoding. The knowledge exploited in the efficient encoding of unfamiliar voices presumably accrues from experience with people, as does knowledge relevant to face encoding. Thus voice encoding shares some aspect of both neural substrate and common environmental influences. In two groups of children, using slightly different voice-encoding tasks, the target curve was obtained (see figure 5.7 for data pooled from both groups). This result cannot, of course, by itself provide evidence for a maturational component to the development of face and voice encoding. The sharp improvement up to age ten could reflect the development of encoding schema for both faces and voices based merely on increased experience with people. Similarly, the dips common to both developmental histories could have a common nonmaturational source, such as a temporary reliance on superficial cues in the course of systematizing encoding strategies for both faces and voices. If, however, the common developmental histories do reflect, in part, the same maturational influences, these results establish that their locus is not restricted to areas of the brain that subserve only face encoding or even complex visuospatial processing.

Finding the target curve for the development of voice encoding—a capacity that shares aspects of both neural substrate and environmental history with face encoding—encouraged us to proceed in our search. We sought developmental norms for tasks that had been used with children in the age range six to sixteen. From our own work we already knew that not all encoding tasks involving complex visual stimuli show this pattern; encoding of inverted faces does not, nor does encoding of upright or inverted houses (Carey, Diamond, and Woods, in press). Similarly, Leehey showed that while the magnitude of right-hemisphere advantage for face encoding displays the target curve, the extent of left-hemisphere ad-

5.7
Performance on voice encoding (from Mann, Diamond, and Carey, 1979)
Solid line: experimental items (all women, all American accents). Dashed
line: practice items (men and women, various foreign accents).

vantage for recognizing words does not, as it increases steadily from
age eight to fourteen (Leehey, 1976).

Evidence for the maturational hypotheses would consist of a
match to the target curve in a capacity which in adults is impaired
by focal brain lesions that also impair face encoding. Further, such
a capacity must not share with face encoding an obvious experiential base. If maturational factors limit the development of these
capacities, children under nine or ten should perform no better than
patients with injury to the relevant areas of the brain. These considerations led us to search the literature for developmental norms
on tasks known to be impaired by focal lesions in adults. It was important to include tasks that implicate areas of the brain other than
the right posterior hemisphere, so that the area of neural substrate
tentatively assigned as the site of the hypothetical maturational

influences might be extended, if required, or the assignment disconfirmed.

The difficulty of the project immediately became apparent. The tasks used to diagnose focal injury in adults often have not been studied developmentally; when they have, they have seldom been presented to children throughout the age range of interest in the same form as that used with adults. Developmental data that have been collected are often unpublished or available only in the manuals for the tests and frequently extend only to ages ten, eleven, or twelve or else are grouped too coarsely for our purposes. Despite these difficulties, data from a total of over forty tasks have been examined so far (many with multiple parts). Despite problems of incompleteness, several results have already emerged.

Most of the developmental norms scrutinized do not resemble the pattern found for face encoding (table 5.1). Certain generalizations

Table 5.1
Developmental norms available to date

Instrument	Source
Not the target curve	
a	

Tasks for which data are complete through adolescence and which show steady improvement throughout

Embedded figures	Witkin, Goodenough, and Karp, 1967
Rod and frame	Witkin, Goodenough, and Karp, 1967
Body adjustment	Witkin, Goodenough, and Karp, 1967
Clip pinching	Connolly and Stratton, 1968
Hand to feet	Connolly and Stratton, 1968
Finger lifting	Connolly and Stratton, 1968
Finger tapping (variability)	Wolff and Hurwitz, 1976
Tapping (score)	Knights and Moule, 1967
Maze	Knights, 1970
Progressive holes	Knights, 1970
Pegboard	Knights, 1970
Auditory closure	Knights, 1970
Sentence memory	Knights, 1970
Verbal fluency	Knights, 1970
Target	Knights, 1970
Stereognosis	Spreen and Gaddes, 1969
Trail making	Spreen and Gaddes, 1969
Category test	Spreen and Gaddes, 1969
Closure	Mooney, 1951

b

Tasks for which data extend through age eleven, twelve or thirteen without evidence of a plateau or decline

Embedded figures	Immergluck and Mearini, 1969
Finger tapping (total score)	Spreen and Gaddes, 1969
Dynamic visual retention	Spreen and Gaddes, 1969
Lateral dominance exam	Spreen and Gaddes, 1969
Speech perception	Spreen and Gaddes, 1969
Tactual performance (time)	Spreen and Gaddes, 1969
Tactual performance (memory)	Spreen and Gaddes, 1969
Three-dimensional con-structional praxis (fifteen blocks)	Spreen and Gaddes, 1969

c

Tasks that show steady improvement until a plateau is reached, as early as age eight or nine

Three-dimensional con-structional praxis (six blocks)	Spreen and Gaddes, 1969
Tactual performance test (location)	Spreen and Gaddes, 1969
Von Frey hairs	Spreen and Gaddes, 1969

Good candidates for the target curve

d

Tasks in which a period of improvement is followed by an apparent plateau beginning at age ten or eleven

Reaction time	Spreen and Gaddes, 1969
Sentence repetition	Spreen and Gaddes, 1969
Right-left orientation	Spreen and Gaddes, 1969
Map walking	Denckla, Rudel, and Broman (chap. 4, this volume)

e

Tasks that exemplify the target curve

Seashore tonal memory	Spreen and Gaddes, 1969

can be made about tasks that do not yield the target curve. First, tests of motor neurological signs, in addition to showing steady improvement through the age range, are also performed better by girls at all ages (Connolly and Stratton, 1968; Wolff and Hurwitz, 1976). This sex difference, which is not found in our face- and voice-encoding tasks, probably reflects the maturational precocity of girls throughout childhood and adolescence. Second, tests that are used to measure field dependence (rod and frame test, embedded figures) and the spatial tasks that are highly correlated with them also do not show the target curve. Progress is made steadily throughout adolescence, and males usually do better at all ages (Witkin, Goodenough, and Karp, 1967). These are the same tasks for which performance is related to maturational rate (Waber, chapter 2, this volume). That is, late maturing children do better than early maturers. Finally, recognition of common objects with their contours obscured (Gollin figures, Mooney figures, and Street figures; the noncanonical views of objects presented by Warrington and Taylor, 1973) do not show the target curve, even though an intact right posterior cortex is required for normal performance in adults. The developmental norms for these tasks deviate from the target curve in either of two respects. Either the adult level of performance is reached very early and maintained through adolescence, or whatever gain remains after age six or seven is achieved steadily throughout adolescence.

The first outcome from our search, then, is encouraging, although it must be accepted with extreme caution; most tasks used in the diagnosis of brain damage do not show the target curve. The second outcome is that we found one clear case of a task that shares the developmental course of face- and voice-encoding—the seashore test of tonal memory (figure 5.8). This task requires listening to a sequence of three to five tones which is repeated with one tone changed. The subject must indicate which tone was changed. These children's norms, from Spreen and Gaddes (1969), extend through age fifteen. Milner (1962) showed that performance on this task is badly impaired by right posterior injury (right temporal lobectomy). Those patients perform slightly better than eight-year-olds (figure 5.8). Thus the pattern found on the tonal memory task supports our maturational hypotheses. Tonal memory shares an aspect of neural substrate with face- and voice-encoding, children under nine resemble patients with right posterior damage, and there is no

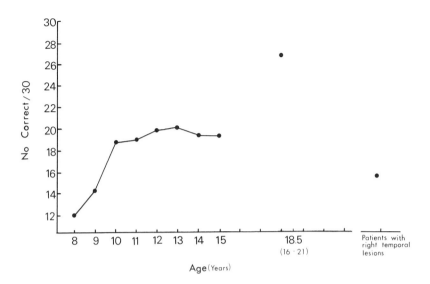

5.8
Age-related performance on Seashore Test of Tonal Memory, compared to performance of right hemisphere damaged patients

obvious common experiential influence on tune encoding and person encoding.

We have identified four other tasks that are potential candidates for the target curve (table 5.1, section d) for which data are incomplete. In some cases an apparent plateau begins at age ten or eleven, but available norms do not extend to age fifteen or sixteen. In addition, appropriate adult norms for these instruments have not yet been found. Therefore we do not yet know whether there is a significant increase between the level of performance of fourteen-year-olds and that of adults.

Data already obtained on one of these four tasks, map walking, illustrate how behavioral data might be used to refine the maturational hypotheses. Map walking is sensitive to right parietal injury in adults (Semmes et al., 1955). Figure 5.9 gives data for ages six to twelve, although the task used was not exactly the same as that used for adults (Denckla, Rudel, and Broman, chapter 4, this volume). It appears possible that the development of map walking may match the target curve. Although the apparent plateau between ages eight and ten is not typical of the target curve, there also appears to be a plateau or dip beginning at age twelve. To confirm that map walk-

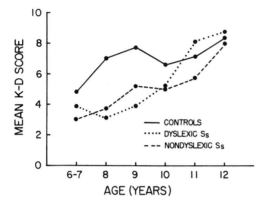

5.9
Relationship of age to Kohn-Dennis route-walking scores for learning-disabled subjects and controls (from Denckla, Rudel, and Broman, chapter 4, this volume)

ing shows the target curve, we must verify that the plateau extends to age thirteen or fourteen and that there is a significant increase to the adult level by age sixteen. We are currently collecting these data. Suppose that the target curve is found. As in the case of the Benton and Van Allen task of face encoding (figure 5.6), the plateau would be interpreted, tentatively, as reflecting the interaction of a decline during ages twelve to fourteen of map-walking skills with an increase during ages ten to sixteen in some other component of the task. Data from a population of dyslexic children, reported in chapter 4, this volume, are relevant to this interpretation of the plateau and also to hypothesis B—that the decline in the target curve during adolescence reflects disruptive effects of events associated with onset of puberty.

Two general types of disruptive mechanisms can be distinguished. First, physiological events may interfere directly with the efficiency of neural functioning in the right posterior cortex. Perhaps, for example, this area is particularly vulnerable to the massive hormonal infusions accompanying puberty. Second, physiological events may temporarily change the balance of right- and left-hemisphere involvement in a number of tasks. If predominance of right-hemisphere functioning is optimal for the map-walking task, greater left-hemisphere involvement could produce the interference reflected in the dip or plateau. How might data from dyslexic children help decide between these two types of mechanisms? We must assume that dyslexic children have normally functioning right hemispheres but abnormally functioning left hemispheres. As reviewed by Denckla et al. in chapter 4, this is not an unreasonable assumption, at least for some dyslexic populations. If the events at puberty that interfere with steady improvement on the map-walking task involve only the right hemisphere, then dyslexic children should also show the target curve. However, if the slowing of development is due to interference from the left hemisphere, children with abnormal left hemispheres might not show the target curve. Data from a group of familial dyslexic children is shown in figure 5.9. At ages beyond ten the scores of these children exceed those of normals; more important, they do not show the beginnings of a plateau. Rather, their performance continues to improve. These results support the second kind of maturational mechanism—disruption at puberty due to a temporary change in the balance of left- and right-hemisphere functioning in normal children. They also support our interpretation of the plateau in map walking as reflecting actual interference with a component of the task.

Because we do not know how older normals and older dyslexics behave in the map-walking task, this discussion is quite speculative. We must confirm that normals show the target curve for this task and then determine whether dyslexic children reach the normal adult level without showing a plateau at puberty. Furthermore, these results bear replication and should be extended to tonal memory and to face- and voice-encoding tasks. We also need to understand why only the familial dyslexics show this pattern. Nonetheless, whatever the final outcome, the example illustrates how data from special populations for tasks that in normals fit the target curve could support and refine the maturational hypotheses.

We are continuing our search for the target curve. Our expectation at this point remains that capacities showing this pattern will implicate the posterior portion of the right hemisphere, as do face encoding, voice encoding, tonal memory, and map walking. However, it is possible that whatever common neural substrate among these capacities there may be is not confined to the right hemisphere. Of course it is also possible that the eventual class of capacities showing the target curve cannot be related to a common neural substrate. By including for evaluation tasks that are sensitive to focal lesions in all areas of the brain, we are searching for data that will disconfirm the maturational hypotheses.

In summary, the results from the first approach—the search for the target curve—so far support hypotheses A and B. In addition, we know that not all capacities that require an intact right posterior hemisphere show the target curve. One goal for further research is to characterize both in terms of neuropsychology and information-processing considerations, the right-hemisphere capacities that show the target curve during development and those that do not.

The Relation between Maturational Status and the Decline
The second approach to a maturational component to the development of face encoding is a direct attack on hypothesis B—the possibility that events associated with the onset of puberty disrupt face encoding. The implication is that children in whom these events are fully under way should encode faces more poorly than those who are prepubescent or who are postpubescent. One would expect, if this were so, that the decline in face encoding after age ten should occur earlier in girls than in boys, producing a sex difference in performance levels in early adolescence. While we found no sex differences at any age, our own samples may have been too small for such effects to be observed. In one lateral field study in which twenty boys and twenty girls were tested at each age, the left visual field advantage in encoding faces was lost two years earlier in girls than in boys (Leehey, 1976). This discrepancy is consistent with the two-year-earlier onset of puberty in girls (Marshall and Tanner, 1969; 1970) and thus with hypothesis B.

Since there is considerable overlap between the sexes for age of onset of puberty, a more direct test of the hypothesis is to compare groups of children matched for age and sex but differing in maturational status. Prepubescent or postpubescent children should perform better on face-encoding tasks than children of the same age who are in the midst of the changes associated with reaching puberty. This means that if tested early in the adolescent period (around age eleven for girls, age thirteen for boys), early maturers should do worse than late maturers, since late maturers will be prepubescent. If tested late in the adolescent period (around age thirteen for girls, age fifteen for boys), in contrast, early maturers should do better than late maturers, since late maturers will be in the midst of pubertal change and early maturers will be postpubescent. This predicted pattern of results should be contrasted with those of Waber (chapter 2, this volume), who showed that individual differences in maturational rate were associated with stable individual differences in the patterning of certain cognitive abilities. On a number of spatial tasks on which males characteristically perform better than females, Waber showed that regardless of time of testing early maturers of both sexes performed worse than late maturers.

As an initial test of hypothesis B we carried out a small pilot study on early and maturing children of one sex and one age. We chose to work with ten- and eleven-year-old girls because their maturational status may be estimated, at least crudely, from measures of height and weight, which are easier and cheaper to obtain than evaluations based on full physical examinations. These girls were tested on three different types of task: tasks that display the target curve (face encoding and tonal memory), tasks on which early maturers perform stably worse than late maturers regardless of stage of pubescence at time of testing (the embedded figures test, one of Waber's spatial tasks), and tasks for which there is no reason to expect maturational status or maturation rate to influence performance (Stroop color naming). Hypothesis B would be supported if early maturers performed worse at face encoding and tonal memory than late maturers, who are prepubescent at these ages. The embedded figures test was included in an attempt to replicate Waber's finding that early maturers perform worse on this task than late maturers. If replicated, this result would also confirm that our method of assigning girls as early and late maturers on the basis of height and weight measurements alone was consistent with Waber's assignment of children on the basis of full physical examinations using the Marshall and Tanner norms (Marshall and Tanner, 1969, 1970). Waber also showed that early and late maturers did not differ on the Stroop color-naming test. We therefore included this task to attempt to confirm this finding. Absence of a difference between our early and late maturing ten- and eleven-year-olds on color naming would also provide evidence that the groups do not differ in some respect that confounds the difference in maturational status.

The assignment of maturational status depended on the fact that early maturing children are taller and heavier than late maturing children at the same preadoleslcent age and that the weight-for-height distributions of the two groups also differ (Marshall and Tanner, 1969, 1970). These relationships are particularly marked for girls (Frisch, Revelle, and Cook, 1973). An index of the increasing weight relative to height that accompanies onset of puberty is total body water (TW). This measure is a constant fraction of lean body weight. It can be calculated from height and weight measurements, using the formula of Mellits and Cheek (1970, p. 15), and has been shown in girls to decrease from 60.4 ± 0.28 at initiation of the adolescent growth spurt to $55. \pm 0.27$ at menarche (Frisch, Revelle, and Cook, 1973). These relationships make it possible to estimate the maturational status of girls from height and weight measurements alone. Twenty-seven girls attending the MIT summer day camp were weighed and measured for height when they were dressed for swimming, and TW/total weight was calculated. Using the norms provided by Frisch, Revelle, and Cook (1973), we were able to assign seven of the girls as early maturers (roughly Marshall-Tanner stage 3) and six of the girls as late maturers (roughly Marshall-Tanner stage 1). We used four tasks:

• *Face-encoding task.* The child was shown a series of forty-eight photographs taken from a recent college yearbook and then provided forty-eight forced-choice recognition items. The set size is one for which ten-year-olds are not at ceiling (Carey, Diamond, and Woods, in press).

• *Seashore tonal memory test.* The child listened to a sequence of three, four, or five tones. The sequence was then repeated with one tone changed, and the child indicated which tone had been changed. There is a standard tape of materials.

• *Embedded figures test.* The child was shown a simple line drawing which was then removed. A colored design with the simple figure embedded in it was presented and the child asked to find the simple figure. There is a standard set of materials to be timed.

• *Stroop color naming.* The child was asked to say the names of the colors of a random sequence of red, green, and blue patches as quickly as possible. There is a standard set of materials to be timed.

Table 5.2 gives the names for early and late maturers on all four tasks. Early maturers did worse on the embedded figures test than late maturers ($t=2.22$, $df=10$, one-tailed $P < 0.05$). The groups did not differ in the Stroop color-naming task. Early maturers performed more poorly on the face-encoding task than late maturers ($t=1.86$, $df=11$, one-tailed $P < 0.05$). While the results for tonal memory did not reach significance, they were in the direction of a disadvantage for early maturers.

The finding that early maturers performed worse on the em-

Table 5.2
Performance of early and late maturers

Task	Early maturers	Late maturers
Stroop color naming (time)	69 sec	66 sec
Embedded figures test (time/item)	101 sec	58 sec
Face encoding (percentage correct)	70	81
Tonal memory (percentage correct)	73	80

bedded figures test than late maturers replicates Waber's results and confirms our division of subjects into early and late maturers. The fact that her finding could be replicated with so few subjects (seven early maturers, five late maturers; one late maturer was not tested on the embedded figures test) and with our crude method of estimating maturational rate attests to the robust nature of the relationship she demonstrated.

Our main prediction, that children in the midst of the changes accompanying puberty would do worse on face encoding than pre-pubescent children, was also confirmed. Obtaining this result on a sample of thirteen children whose maturational status was only approximately known suggests that this result, too, is robust. The results for the tonal memory task did not confirm our predictions. The 7 percent difference between early and late maturers, while in the predicted direction, was not significant. For the present, we assume that a larger sample would reveal a significant difference in favor of the late maturers in this case as well.

The early maturers' poorer performance on the face-encoding task could have two explanations. One is the validity of hypothesis B—that face encoding is temporarily disrupted at onset of puberty. Since early maturing girls at age ten to eleven are in the midst of the pubescent period, their performance would maximally show this disruption. The other possibility is that face encoding, like the embedded figures test, is sensitive to maturational rate rather than maturational status. If so, then early maturers will be worse on face-encoding tasks than late maturers regardless of when during adolescence the groups are tested. We do not think the latter possibility is likely, since there are no stable sex differences on face-encoding tasks in adults. On the embedded figures test, males (on the average later maturers than females) are consistently better. A direct test of the matter, of course, is to examine adolescent children at an older age, when late maturers are in the midst of reaching puberty and early maturers are postpubescent. If maturational status at the time of test accounts for the difference between groups, then the relation on table 5.2 should be reversed; late maturers should perform worse than early maturers on tasks that show the target curve. We plan to carry out such a study, using girls at ages eleven and thirteen and boys at thirteen and fifteen. Our design is longitudinal, so we will be able to verify the dip within individual children.

Clearly the pilot study provides only the most tentative support for hypothesis B, resting as it does on the data from thirteen girls. But its logic is clear. A dissociation, in the full study, between tasks that show the target curve and those that do not (table 5.1), such that only the former are impaired when the subject is in Marshall-Tanner stages 2–3, would provide strong support for hypothesis B.

SUMMARY AND CONCLUSIONS

The results of both approaches we have taken to bring empirical considerations to bear on our maturational hypotheses have so far supported those hypotheses. We have worked from behavioral data from a variety of sources—brain-damaged patients, normal and abnormal children, and normal adults. And while we have not yet made much progress toward formulating hypotheses about actual maturational mechanisms, this remains our goal. We have attempted to delimit the sites of the maturational influences by sampling tasks impaired by focal lesions implicating known areas and by relating the performance of patients to that of children. We have found tentative evidence that the disruption of performance at ages twelve to fourteen may be due to interference from the left hemisphere rather than from direct maturational influence on the neural substrate of face encoding. Further research will specify exactly when in adolescence, in terms of maturational status, the decline occurs and over what range of tasks. Firm behavioral data relevant to these issues will further constrain hypotheses about maturational mechanisms. Eventually, we hope, contact will be

made with what is known about the neuropsychology of development of the human brain.

REFERENCES

Assal, G., Zander, E., Kramin, H., and Buttet, J. 1976. Discrimination des voix lors lesions du cortex cerebral. *Archives Suisse de Neurologie, Neurochiurgie, et Psychiatry.* 119: 307–315.

Bahrick, H. P., Bahrick, P. O., and Wittlinger, R. P. 1975. Fifty years of memory for names and faces: A cross-section approach. *J. Exp. Psychol. General* 104: 54–75.

Benton, A. L., and Van Allen, M. W. 1968. Impairment in facial recognition in patients with cerebral disease. *Cortex* 4: 344–359.

Blaney, R. L., and Winograd, E. 1978. Developmental differences in children's recognition memory for faces. *Developmental Psychology* 14: 441–442.

Bower, T. G. R. 1976. Repetitive processes in child development. *Scientific American* 235: 38–47.

Bower, G. H., and Karlin, M. B. 1974. Depth of processing pictures of faces and recognition memory. *J. Exp. Psychol.* 103: 751–757.

Carey, S. 1978. A case study: Face recognition. In *Explorations in the biology of language,* ed. E. Walker. Montgomery, Vt.: Bradford Books.

Carey, S., and Diamond, R. 1977. From piecemeal to configurational representation of faces. *Science* 195: 312–314.

Carey, S., Diamond, R., and Woods, B. The development of face perception: A maturational basis? *Developmental Psychology,* in press.

Chomsky, N. 1974. *Reflections on language.* New York: Pantheon.

Connolly, K., and Stratton, P. 1968. Developmental changes in associated movements. *Developmental Medicine and Child Neurology* 10: 49–56.

De Renzi, E., Faglioni, P., and Spinnler, H. 1968. Performance of patients with unilateral brain damage on face recognition tasks. *Cortex* 4: 17–34.

De Renzi, E., Scotti, G., and Spinnler, H. 1969. Perceptual and associative disorders of visual recognition: Relationship to the side of the cerebral lesion. *Neurology* 19: 634–642.

Diamond, R., and Carey, S. 1977. Developmental changes in the representation of faces. *J. Exp. Child Psychol.* 23: 1–22.

Ellis, H. D., and Shephard, J. W. 1975. Recognition of upright and inverted faces presented in the left and right visual fields. *Cortex* 11: 3–7.

Epstein, H. T. 1974a. Phrenoblysis: Special brain and mind growth periods. I: Human brain and skull development. *Developmental Psychobiology* 7: 207–216.

———. 1974b. Phrenoblysis: Special brain and mind growth period. II: Human mental development. *Developmental Psychobiology* 7: 217–224.

Fish, D. 1976. Upright and inverted landscapes. Working paper, Psychology Department, Massachusetts Institute of Technology.

Fontenot, D. J. 1973. Visual field differences in the recognition of verbal and nonverbal stimuli in man. *J. Comp. Physiol. Psychol.* 85: 564–569.

Frisch, R. E., Revelle, R., and Cook, S. 1973. Components of weight at menarche and the initiation of adolescent growth spurt in girls: Estimated total water, lean body weight, and fat. *Human Biology* 45: 469–483.

Geffen, G., Bradshaw, J. L., and Wallace, G. 1971. Interhemispheric effects on reaction time to verbal and non-verbal stimuli. *J. Exp. Psychol.* 87: 415–422.

Ghent, L. 1961. Form and its orientation. A child's eye view. *Am. J. Psychol.* 74: 177–190.

Ghent, L., Bernstein, L., and Goldweber, A. M. 1960. Preferences for orientation of form under varying conditions. *Perceptual and Motor Skills* 11: 46.

Goldstein, A. G. 1965. Learning of inverted and normally oriented faces in children and adults. *Psychonomic Science* 3: 447–448.

Goldstein, A. G., and Chance, J. E. 1964. Recognition of children's faces. *Child Development* 35: 1129–136.

———. 1965. Recognition of children's faces. II: *Perceptual and Motor Skills* 20: 547–548.

Gross, N. M. 1972. Hemispheric specialization for processing of visually presented verbal and spatial stimuli. *Perception and Psychophysics* 12: 357–363.

Hilliard, R. D. 1973. Hemispheric laterality effects on a facial recognition task in normal subjects. *Cortex* 9: 246–258.

Hochberg, J., and Galper, R. E. 1967. Recognition of faces. I: An exploratory study. *Psychonomic Science* 9: 619–620.

Immergluck, L., and Mearini, M. C. 1969. Age and sex differences in responses to embedded figures and reversible figures. *J. Exp. Child Psychol.* 8: 210–221.

Kagan, J., and Klein, R. E. 1973. Cross cultural perspectives on early development. *American Psychologist* 28: 947–961.

Kimura, D. 1963. Right temporal lobe damage: Perception of unfamiliar stimuli after damage. *Arch. Neurol.* 8: 263–271.

Klein, D., Moscovitch, M., and Vigna, C. 1976. Perceptual asymmetries and attentional mechanisms in tachistoscopic recognition of words and faces. *Neuropsychologica* 14: 44–66.

Knights, R. M. 1970. Smoothed normative data on tests for evaluating brain damage in children. Department of Psychology, Carleton University, Ottawa, Ontario.

Knights, R. M., and Moule, A. D. 1967. Normative and reliability data on finger and foot tapping in children. *Perceptual Motor Skills* 25: 717–720.

Leehey, S. 1976. Face recognition in children: Evidence for the development of right hemisphere specialization. Doctoral dissertation, Massachusetts Institute of Technology.

Leehey, S., Carey, S., Diamond, R., and Cahn, A. 1978. Upright and inverted faces: The right hemisphere knows the difference. *Cortex* 14: 411–419.

Levy, J., Trevarthen, C., and Sperry, R. W. 1972. Perception of bilateral chimeruc figures following hemispheric deconnexion. *Brain* 95: 61–78.

Lenneberg, E. H. 1967. *Biological foundations of language.* New York: John Wiley and Sons.

——— . 1974. Language and brain: Developmental aspects. *Neurosciences Research Program Bulletin* II.

Mann, V. A., Diamond, R., and Carey, S. 1979. Development of voice recognition: Parallels with face recognition. *J. Exp. Child Psychol.*

Marshall, W. A., and Tanner, J. M. 1969. Variations in the pattern of pubertal changes in girls. *Archives of Disease in Childhood* 44: 291–303.

——— . 1970. Variations in the pattern of pubertal changes in boys. *Archives of Disease in Childhood* 45: 13–23.

McKeever, W., and Huling, M. 1970. Right hemisphere superiority in graphic production of briefly glimpsed dot figures. *Perceptual Motor Skills* 31: 201–202.

Mellits, E., and Cheek, D. B. 1970. The assessment of body water and fatness from infancy to adulthood. *Monogr. Soc. Res. Child Devel.* 35: 12–26.

Milner, B. 1962. Laterality effects in audition. In *Interhemispheric relations and cerebral dominance,* ed. V. B. Mountcastle. Baltimore, Md.: Johns Hopkins Press.

——— . 1968. Visual recognition and recall after right temporal lobe excision in man. *Neuropsychologia* 6: 191–209.

Mooney, C. M. 1957. Age in the development of closure ability in children. *Canadian J. Psychol.* 11: 219–227.

Paterson, A., and Zangwill, O. L. 1944. Disorders of visual space perception associated with lesion of the rigid cerebral hemisphere. *Brain* 67: 331–358.

Rizzolatti, G., Umilta, C., and Berlucci, G. 1971. Opposite superiorities of the right and left cerebral hemispheres in discriminative reaction time to physiognomic and alphabetical material. *Brain* 94: 431–442.

Robertshaw, S. and Sheldon, N. 1976. Laterality effects in judgment of the identity and position of letters: A signal detection analysis. *Quart. J. Exp. Psychol.* 28: 115–121.

Rock, I. 1974. The perception of disoriented figures. *Scientific American* 230: 78–86.

Saltz, E., and Sigel, I. E. 1967. Concept overdiscrimination in children. *J. Exp. Psychol.* 73: 1–8.

Scapinello, K. F., and Yarmey, A. D. 1970. The role of familiarity and orientation in immediate and delayed recognition of pictorial stimuli. *Psychonomic Science* 2: 329–331.

Semmes, J., Weinstein, S., Ghent, L., and Teuber, H. L. 1955. Spatial orientation in man after cerebral injury. I: Analysis by locus of lesion. *J. Psychol.* 39: 227–244.

Shepard, J. W., Deregowski, J. B., and Ellis, H. D. 1974. A cross-cultural study of recognition memory for faces. *Int. J. Psychol.* 9: 205–212.

Spreen, O., and Gaddes, W. H. 1969. Developmental norms for 15 neuro-psychological tests age 6 to 15. *Cortex* 5: 170–191.

Strauss, S. 1977. *U-shaped curves in development.* Report to the Ford Foundation, September.

Warrington, E. K., and James, M. 1967a. An experimental investigation of facial recognition in patients with unilateral cerebral lesions. *Cortex* 3: 317–326.

——— . 1967b. Tachistoscopic number estimation in patients with unilateral cerebral lesions. *J. Neurol. Neurosurg. Psychiat.* 30: 468–474.

Warrington, E. K., and Taylor, A. M. 1973. The contribution of the right parietal lobe to object recognition. *Cortex* 9: 152–164.

Witkin, H. A., Goodenough, D. R., and Karp, S. A. 1967. Stability of cognitive style from childhood to young adulthood. *J. Personality and Social Psychol.* 7: 291–300.

Wolff, P. H., and Hurwitz, I. 1976. Sex differences in finger-tapping: A developmental study. *Neuropsychologia* 14: 35–41.

Yarmey, A. D. 1971. Recognition memory for familiar "public" faces: Effects of orientation and delay. *Psychonomic Science* 24: 286–288.

Yin, R. K. 1969. Looking at upside-down faces. *J. Exp. Psychol.* 81: 141–145.

———— . 1970a. Face recognition: A special process. Ph.D. thesis, Psychology Department, Massachusetts Institute of Technology.

———— . 1970b. Face recognition by brain injured patients: A dissociable ability? *Neuropsychologia* 8: 395–402.

II

Studies of Language Development

6

Linguistic Perspectives on Language Development

David Caplan
and
Noam Chomsky

The papers in part 2 deal with biological mechanisms underlying the acquisition of language. Approaches to this field involve direct physiological and anatomical observations, experimental studies of behavior, and analysis of behavior and judgments in an effort to determine the conditions that must be met by physical mechanisms. These introductory remarks outline an approach to language acquisition derived from the study of linguistic phenomena and suggest some conclusions about the properties of organic mechanisms responsible for this process.

Empirical observations of the most casual sort, as well as more careful studies, suggest an obvious point of departure for theories of language development. First, there is a superficial diversity of languages to which children are exposed, and the child learns the language of his speech community. Second, there is a radical and qualitative difference between the highly articulated and specific properties of the language acquired and the evidence on the basis of which it is attained.

To cite just one example to illustrate the latter point, consider the following sentences:

1. John believes he is incompetent.
2. John believes him to be incompetent.
3. John wants him to win.
4. John wants Bill to see him.

Part of the shared knowledge common to all English speakers is that in sentences 1 and 4, *John* and *he/him* can refer to the same person, though they need not, whereas in 2 and 3 they cannot. Thus sentence 3 means that John wants someone other than John to win, whereas sentence 1 might mean that John believes that he himself is incompetent. It is hard to imagine that children receive specific training to establish this shared knowledge or even that this knowledge is derived inductively from experience. It is still more difficult to imagine that all speakers of English are provided with evidence that provides an inductive basis for this shared knowledge. Yet these are quite trivial facts about coreference in English, evident from the consideration of extremely simple sentences. When we consider structures of greater intricacy, the discrepancy between the detail and specificity of the knowledge acquired, on the one hand, and the nature of the child's exposure to language, on the other, becomes still more striking.

These general observations suggest at once that there is a language-related faculty of mind that has available to it a wide variety of options for realization but which produces specific, intricate linguistic structures once committed to a particular line of development. Suppose that we have a rich system of principles framed in terms of a certain descriptive vocabulary with conditions on the realization of these principles, and furthermore a number of variables that can take on particular values as a function, inter alia, of linguistic exposure. If the system's deductive structure is rich enough, then small modifications in the specification of the variables may lead to what appear to be gross differences in the resulting system, and each of the possible end states attained as the variables are determined by experience will be remote from the available data. Each end state will be one of the systems compatible with the system of principles, but there is no reason to expect that the resulting end state is derived inductively (or by any general procedure) from the data that trigger and shape language development. In a roughly comparable way, embryological development involves the unfolding of a genetically determined program to an end state that is not derived by any general "growth principle" from the environmental inputs, and slight changes in the program—say, in the timing of regulatory mechanisms—can lead to radically different organisms.

This approach to language assumes that two immediately obvious properties of language—its richness of structure and detail, its wide diversity—reflect specific, genetically determined mechanisms pertaining to language and are not the results of general learning mechanisms applied to the data of experience. The legitimacy of this move seems apparent, given the vast discrepancy that empirical inquiry reveals between the complexity of the rule systems uniformly acquired in a given speech community and the limited character of the evidence available to the language learner. For the biologist investigating language, this is an optimistic conclusion. The biologist should have made a kind of Pascal's wager that this is the case, for otherwise the emerging system would reflect properties of the environment rather than those of the biological entity under study and would correspondingly be less important for the study of this organism.

The conceptual framework we are suggesting was well developed in the seventeenth century by Descartes and his successors, who adapted a classical argument in the theory of knowledge that we might call the argument from poverty of the stimulus. Everyone takes for granted (then as now) that physical development is to be explained in terms of the unfolding of intrinsic properties of the organism, a genetic program in modern terms. This is assumed even without direct evidence, and for very good reasons. The environment for growth of the organism is far too undifferentiated, impoverished, and unspecific to account for the particular course of growth and the end states it attains. There is nothing in the environment of the human embryo that could determine the growth of arms rather than wings. Descartes drew the same conclusion with regard to the mind. He suggested, for instance, that a child presented for the first time with a graphic representation of a (more or less) closed three-sided figure with (more or less) straight lines would see the item as a flawed example of a triangle and not as a perfect example of whatever it is. Consideration of such gedanken experiments leads to the conclusion that the mind is organized essentially in terms of principles of Euclidean geometry and constructs mental representations of straight lines, triangles, squares as examplars for the construction and interpretation of immediate experience. On similar grounds, one might anticipate that a child without relevant experience would predict trajectories along certain curves (parabolas), but not others, as a function of the intrinsic organization of mental (ultimately physical) structures that are part of the human biological endowment. Our approach to language development is similar to the Cartesian view of interpretation of geometrical form. In both cases, as in the case of physical growth where the point is uncontroversial, it seems to us that the argument from poverty of the stimulus can be effectively applied to reveal the basic character of the knowledge attained as a reflection of the intrinsic mental capacities of the organism, with variation of end states attained attributable to choice of parameter, fixed by experience, resulting in systems of considerable internal complexity.

This view of the mechanisms involved in language development is quite typical of our understanding of other biological systems. The regular processes of embryological development, seen in the differentiation of cell types, organelles, organs, and systems within a species are under genetic control, and relatively small differences in control mechanisms have major phenotypic effects. It seems to us that much the same is true of language, which can thus be regarded as a kind of mental organ, ultimately to be understood in terms of the physical mechanisms having the properties outlined in the more abstract studies that are feasible today.

Much contemporary work in linguistics has been concerned with the characterization of systems that might account for the process of language growth. Models are beginning to be developed which have the necessary detail and structure (Chomsky, 1970, 1971, 1976, 1977). We believe that success in these studies would mark an important step forward in the understanding of human mental endowment and mental development and would contribute to, while at the same time drawing from, the study of the organic mechanisms underlying physical development.

We will not attempt to outline such theories here but will simply present some examples to indicate directions that have been profitably pursued. Consider the following sentences.

5a. The boat that you believe John painted is a yawl.
5b. The boat that you believe the claim that John painted is a yawl.
5c. The boat that you asked who painted is a yawl.

Despite the parallels in syntactic structure, only 5a is an acceptable sentence in English. The problem is not that 5b and 5c are meaningless; if they were well-formed sentences, their meaning would be clear enough. Thus 5b and 5c could be paraphrased in the artificial semi-English of logic or mathematics as 5b' and 5c', respectively.

5b'. The boat, such that you believe the claim that John painted it, is a yawl.
5c'. The boat, such that you asked who painted it, is a yawl.

In fact, there are languages that use devices comparable to 5b' and 5c', and in these languages the "translations" of sentences 5b and 5c are well-formed sentences. The difference between these two categories of language derives from differences in the mechanism for establishing the relationship that obviously holds between the subject of the main clause, *the boat*, and the direct object of the verb *painted* of the subordinate clause. In a language that uses devices such as those of the examples 5b' and 5c', the relationship is established by a rule of interpretation that associates the subject of the main clause with an overt pronominal element (*it* in 5b' and 5c'). In a language such as English the relationship is established by a rule of a different sort that moves the direct object of the subordinate clause to the front of the clause, or beyond, as seen overtly in such sentences as the following:

6. The man whose picture you painted is a friend of mine.

The ill-formedness of the sentences 5b and 5c in normal English results from a certain general condition of locality (called subjacency in the technical literature) that holds generally for movement rules but not for other kinds of rules, so it appears.

To explore the matter further let us assume, following Bresnan (1970), that the basic structure of a clause is bipartite, with a "complementizer" (COMP) and a propositional content, as in the following sentence:

7. The claim [that John painted the boat] is false.

In 7 the embedded clause is "that John painted the boat." Its COMP is *that*, and the propositional content is *John painted the boat*. In standard terminology the propositional content is assigned to the category S (sentence) and the full clause to the category $\bar{S}$, for reasons having to do with general properties of phrase structure systems. Thus among the basic rules of English grammar, themselves special cases of principles of greater generality, are those represented in 8, meaning that a clause is analyzed as a complementizer followed by a propositional content, which in turn consists of a noun phrase (NP) subject and a verb phrase (VP) predicate.

8a. $\bar{S} \longrightarrow$ COMP S
8b. S $\longrightarrow$ NP VP

We assume further that the movement rule places the *wh*-phrase (*who, which, whose picture*) in the COMP position. Thus 6 has the form 9, where we use the symbol *t* (read "trace") to stand for the position from which the *wh*-phrase has been moved by the movement rule.

9. The man [$_{\bar{S}}$ [$_{COMP}$ whose picture] [$_S$ you painted t]] is a friend of mine.

In 9 we indicate phrase structure by paired brackets, where the subscript on the left-hand member of the pair indicates the category of the phrase contained within the brackets.

The *wh*-phrase may be overt, as in 9, or it may be deleted (lexically empty) as in 5a, which has the following form.

10. The boat [$_{\bar{S}}$ [$_{COMP}$ that] [$_S$ you painted t]] is a yawl.

The abstract representation, including the deleted *wh*-phrase that does not appear phonetically, is as follows.

11. The boat [$_{\bar{S}}$ [$_{COMP}$ which that] [$_S$ you painted t]] is a yawl.

Earlier varieties of English actually allowed structures like 11.

Suppose that we now characterize 5b and 5c along the lines of 11. We then have 12 (corresponding to 5b) and 13 (corresponding to 5c).

12. The boat [$_{\bar{S}}$ [$_{COMP}$ which that] [$_S$ you believe [$_{NP}$ the claim [$_{\bar{S}}$ [$_{COMP}$ that] [$_S$ John painted t]]]]] is a yawl.

13. The boat [$_{\bar{S}}$ [$_{COMP}$ which that] [$_S$ you asked [$_{\bar{S}}$ [$_{COMP}$ who] [$_S$ t_1 painted t_2]]]] is a yawl.

In case 13, t_1 is the trace of *who* and t_2 is the trace of *which*. The subjacency condition asserts that a movement rule—a rule relating an element (which may be phonetically null) to its trace—cannot be separated by more than one bounding node, where the bounding node for English is S. In case 5a, the acceptable sentence, *which* and its trace are separated by only one occurrence of S, as we can see in 11. In 5b and 5c, *which* and its trace are separated by two occurrences of S, as we can see in 12 and 13. Thus the principle of subjacency accounts for the distinction. Recall that in a language that formed relative clauses without movement (as in 5b′, 5c′), the principle would not apply, so that the corresponding sentences are well formed.

Choice of bounding node appears to be a parameter that can vary from language to language. Luiji Rizzi (1977) has argued persuasively that for Italian (and many other languages, including some dialects of English) the bounding node is S̄ rather than S. In all languages NP is a bounding node, however. Consider, then, the analogues of the sentences of 5 (namely, 11–13) in such a language. Sentence 5a (=11) is still well formed. Similarly, sentence 5b (=12) is not well formed, since *which* and its trace are separated by two bounding nodes, S̄) and NP. However, sentence 5c (=13) is now well formed, since only one occurrence of a bounding node (namely, S̄) separates *which* and its trace t_2.

Thus a slight change in parameter leads to a different array of well-formed and ill-formed sentences. As Rizzi further shows, a complex range of consequences follows from this change, and interaction with other choices of parameters leads to a still more intricate set of consequences, which are borne out by empirical investigation of several languages.

This example illustrates the situation that we expect to find if our earlier assumptions are correct. Certain general principles, such as subjacency, hold for certain categories of rules, and these principles have certain parameters to be set by exposure to linguistic data. Furthermore, there are very general conditions on rules that permit such rule systems as 8 but not others and permit *wh*-movement to COMP but not other types of movement. Fixing the parameters, we have systems of considerable complexity and intricacy, each with a certain range of empirical consequences. The consequences do not match cross-linguistically point by point, because of the intricacy systems in which they are embedded, but in a deeper sense the resulting languages are still cast from the same mold. Furthermore, each of the resulting languages—each end state of the process of language growth—may be quite remote in character from the input data that set the process of growth in operation; each such end state reflects the basic biological endowment that establishes a schematism for the growth of language. The child learning English or Italian, for example, need not be exposed to anything like the full range of consequences. Rather, the child needs evidence about the choice of parameters such as bounding node, and the full range of consequences then follows from the structure of the language faculty itself.

There are now preliminary data indicating that children manifest abilities implying their appreciation of conditions of this sort. Roeper (1978) has reported experiments in which children were asked to demonstrate the situations in 14 and 15.

14. Can you show Mary jumping?
15. Can you show Mary the jumping?

In 14 *Mary* is the subject of *jumping*; in 15 *the jumping* is a noun phrase and *Mary* cannot be the subject of *jumping*. Roeper found that three- and four-year-old children demonstrated clear-cut differences in interpreting these sentences, assigning the adult pattern to the relationship between *Mary* and *jumping*. Once sensitive to the distinction between noun phrase and verb phrase, marked by the presence or absence of the article, these children demonstrated capacities relating to the properties of rules determining relationships between elements inside and outside these structures. Roeper interprets his results within a framework for language development that makes central use of grammatically based mechanisms and in which the principles we have mentioned concerning relative clause formation are largely borne out (though in a different domain). The child need only find evidence pertaining to a restricted number of parameters of the linguistic structures he hears (bounding nodes, NP/VP markers), and a large number of constructions are mastered as a consequence of the way that this determination fits into what the child already knows about language, by virtue of biological endowment.

There is an empirical problem of considerable magnitude in relating these sorts of abstract (mentalist) accounts to organic structures (see Marshall, chapter 7, this volume). The most reasonable assumption, we believe, is to view linguistic capacities as the result of the functioning of genetically determined neural structures. The approach we have presented cannot serve to constrain the physical mechanisms involved in a narrow way, but it does argue that a high degree of environment-independent structure coupled with a very specific type of plasticity (to use a term popular in neurophysiology) must characterize this system. Furthermore, this abstract (mentalistic) approach can specify many of the conditions that the physical mechanisms must satisfy. Systems lacking these properties are not candidates for consideration as neural mechanisms underlying language development. It seems to us possible, in the current state of our understanding, to reach conclusions with regard to functional plasticity and specific roles for the environment in language development that might well be of considerable interest in the study of neurological mechanisms.

We have concentrated on a brief outline of one aspect of the language development process, ignoring many interesting areas, such as the specificity for language of the mental (and organic) processes involved and the role of nongrammatically based processes in language development. Our intention has obviously not been to review the entire field but to present a general approach that seems to us promising and suggestive for the understanding of language development. Limited but significant inferences can be drawn from these studies regarding organic mechanisms and processes. We believe that such an approach provides a natural framework for study of the basis and nature of human intellectual capacities and that it can be fruitfully integrated with other related inquiries.

REFERENCES

Bresnan, J. 1970. On complementizers: Towards a syntactic theory of complement types. *Foundations of Language* 6: 297–321.

Chomsky, N. 1970. Remarks on nominalization. In *Readings in transformational grammar*, ed. R. Jacobs and P. Rosenbaum. Boston: Ginn and Co.

———. 1971. Deep structure, surface structure, and semantic interpretation. In *Semantics: An interdisciplinary reader in philosophy, linguistics, and psychology*, ed. D. D. Steinberg and L. A. Jakobovits. Cambridge: Cambridge University Press.

———. 1976. Conditions on rules of grammar. *Linguistic Analysis* 2: 303–351.

———. 1977. On Wh-Movement. In *Formal Syntax*, ed. A. Akmajian, P. Culicover, and T. Wasow. New York: Academic Press.

Rizzi, L. 1977. Violations of the Wh-island constraint in Italian and the subjacency condition. Scuola Normale Superiore, Pisa.

Roeper, T. 1978. Linguistic universals and the acquisition of gerunds. In *Papers in the structure and development of child language*, ed. H. Goodluck and L. Solan. University of Massachusetts Occasional Papers in Linguistics No. 4, Amherst, Mass.

7

On the Biology of Language Acquisition

John C. Marshall

BLIND BOTANISTS

It will be as well to admit at the outset that the title of this chapter is certainly premature and probably presumptuous.[1] My only excuse lies in the hope that gaining some idea of why it is premature may help to hasten the day when a full-term birth takes place. The primary responsibility for our underdeveloped understanding does not rest with the biologists. They have accumulated a vast body of knowledge concerning the gross anatomy of the parts of the central and peripheral nervous system that seem to be implicated in the acquisition and exercise of linguistic abilities. Some knowledge is even available about the slightly less gross physiology of the relevant brain areas. Nor does primary responsibility rest with the students of developmental psycholinguistics. They too have amassed alarming amounts of data on the progression from the birth cry to the multiply embedded relative clause. The problem is rather that no one knows how to relate these two domains of inquiry to each other. To misquote Wittgenstein, behavior and physiology pass each other by.

We have so far failed to construct functional process models (psychological theories) that can mediate between noun phrases and neurones. In his seminal work on the aphasias, Freud (1891) asked rhetorically, "Is it justified to immerse a nerve fibre, which over the whole length of its course has been only a physiological structure subject to physiological modifications, with its end in the psyche and furnish this end with an idea or memory?" (p. 55). The task that Freud set himself—building a psychology for neurologists—is still with us. The metaphors of representation and computation that were intended to solve or at least bypass the mind-body problem have not brought anatomy and action together. Thirty-five years after McCulloch and Pitts (1943) proposed "a logical calculus of the ideas immanent in nervous activity," Freud's question echoes as loudly as ever:

> To mix hardware and program descriptions ("that transistor has a missing right parenthesis") is to make a category mistake. The conceptual distance between symbolic rules and neurons is so great that it is difficult to propose how knowledge about one might contribute to knowledge of the other (Colby, 1978, p. 7).

We have not found and systematically developed an appropriate level of theory construction, a level that would permit the output of hypothesized mechanisms to be checked for compatibility with linguistic generalizations, and the mechanisms themselves to be evaluated in terms of physiological plausibility. Consequently, our knowledge of the physical "instantiation" of language capacity and use is piecemeal at best. The nature of the organizing principles, the structure of the system eludes us. Despite Jackson's protestations, we continue to confuse the location of functions with the location of damage that impairs particular functions (Jackson, 1874).

With specific respect to acquisition processes, we have little idea of how to represent forms of interaction between innate and environmental variables in the development of complex systems.

A fundamental question concerns the extent to which available models give insight into developmental processes rather than merely specifying developmental stages as discrete time slices. Once more we see a number of (often extremely good) descriptions but little in the way of a mechanism that could move the child through the ever more complex structures over which he gains control. The very idea of stages seems to presuppose an underlying unity of process, a set of parameters that make stages the stages of a single organism.[2] It is here that the metaphors of embryogenesis and maturation capture the imagination. George Henry Lewes (1897) wrote, "Just as birds have wings, man has language. The wings give the bird its peculiar aptitude for aerial locomotion. Language enables man's intelligence and passions to acquire their peculiar characters of intellect and sentiment" (p. 143). Lewis is no doubt correct in his supposition, but can we turn the biological metaphor into a formal model with real power and depth?

It is not, of course, in dispute that acquisition of a native language in some sense depends on an intact and peculiarly human central and peripheral nervous system whose general plan is innate. Neither is it a matter of controversy that adequate exposure to a linguistic environment is required in order to transform capacity into skill. But *innate* and *exposure* are notorious weasel words; I shall therefore try to outline some of the radically different ways in which investigators have used such concepts. If some of these definitional tangles can be unraveled, we can then move to the more substantive issue of attempting to specify the range of nature-nurture possibilities that are compatible with learning to become and remain a mature, fluent language user. I shall then conclude with some speculations about the form that an adequate theory of language acquisition might take; obviously, the crucial question concerns the extent to which our fragments of knowledge can be used to constrain theories of the acquisition device.

WHAT IS INNATE?

It is well known that ethologists have as many concepts of *innate* as Eskimos purportedly have words for snow. Here I shall concentrate on just two usages. In one usage innate can be predicated of an anatomical structure that is present and functioning at birth. The current popularity of this notion is due largely to the reports of the last ten years or so that anatomical right-left asymmetries in the human brain are associated with some of the classical speech areas (Geschwind and Levitsky, 1968).

Classical speech areas are the cortical areas damage to which in right-handed adults typically produces aphasic manifestations.[3] The most important of these regions are the left inferior frontal gyrus (Broca's area), the posterior part of the left temporal lobe (Wernicke's area), and parts of the left parietal lobe, including especially the angular gyrus. Although controversy exists over the precise delimitation of these areas (vide infra), and indeed over whether the very notion of strictly demarcated regions is sensible (Bogen, 1976a), there is little doubt that the integrity of these brain areas is crucial for normal linguistic functioning in most adults. That these regions are implicated in language processes is also shown by EEG studies, although methodological problems complicate the picture (Donchin, Kutas, and McCarthy, 1977), and by measurement of regional blood flow (Ingvar, 1976).

It is against this background that anatomical asymmetries, favoring the left side, are to be interpreted. Some of these structural differences are apparently present at birth (Wada, Clark, and Hamm, 1975; Teszner et al., 1972), and indeed some can be observed as early as thirty-one weeks of gestation (Chi, Dooling, and Gilles, 1977). The account of Witelson and Pallie (1973) is very clear.

The finding that seems most reliable and has occasioned most comment is that the left temporal plane (a part of auditory association cortex) is generally bigger, sometimes substantially so, than the right. However, it does not seem true that all the gross morphological asymmetries in areas that form part of the neurological substrate for language show greater development of the left side. Campain and Minckler (1976) and Chi, Dooling, and Gilles (1977) have shown that the transverse temporal gyri are on average larger or more numerous in the right hemisphere. Wada, Clarke, and Hamm (1975) found that the frontal operculum is larger in the right, although measurement problems concerned with convolutional packing make them suspect that the opposite is the case. Akesson, Dahlgren, and Hyde (1975) report that the superior temporal gyrus, on some accounts a part of Wernicke's area, is larger in the right. Rubens (1977) claims that the retro-Sylvian parietal region, which includes the angular gyrus, is usually larger in the right. According to the classical lesion-derived model, all these areas are involved in language functions. There are, however, serious problems involved in measuring areas in objects whose landmarks are as complex and variable as those of the human brain. Inferences from surface area to volume are similarly fraught with difficulties. As Rubens, Mahowald, and Hutton (1976) point out, one will feel happier when gross morphological asymmetries have been correlated with the extent of cytoarchitectonic regions. Some preliminary, albeit very encouraging, results in which this has been undertaken are reported by Galaburda et al. (1978). Nonetheless, an eminent, skilled, and highly experienced neurosurgeon has seen fit to ask, Where is Wernicke's area? and give no (unique) answer (Bogen and Bogen, 1976). Lest this seem merely perverse on the Bogens' part, I note that Ojemann (1977) has written in the same vein.

One need only consult a number of standard neuroanatomical texts to find that although the angular gyrus is placed where Dr. Greenblatt has put it by the majority of authorities, and specifically by such experts in cytoarchitectonics as Von Economo, it is certainly not placed there by all. Krieg, for example, puts the angular gyrus in the posterior part of the temporal lobe rather than in the parietal lobe! (p. 14).

A brief but useful review of individual variation in brain structure can be found in Selnes and Whitaker (1977).[4]

The presence of morphological asymmetries at birth does not in itself demonstrate that functional asymmetries are in operation from an early age. Independent evidence, however, suggests that some language- or speech-related behavioral asymmetries can be detected in the infant. This can be demonstrated with electrophysiological techniques. Thus Wada and Davis (1977) have measured auditory evoked potentials to simple visual (flashes) and auditory (clicks) stimuli in babies of five weeks and have shown hemispheric asymmetries in coherence and power spectra. Molfese, Freeman, and Palermo (1975) have reported that in infants a late component of the averaged evoked response is larger over the left hemisphere for syllables and words and larger over the right hemisphere for noises and tones. Gardiner and Walter (1977) have noted asymmetries in EEG power distributions for speech and music with six-month-old babies. These same asymmetries for speech sounds and musical notes have been found by Glanville, Best, and Levenson (1977) with three-month-olds; their technique involved dichotic listening, and the behavioral measure was recovery from habituation of the cardiac response when a novel stimulus was presented to either the left or the right ear. Similar results are reported by Entus (1977), using an equivalent design that combined dichotic listening with a nonnutritive sucking response. Given the basic consistency of the data across a number of different paradigms, one could, at the very least, rationally conjecture that some of these behavioral asymmetries might be correlated with the morphological asymmetries that are currently being discovered (or rediscovered). On the other hand, it is far from clear how we are to relate the patterns of behavioral laterality that can be observed in the infant to those that we see in the language-proficient child or adult (Witelson, 1977).[5] No mechanism has yet been proposed that would serve to constrain language learning to those left-hemisphere areas that seem to constitute the neural substrate for language skills.

The suggestion that the two types of data—anatomical and behavioral—are related involves the assumption that (morphologically) bigger equals better. Geschwind (1972) seems fully prepared to embrace this conclusion: "What happens to the child whose brain shows a bilateral right-sided pattern of the planum temporale? What is that child like as compared to one who has a huge left planum and a small one on the right side? In other words, there are many different variations here which may well correspond to differences in talent." In addition to the range of normal variation in aptitudes, Galaburda et al. (1978) suggest that the extent of asymmetries might also account for individual differences in recovery from aphasia and for some childhood learning disorders. Franz Joseph, thou shouldst be living at this hour!

All we can confidently maintain is, that, *caeteris paribus*, a person who has this organ large, will be more easily induced to commit homicide, than one not naturally disposed to it by his organization (Gall, 1835), p. 42).

As for murder, so for language. Now, while Gall's hypothesis is perfectly reasonable, the history of phrenology shows that this game must be played according to the very strictest rules (Young, 1970). The basic problem was that many phrenologists looked only for confirming cases; little attention was paid to examples where a large bump was associated with limited talent or a small bump with exceptional performance. When counterexamples could not be ignored, ancillary hypotheses were invoked. For example, a large bump was said to be "inhibited" by some other bump, or a small bump for a particular faculty was believed to be supplemented by a bump that represented an alternative strategy for expression of an aptitude. Even worse, an appropriate education was deemed capable of modifying the expression of an innate propensity! Ceteris paribus indeed. One hopes that we are not going to repeat this fashion of playing tennis with the net down.[6]

One suspects that having a large left temporal plane is neither a necessary nor a sufficient precondition for becoming a linguistically fluent animal. Women (McGlone, 1977) and many left-handed men (Marshall, 1973) seem to manage quite nicely with little or no cerebral dominance for language.

Let us now turn to another sense of innate. In a number of publications Chomsky (and many other linguists) have made claims of the following nature: "A human language is a system of remarkable complexity. To come to know a human language would be an extraordinary intellectual achievement for a creature not specifically designed to accomplish this task. A normal child acquires this knowledge on relatively slight exposure and without specific training"

(Chomsky, 1976a). I shall defer consideration of the truth of the last sentence and concentrate here on the general form of the argument. First, some variant of such an argument must be true. It is close enough to a truth of logic (and materialism) that no animal can learn that which its central nervous system (and gross anatomy) does not permit it to learn. No circus Skinnerian would attempt to teach pigs to fly (except perhaps on a trapeze, although even here their tails may be a trifle small for them to achieve real proficiency). The only issue, then, is how strong a form of the linguist's "innate" argument can be constructed. "The question is not whether learning presupposes innate structure—of course it does; that has never been in doubt—but rather what these innate structures are in particular domains" (Chomsky, 1976a).

The "biologism" in question here is highly abstract. Lewes, as always, expresses the philosophy very clearly.

Different seeds and different soils yield different plants, but all have the same fundamental substance and the same constituent forms. A speculative botanist extracting these common forms may present them as *à priori* conditions and call them Nature's innate ideas; following thus in the track of speculative psychologists. The psychologist admits that all knowledge arises *in* experience, though not *out* of it. The botanist admits that all plants arise in earth or air, but not all out of them. There are conditions and pre-conditions of experience, as there are conditions and pre-conditions of plant life (Lewes, 1879, p. 18).[7]

As an example of a constraint on learning, Chomsky discusses the hypothesis that universal grammar contains the principle that a certain class of rules must be structure dependent. The specific exemplar given concerns one of the rules for the formation of questions in English. Chomsky claims that given a sentence such as "The man who is tall is in the room," the child will "unerringly" form questions of the type "Is the man who is tall in the room?" and will not ("if he can handle the example at all") produce such erroneous versions as "Is the man who tall is in the room?" Chomsky claims that "children make many mistakes in language learning, but never mistakes such as exemplified in [the last form]." The virtue of this and related discussions in the literature is that they make good, solid, empirical predictions, although testing them may not be quite the simple matter that Chomsky assumes. By the time the child "can handle the example at all," he will be quite old, and we are unlikely to know whether he is meeting the class of example for the first time. But this is clearly a technical difficulty rather than a principled objection. It does, however, leave open the possibility that at a much earlier age the child has learned the principle from simpler examples. I am aware that this remark is mere hand waving, but in the absence of studies of young children in which errors inconsistent with universal grammar have been specifically looked for, so is much else in this area.

Another issue is the extent to which such general principles as the notion of structure dependence are specific to language. Psychologists have tended to assume—without an excess of argument or data—that any principle of this sort must cover a much larger domain than linguistic knowledge. One popular version of this viewpoint is the claim that any universals of language are really universals of cognition.[8] It is not totally clear what has been gained by this stratagem. In theoretical accounts what has typically happened is this: A set of innate universals of cognition is postulated, and manifestations of structures that obey them are expressed in a formalism that is a vague variant of those found in linguistics (or worse, in predicate calculus). Since the structures found in cognition are then seen to have a surprisingly simple mapping to the (simplest) sentences of a natural language, the conclusion is drawn that innate linguistic principles are unnecessary. This is yet another disguise for our old friend who plays tennis without a net. There is, of course, an empirical claim involved, but it is difficult to obtain good evidence that bears on it (but see McNeill, 1971).

Whatever the eventual outcome, it is clear that there is a huge set of interesting problems here. I shall mention just a few. What are the psychological implications of the distinction between formal and substantive universals (Chomsky, 1965)? Should (one-time) universals such as the A-over-A principle, the complex-noun-phrase constraint, or the subjacency principle (which certainly do not look like cognitive universals) be interpreted as linguistic constraints in the sense of constraints on possible rules of grammar, or should they be regarded as arising from constraints on the processing machinery involved in the child's production and perception of language (Bever, 1970)? How can we build the constraints into a learning device, rather than regarding them merely as constraints on the states that the device can end up in (Wexler, 1978)? We are still a long way from formulating a clean set of principles of universal grammar, and we may find it far from easy to test putative candidates by observation of the classes of extrapolation errors in both comprehension and production that the child does or does not make. Nonetheless, it should be obvious that the research-program is at least pointing in the right direction.

It should be equally obvious that the two concepts of innate that I have briefly outlined are noncommensurate. Knowledge of the relative sizes of different cortical areas cannot constrain hypotheses concerning the principles of universal grammar or vice versa.[9] A theoretical physiology might make contact with psychology, but gross anatomy will surely not.

WHAT DOES EXPOSURE DO?

I turn now to the complementary problem of interpreting the environmental factors that serve to change structural capacity into functional skill. Here the issues are different from those involved in studying the (so far) noncommensurate concepts of innate prerequisites for the emergence of language. We know approximately what exposure to a linguistic environment is, but we do not know in any theoretically cogent fashion what it does or how it does it.

We can, however, clear away a few preliminaries fairly speedily. Modern-day children, isolated from human contact, do not spontaneously invent Hebrew, Lallans, or Phrygian (Stam, 1976), although they may invent some quite sophisticated manual languages (Goldin-Meadow and Feldman, 1977); neither do they invent Turkish if brought up in a monolingual English-speaking environment, although they may change pidgins into more complex languages quite rapidly (Sankoff and Laberge, 1974). But at least some arguments about the universal language are fortunately long dead and gone. God's own language has been replaced by the mysteries of natural selection, a concept that is itself not entirely lacking in theological undertones. As Marshall and Wales (1974) note, "If one cannot conceive of a *mechanism* whereby a particular ability came into existence, one claims that it took a long time to evolve."

No doubt a linguistic environment also motivates children to acquire speech, although one group of investigators (Lovaas et al., 1977) appear to have been mildly surprised to discover that, once having learned to talk, some children actually say more when left to themselves than when provided with "social reinforcement." It is, of course, a tribute to the inextinguishability of operant philosophy that this result should have an immediate interpretation in terms of the self-reinforcing nature of speech.[10]

But to more serious matters. What is the form and function of the utterances to which a child is exposed? What has purportedly been shown about the characteristics of the environment in which language learning takes place? In the heyday of "nativist" accounts of language acquisition (the early 1960s) it was widely assumed that the speech heard by children was a haphazard collection of sentence fragments, mistakes, backtrackings, throat clearings, and other kinds of unintelligible gibberish. This assumption appears to have been derived from analyses of adults talking to each other at psycholinguistic conferences. There is now, of course, a considerable body of evidence showing that the speech addressed to young children is typically very different from that addressed to older children and adults. Many of these variations are structural and seem to reflect something other than differences in topic and semantic content. Mothers, some at least (and other adults), frequently speak slowly to children, leave physical gaps between words or phrases, use an extended pitch range, give very heavy stress to lexical items, use short sentences, simplify the syntax, expand and even correct their children's utterances (Snow and Ferguson, 1977).

Although speech to children is often dramatically different from speech to adults, one could still argue that this is irrelevant to language acquisition, that it has no effect. One might even suggest that "motherese" has a deleterious influence on language learning. It is indeed not an a priori truth that restricting a child's access to certain grammatical constructions, for example, is the best way of teaching him the structure of his mother tongue. The issue at stake is, Which aspects of "motherese" are useful, which are irrelevant, and which are positively harmful?[11]

Let us look at this a little more closely and consider the form that studies of the role of the environment have typically taken. In a well-known paper, Brown, Cazden, and Bellugi (1969) report on a naturalistic (not experimental) investigation that showed a correlation, albeit a rather weak one, between rate of grammatical development and the frequency with which a mother expanded her child's utterance when responding to something the child said. That is, when the child says "Daddy sock," the mother responds with an utterance such as "Yes, indeed that sock does belong to your father." Brown, Cazden, and Bellugi are well aware of the interpretive difficulties attendant upon such naturalistic, between-child comparisons. In particular, there is the standard objection that one cannot infer causation directly from correlation. We cannot tell whether it is rate of expansion that stands in a causal relationship to grammatical development or vice versa. (Perhaps the child's rapid acquisition of language somehow inspires the mother to expand utterances. After all, children do become more interesting to converse with as they acquire greater facility in conversing.) Likewise, in a descriptive study one cannot rule out the possibility that some unknown, hidden variable (perhaps intelligence or personality) is responsible for both rate of acquisition and rate of expansion. Perhaps mothers who expand are likely to have children who are quick learners. Similarly, in a naturalistic setting one cannot fully unconfound and statistically partial out the numerous other parameters of maternal speech that may be associated with expansion rate. Clearly, experimental manipulation of the experiential factors hypothesized to be related to acquisition rate is called for, within the limits imposed by ethical considerations.

Early studies of experimental manipulation (Cazden, 1965; Slobin, 1968) were not very encouraging to the environmentalist position as it was then being formulated. But while Cazden and Slobin were themselves quite scrupulous in pointing out the preliminary, limited nature of their conclusions, it seemed regrettably easy for others to interpret such papers as showing that specific environmental factors (variables other than the sheer presence of talking adults) had little or no effect on language acquisition. A number of popularized textbook accounts interpreted such results as supporting the hypothesis of an innate language acquisition device of the type purportedly patented by Chomsky.

More recent work, however, has begun to suggest that some aspects of motherese are causally related to rate of acquisition. For example, in a study that assigned children to different experimental conditions, Nelson, Carskaddon, and Bonvillian (1973) have shown clear gains, in thirty-two- to forty-month-olds, as a result of adults' responding to the children's utterances with "recast sentences that maintained the same basic meaning but provided new syntactic information." Related work concerning the acquisition of new verb forms and new question structures is reported in Nelson (1977), and again the conclusion is that environmental manipulation may facilitate acquisition. A sensible discussion of the pattern of adult-child language interactions can be found in De Paulo and Bonvillian (1978) and in Bruner (1978).

I have intentionally quoted authors who have drawn fairly modest and reasonable conclusions from studies in which environmental modification was, in some sense, efficacious. But one does come across increasing numbers of writers who conclude that the effectiveness of motherese is inversely proportional to the plausibility of an innate language acquisition device.[12]

I have always suffered from cold shivers whenever I hear such arguments, but it was only recently that I finally realized why I had been so unhappy with the interpretation. The triggering factor was the paper by Munsinger and Douglass (1976), "The Syntactic Abilities of Identical Twins, Fraternal Twins, and Their Siblings." Although the contents of the paper are highly predictable from the title, I shall briefly describe them.

In their first paragraph they set up a conflict between Chomsky's approach to language development and Skinner's environmental "theory" of language acquisition, a viewpoint that "assumes that language is just another example of human behavior and that verbal behavior can be predicted and controlled by a few basic principles of operant conditioning." By contrast, Chomsky's theories "stress genetic mechanisms and maturation as the causes of language development and minimize the importance of social or cultural events." So far, so bad. Munsinger and Douglass's second paragraph must be quoted in its entirety if the full flavor is to come across.

Chomsky and Lenneberg are not specific about their innate language acquisition device, but they do say that it is genetically determined and deals with the basic rule system or syntax of natural languages rather than the surface utterances of children. These two assumptions imply that there should be a connection between the similarity of children's syntactic comprehension and the closeness of their family relations. Specifically, identical twin pairs should be most alike in language comprehension, followed in descending order of language similarity by fraternal twins and sibs, half sibs, cousins, and so on. Several methodological problems, such as the confounding of genetics and environment in most naturally occurring families, the determination of zygosity, and the reliable and valid measurement of language comprehension, independent of age, sex, and IQ variation, must be solved before these competing theories can be tested. But the basic logic of behavior genetic analysis offers some promise of settling this important theoretical dispute (p. 40).

What happens now? Munsinger and Douglass find some fairly reliable tests of syntactic comprehension; they select a group of 206 children in such a way that genetic-environmental confounding is minimized; they partial out the correlation of nonverbal IQ with comprehension scores; they compute $h^2 = 2(r_{mz} - r_{dx})$ and so on; and they conclude that "the heritability of children's language abilities is .79, and that the total environmental effect on language skills cannot be much over .10." This, I presume, is how "the basic logic of behavior genetic analysis" is intended to settle an "important theoretical dispute."

I do not want to argue the validity of heritability coefficients. We have been over this issue ad nauseam in the IQ and race debates. All that I am now concerned with is that results such as theirs are totally irrelevant to the universal grammar hypothesis. And I hold that this claim is correct quite irrespective of the intrinsic validity and meaningfulness (or otherwise) of the heritability estimates themselves.

What many students of the effects of the environment have done is to confuse two distinct genetic concepts. One of these notions (the one that Chomsky, I think, has in mind) is that the genome, its cytoplasmic environment, and whatever maturational processes it is involved in lay down the plan of a species-specific central nervous system. In the human case the intrinsic structure of the central nervous system both permits language acquisition and constrains the nature of what is learned from exposure to a linguistic environment. The other genetic notion—the one employed in behavior-genetic analysis—is that for a particular fixed gene pool and a particular fixed set of environments, genotypic differences account for a certain proportion of the observed variability between the individuals of a common species. Nothing but theoretical chaos can result from conflating these two notions.

In the case of Munsinger and Douglass's paper the observed variation in question is variation in the rate of acquiring the language—exactly the parameter that is measured in practically all studies that manipulate experimentally the extent to which and fashion in which mothers (and others) modify their speech when talking with young children. But irrespective of the rate at which they do so, what are all those children in Munsinger and Douglass's study acquiring upon exposure to English? Why, English, of course, just as if with exposure to Dutch they would have acquired that language. It is this remarkable ability to which Chomsky's speculations are addressed.

I think that we have fallen into this confusion because of our loose talk about the rapidity and ease with which the normal child acquires language on relatively slight exposure. To some extent Chomsky must himself bear the responsibility for the confusion, for he has repeatedly (and correctly no doubt) stressed the naturalness and facility of the child's language learning. But imagine that in the same kind of environment one child takes twice as long as another before it produces utterances that have the basic syntactic structure of English. For Chomsky's notion of innate it would obviously be a simple category mistake to argue from this that the properties of universal grammar are twice as innate in the first child as in the second. But the logic of behavior-genetic analysis dictates that, given an ideally identical environment, the differences between the children must be due to innate factors. Yet to say that some children learn faster than others or to point out that linguistic deprivation is not conducive to language learning is not to provide evidence against innate universals as constraints on learning.

In any case the environmentalist has yet another option if he wishes to prove that specific exposure is all important. The demonstration can even be conducted within the confines of behavior-genetic analysis. One simply performs the following experiment. Take 206 children of Chinese extraction and bring them up in a monolingual English-speaking environment, 206 children of Danish extraction placed in a Turkish environment, 206 English children placed in a monolingual Arabic-speaking environment, and so forth. It will surely be discovered that most of the variance concerning which language the different children speak is determined by their environment not by their inheritance.

All this simply serves to make the trivial point that however much weight one places on the role of innate constraints on what is learned, normal linguistic surroundings will always be rich enough in peculiarities to satisfy the most ardent environmentalist. Everything that distinguishes Dutch from Japanese is there, and it is after all Dutch or Japanese or whatever that the child must acquire. Clearly, it has to be exposure that determines which language, with all its idiosyncrasies, is eventually learned.

Believers in analogical learning can look at the child's overgeneralization of the particular morphological paradigms of the language to which he is exposed. Students of induction can see how long it takes the child to understand that attributive adjectives come before

the head noun in English but typically after it in French. Enthusiasts
of associative learning can observe how the (English) child comes to
acquire the (absolutely unprincipled) information that a certain type
of loud, high-pitched noise is called a scream, or/ki : m/ as the
children of generative phonologists pronounce it (Smith, 1973). De-
votees of one- (or few-) trial learning can attempt to explain Carey's
beautiful observations (Carey, 1978) on how easily children pick up
the meaning of new words heard in context. In brief, scholars who
disapprove of universal grammar will never be short of work. We
can even provide a lower bound for the amount of exposure that is
required. The child must have at least one exposure to each example
of every rule that is not universal but occurs in the language he is
learning; he must furthermore have at least one exposure to every
example of any exception to each rule of the language. As Chomsky
and Lasnik (1978) remark, "languages do contain idiosyncratic properties that must simply be learned and stated in particular grammar"
(p. 274). Having tidied up a few distinctions I shall now turn to
more substantive issues regarding the anatomical and physiological
substrate for language.

WHAT DOES ANATOMY MEAN?

In the last section I concluded that behavior-genetic analysis may
not be the best way to elucidate the biological foundations of language. But behavior-genetic analysis hardly exhausts the methods
and concepts of the biological sciences. Thus although I have also
been mildly skeptical of certain Gallist assumptions about size and
proficiency I want now to return to this issue, expanding the topic
to cover more general anatomical arguments.

   Let us grant that there are individual differences in the relative
sizes of the left and right temporal planes and that in a majority of
instances this asymmetry favors the left. What are we to make of
this? Within what kind of theoretical framework should we interpret
such findings? The first possibility that springs to mind is the null
hypothesis that the behavioral significance of the asymmetry is zero.
After all, within quite wide limits the total volume of the adult human brain seems to make little behavioral difference (but see Jerison,
1977).[13] But imagine that Gall was right, that absolute and relative
brain size is, ceteris paribus, a parameter with functional consequences. When taxed with naivety, Gall countered that on the whole one

would expect the larger of two cart horses to be the stronger. More recently Witelson (1977) has written,

Although a bigger area does not necessarily mean that it is more important for a particular function there are precedents in neural organization to indicate that size of cortical representation of function is positively correlated with degree of function. For example, the sensory and motor cortical representations for the hands are much larger than for the entire trunk of the body (p. 340).

It seems, however, that a straightforward interpretation of size and relative efficiency presupposes that the computational logic of the left temporal lobe (or its relevant subparts) and the homologous area of the right hemisphere should be identical. It could then follow that having more language-learning elements is what makes the left temporal plane a better linguistic processor than the right. But of course this model in which the left and right hemispheres do the same thing but the left does it better is false (Jackson, 1876). A variety of visual, visuospatial, and mainpulative skills are known to be more impaired as a result of right rather than left posterior lesions (Newcombe, 1969). If the right temporal plane is the natural substrate for some skill other than language, why does that skill not also require an extensive anatomical basis? The literature contains a few speculations on such issues. Thus Galaburda et al. (1978) suggest that "a larger right planum might signify a high degree of musical potential," thereby contradicting Gall who, on the basis of casts of the heads of Beethoven, Mozart, Haydn, Gluck, Liszt, Rossini, and many others, was inclined to place that faculty just over the Sylvian fissure. Chi, Dooling, and Gilles (1977) suggested that auditory association cortex may be more extensive on the left whereas primary auditory cortex may be larger on the right side. This leads them to wonder whether the "larger left temporal plane thus may provide more potential space for receiving and processing visual, somatosensory, and motor impulse to be integrated with auditory association areas in the left temporal lobe from which there may be outflow to other regions." We can be sure that despite (or perhaps because of) the conceptual problems involved, this whole area will continue to flourish over the next decade. Recent development in computerized tomography and related techniques might even permit experimental rather than observational studies to be conducted, thereby allowing hypotheses to be stated ahead of time.

It is certainly to be hoped that technological advances will soon allow us to reopen the whole question of localization of functions on a higher plane than currently obtains. Yet technique alone will not overcome conceptual confusion. As Vygotsky (1965) remarked, classical investigations "failed to arrive at an adequate solution of the problem because of the lack of structural-psychological analysis of the functions they try to localize." Vygotsky's summary is exactly to the point: "the problem of *what* can be localized is not at all irrelevant to the problem of *how* it can be localized in the brain." An appropriate *level* of description will presumably be intermediate between Wernicke's centers (or Gall's faculties) and the atoms of sensation and movement invoked by physiological associationists. We are thus led to ask whether the anatomy of language (or rather its psychological decomposition) can be given a theoretical foundation in the same kind of sense that some aspects of the anatomy of vision now seem to make sense (see Marr, 1976).

One would not expect language to be an exception to so many biological and artifactual mechanisms in which anatomy constrains function. After all, the shape of motor cars, the placement of the wheels, the position of the engine, and so on, have some relationship to its performance. Thus Lashley (1937) summarizes the prevailing spirit in his conjecture that "separate localization of functions is determined by the existence of diverse kinds of integrative mechanisms which cannot function in the same nerve field without interference." Interference apart, one might suppose that the finite speed of nervous conduction might itself place strong constraints on what must be next to what. It could be for such a reason that, as Freud (1891) wrote, "the parts of the speech region bordering on the cortical fields of the optic, auditory and motor cranial nerves have gained the significance demonstrated by morbid anatomy which has established them as centres of speech." Yet Lashley (1937) also raised the possibility that the topology of the neurological substrate for higher cortical processes might have no functional significance, arising merely as "an accidental product of the mechanism of embryonic development." Certainly gross anatomical connectivity is too weak a notion to support much theoretical weight, for, as Mark (1974) notes, Szentagothai has suggested that "the density of interconnections throughout the brain is such that one could trace a path via anatomical synaptic connections from any one neurone to any other one by passing through only five intermediate cells" (p. 118).

Can we specify then the domains for which Lashley's first hypothesis might be true? Can we also characterize the range of individual differences for which the precise topology and connectivity of the brain is irrelevant to psychological functioning? Is there more than one way of assembling a language-using machine? The answer to this last question appears to be an emphatic yes. Both pathological evidence from the effects of lesions sustained in adulthood and various indirect measures of laterality (such as studies of dichotic listening or of EEG recordings) have indicated considerable variability in the anatomical substrate for language skills.[14] Many workers have supposed that this variability must be correlated with comparable differences in functional efficiency. Yet efforts to show, for instance, that left-handers or women suffer cognitive impairment as a consequence of failing to follow the conventional blueprint (that of right-handed men without familial sinistrality) have not met with overwhelming success in recent years (Hardyck and Petrinovich, 1977; Fairweather, 1976).[15] Whatever subtle differences refined neuropsychological testing may find, normal girls and normal left-handed boys (where "normal" simply means without demonstrable brain damage) do not, as far as we know, fail to acquire the language of their community, nor do they use that language with noticeably less facility than anyone else. Nonetheless, the evidence from studies of brain damage in adults shows that aphasia from a right-hemisphere injury occurs with some frequency in nonright-handers and that the nature of the aphasia seen in the non-right-handed is frequently unclassifiable in terms of the traditional taxonomies (Gloning, 1977). Likewise, the results of McGlone (1978) indicated that, in contrast with men, "right-handed women did not show selective verbal or performance intellectual deficits after unilateral brain injury." Those impairments that were found were both "less severe and less specific" in women than in men.[16]

I have written that the capacity for language acquisition depends on "an intact (and peculiarly human) central and peripheral nervous system." But the bounds of normality within this general plan may be quite wide; the range of normal variability is apparently extensive (Whitaker and Selnes, 1976). Yet even more striking is that grossly abnormal brain development *can* be compatible with language acquisition and average or better linguistic performance. Thus Nathan and Smith (1950) have described a man of thirty-four with arrhinencephaly (nondivision of the cerebral hemispheres) but apparently normal intellect, temperament, and language. Dennis (1977) has reported that a fourteen-year-old boy suffering from noncommunicating hydrocephalus (with dilated ventricles and EEG abnormalities in the left postcentral region) nevertheless obtained a verbal IQ of 121. Sperry (1968) has studied a twenty-year-old girl with the entire corpus callosum missing. She had been obtaining average grades in a Junior City College while working twenty hours a week as an office clerk.

It is not necessary to claim that these and related conditions are typically asymptomatic with respect to psychological functioning; indeed such a claim would be false. But even solitary examples suffice to demonstrate that some brains with severe embryological malformations can mediate satisfactory language acquisition and adult skill. Naturally, when discussing instances such as these or some cases of recovery from childhood trauma), one talks of developmental compensation and the remarkable plasticity and capacity for reorganization of the immature brain. But such phrases are simply shorthand descriptions of the phenomena in question; they do not incorporate any set of principles that would show why some anomalies and insults can be compensated for while others apparently cannot (Hebb, 1942).[17]

Some of the most striking examples of plasticity are to be found in studies of hemispherectomy and hemidecortication. There is good evidence that if a damaged left hemisphere is surgically removed early in life, then the right can acquire and sustain good comprehension of language, good expressive skills, and an adequate verbal IQ. Indeed Smith and Sugar (1975) have reported one such case in which the right hemisphere maintained language and other intellectual functions that were well above average. However, Dennis and Kohn (1975) and Dennis and Whitaker (1976), while agreeing that a solitary right hemisphere can acquire excellent phonological and semantic abilities, have presented data showing that the syntactic competence of the right hemisphere may be quite restricted. It appears that the right hemisphere compensates for lack of truly syntactic abilities by reliance on semantically based strategies. Deficits of auditory comprehension show up (as errors and long latencies for correct performance) in situations where complex syntactic structure must be analyzed or produced without semantic support. This pattern of performance is not characteristic of the subjects with right hemidecortication, although one of the left hemidecorticate subjects in Dennis and Kohn (1975) is well within the range of the right hemidecorticate subjects.[18]

The conclusions of Dennis and her colleagues are broadly consistent with those reached by Curtiss, Fromkin, and Krashen (1978) on the basis of studies of a child in whom right-hemisphere language was most probably the result of severe environmental deprivation from an early age.

IS THERE A PHYSIOLOGY OF LANGUAGE?

There is at the moment no discipline that could be called the physiology of language and, to the best of my knowledge, no one has ever considered how theories within such a discipline could be constructed or evaluated. That is, we have no principled ideas about how language is coded by the brain. That there are codes whereby the brain represents information is both metaphor and fact. It is fact when we claim that in some parts of the nervous system the intensity of a signal is coded by the frequency of trains of nervous impulses; it is metaphor—but potentially very fruitful metaphor—when Macbeth desires to

Pluck from the memory a rooted sorrow
Raze out the written troubles of the brain

or when Freud (1896) emphasizes that the stages of perception can be likened to a translation of psychical material. Yet if there is to be a physiology of language we must discover how linguistic objects can be instantiated in neuronal nets, and we must discover what forms of linguistic representation can be transmitted by association fibers (granted, that is, the theoretical validity of nerve nets and association fibers). At the moment it would not be too unfair to characterize neuronal modeling as an enterprise that uses a very sophisticated mathematics to analyze the statistical behavior of large masses of nerve cells whose function is to provide statistical regularities that can indeed be so modeled.[19] Even for the simplest systems the majority of the candidate neural codes listed by Perkel and Bullock (1968) are annotated with the remark, "interpretation and biological significance unknown." Perhaps the unknown "codes" are not codes?

In large part, of course, this gloomy state of affairs is due to the enormous difficulty of the problem, especially when we consider language processes. But there is, I think, another reason for our failure to approach a physiology of higher cognitive processes: the

amazing success and insights of the explanatory mode created by
Carl Wernicke and his colleagues in the late nineteenth century
(Eggert, 1977). On the basis of the patterns of loss and preservation
of ability following brain lesions these men devised a theory that
showed how language abilities were organized into functional subsystems that could be disconnected by trauma. It is unnecessary to
dwell on the manifest virtues and extraordinary intellectual accomplishments of these men. The "diagram makers," as Henry Head
(1926) contemptuously referred to them, constructed formal theories
that they represented as finite-state graphs. Their diagrams thus generated, with minimal recourse to intuition, a typology of the
aphasias through injury to postulated centers and the connections
between them. They realized that their notation could, in principle,
"explain" any constellation of symptoms by the simple expedient of
proliferating centers and connections. In the interest of constraining
the theory they accordingly argued that postulation of a new center
or pathway was justified only if it enabled one "to represent the
causation of . . . derangements of speech" (Broadbent, 1878) other
than the one that initially prompted it. A simplicity criterion was
proposed so that 'the better theory" was the one that generated all
and only the observed symptom complexes with the smaller number
of centers and pathways between them.

   Unsurprisingly the black boxes (centers) of the nineteenth century
were very large and very black. Yet the fertility of the approach can
be seen from its reinvention in the second half of the twentieth century. There is a striking kinship between Wernicke's diagrams and
the flowcharts of our modern information-processing psychologists.
Much of the most interesting modern work on the aphasias consists
of attempts to decompose linguistic functions into units of a type
and size that could plausibly find a place in effectively computable
performance models.

   But now we can see the first way in which this mode of theorizing
may have misled us. When such models are "glued" onto the surface
of the brain, with the consequent confusion between localization of
function and of symptom, they seem, erroneously, to provide their
own physiological interpretation. The models attempt to incorporate
psychological theory directly into anatomy and physiology. Students of the philosophy of psychology were quick to spot such
sleight of hand.

Much of what passes for physiological explanation of psychological process is simply the translation of those processes in terms of hypothetical physiology (Lewes, 1879, p. 114).

And William James remarked on how unlikely these interpretations were.

If we make a symbolic diagram on the blackboard of the laws of association between ideas, we are inevitably led to draw circles, or closed figures of some kind, and to connect them by lines. When we hear that the nerve centres contain cells which send off fibres, we say that Nature has realized our diagram for us, and that the mechanical substratum of thought is plain. In some way, it is true our diagram must be realized in the brain, but surely in no such visible and palpable way as we at first suppose (James, 1891, p. 81).

Our flowcharts can reasonably be regarded as specifying "abstract conditions that unknown mechanisms must meet" (Chomsky, 1976b), but they are surely not physiological theories. To put the issue another way, when a classical aphasiologist says that Wernicke's area transmits an auditory form of a linguistic object via the arcuate fasciculus to Broca's area, are we to take the remark literally? And if so, what evidence could be held to support the claim? We all firmly believe that the corpus callosum transmits high-level information from one hemisphere to the other. Would anyone like to guess the properties of the language in which it does so? We have seen interesting correlations between evoked potentials and syntactic-semantic aspects of linguistic stimuli (Teyler et al., 1973; Johnston and Chesney, 1974). Freud (1913) believed that "the interpretation of dreams is completely analogous to the decipherment of an ancient pictographic script such as Egyptian hieroglyphs"; what are the formal properties of the script that emerge from the recording pen attached to surface electrodes? Can current electrophysiological techniques provide data that are interpretable as part of a linguistic system, or are we restricted to collecting correlations with particular stimulus conditions?[20]

A second block to the development of physiological theory for psycholinguists has been the failure of the diagram makers and their modern counterparts to consider any even remotely sophisticated concept of a machine. La Forge (1677) defines a machine as "a body composed of several organic parts which being united conspire to produce certain movements of which they would be incapable if separate." Yet to a considerable extent the model that underlies even the best modern work is one in which the individual components seem, when disconnected, to function in exactly the same manner as when joined together. It was, of course, Hughlings Jackson (1884) who first drew attention to the hierarchical organization of the central nervous system, but although we pay frequent lip service to his notion that damage releases the activity of lower centers from higher control, such ideas have had relatively little effect on the development of theory (but see Pick, 1931). An injection of control theory might help to bring the assembly line up to date (D. E. Broadbent, 1977).

In a serious effort to weaken the hold of the diagram makers Lenneberg (1973) has argued strenuously against the conception of the brain as "a collection of more or less independent apparatus connected to one another by cables." In casting around for an alternative he writes,

Assume that every histologically distinct structure in the brain has its own peculiar activity patterns; add to this the facts that just about every structure of the nervous system has a multiplicity of fibre systems that interconnect it, non-randomly, to several other structures, and that no nervous tissue is ever "idle"; then one is tempted to think that structures are not independent agencies that send messages to one another, but, rather, that the brain and its activities are in constant functional flux. Even when a steady state is reached, in the sense that different activities in different parts of the brain are relatively constant, the equilibrium of the system as a whole would still be precarious equilibrium. Any alteration of activity in any part of the brain would cause chain reactions of new interactions and cross-perturbations that might take a long time to reach a new steady state (p. 129).

This leads Lenneberg to propose that we replace our "switching diagrams" by "a new conception of four-dimensional dynamic patterns." In the new conception "all the specialized activities in all the different parts of the nervous system can be viewed as a single configuration, and the activity patterns of the brain can be seen as a series of moment to moment transitions from configuration to configuration" (p. 130). This is coding with a vengeance, for the problem of individuation within such a system is of horrendous proportions. Lenneberg wanted to characterize the aphasias within this paradigm as new steady states of the whole brain resulting from the malfunctioning of a part. Can we try to carry on from where he left off?[21]

My own feeling about the state of the art (a feeling for which I can offer no compelling rational justification) is this: The paradigm represented by Wernicke and Geschwind is wrong, but it has been and will continue to be supremely fruitful; the paradigm represented by Jackson and Lenneberg is right, but it will be almost impossible to obtain results within its confines. We can individuate the objects of concern within the high-level language of information processing, but Lenneberg seems to be asking what we try to do so in machine code. But then surely physiology is supposed to be the study of the machine code?

LEVELS OF UNDERSTANDING

What then are the prospects for a truly biological theory of language and language acquisition? Is it possible to integrate any of the disparate strands of data that are currently available? Marr and Poggio (1976) have recently produced an extremely lucid outline of some of the steps "from understanding computation to under-standing neural circuitry."

The CNS [central nervous system] needs to be understood at four nearly independent levels of description: (1) that at which the nature of a computation is expressed; (2) that at which the algorithms that implement a computation are characterized; (3) that at which an algorithm is committed to particular mechanisms; and (4) that at which the mechanisms are realized in hardware (p. 1).

With respect to psycholinguistic inquiry we can regard formal theories of universal grammar as putative accounts of what must be computed when utterances are expressed or understood. Chomsky's notion of competence has always had this character (Chomsky, 1955, 1978), although one might note that Marr (1977) has doubted the validity of such a computational theory for natural language.

The fly in the ointment is that while many problems of biological information processing have a Type 1 theory, there is no reason why they should all have. This can happen when a problem is solved by the simultaneous action of a considerable number of processes, *whose interaction is its own simplest discription* (Marr, 1977, p. 38).

While Marr may well be correct in this supposition, the achievements of linguistic theory make it sheer folly to concede the point at this stage.[22]

After a certain amount of backsliding, psycholinguistic studies now seem to have stabilized at a point where it is recognized that there is an essential difference between the theory of a computation and the algorithms that implement the computation. It has also been realized that the first level constrains the second. As Thorne phrases it,

A grammar will provide the most rigorous imaginable series of tests for a performance model; it will specify the results a performance model must give in every case. But the assumption underlying much recent work in psycholinguistics, that the study of the *form* of grammars is the right place to begin the study of performance models, is surely misleading (Thorne, 1966, p. 10).

Some progress has been made toward the formulation of adequate models for language recognition (Thorne, 1968; Marcus, 1977), and we can see in outline at least how experimental data might be brought to bear on them.

Marr and Poggio's third level, at which an algorithm is committed to particular mechanisms, has been the traditional preserve within psycholinguistics of the aphasiologists. The diagram makers' emphasis on the prediction of lesion site from symptom complex (and vice versa) was the first serious attempt to specify centers of integration whose integrity was crucial to normal language functioning. Some effort was even made to motivate the locus of these centers anatomically through Flechsig's concept of developmental (myelogenetic) localization (Flechsig, 1901). I shall not reiterate the problems that arise when localization of functions is confused with localization of symptoms (Caplan and Marshall, 1975) but merely express optimism that detailed studies of aphasic breakdown within an information-processing framework can discover computational units of the right size, that is, a size that can be interpreted as parts of a workable mechanism.[23]

It is at Marr and Poggio's lowest level, "basic component and circuit analysis," that neurolinguistics has thus far achieved the least success. We just do not know whether the neurones, synapses, transmitter substances, patterns of connectivity, and so forth, in the language areas of the brain differ in important respects from those characteristic of other parts.[24] Nonetheless, there seems to be no reason in principle why histological and histochemical studies should not eventually throw more light on these issues. Already we are beginning to see some results, both positive and negative (Galaburda et al., 1978; Oke et al., 1978; Hansen, Perry and Wada, 1972). So far—although not very far—so good. But when we turn to developmental considerations the picture is not an entirely happy one.

Nonetheless, our knowledge is slowly accumulating. The "time slice" approach to the characterization of the child's emerging language abilities is far from exhausted. Indeed it seems that much more detailed information is needed here if we are to cash the claims from universal grammar about the constraints that language acquisition is subject to. Recent developments in identifiability and learnability theory (Wexler, Culicover, and Hamburger, 1975) hold considerable promise that formal grammars can be restricted so that they are accessible to some device (even if not to a child!).

Process models are unfortunately almost unheard of in developmental psycholinguistics, although again experimental and observational data are coming to be seen within a framework that addresses itself to the algorithms that express the child's increasing command over his language (Morton and Smith, 1974; Tyler and Marslen-Wilson, 1978; Slobin, 1978; Roeper, 1978).

Studies of the acquired aphasias of childhood have not received nearly the attention that has been devoted to adult aphasia. We accordingly have totally inadequate accounts of the types of symptom complexes that an injured brain displays at different maturational stages. It is, of course, widely believed that the immature brain breaks down as a whole, rather than showing the very restricted patterns of impairment that can (sometimes) be observed in the adult. No doubt there is some truth to this observation, but an infant brain does not become an adult brain overnight, and one suspects that much more information can be obtained about the developmental progression as reflected in response to damage. Brown (1977) summarizes the types of observation that must be dramatically extended if progress is to be made.

Early childhood aphasia is characterized by mutism and/or agrammatism. Nonfluent phonemic paraphasia and word-finding difficulty tend to occur in older children. Phonemic paraphasia appears in the context of a non-fluent state, so that the picture of fluent phonemic paraphasia (. . . or "conduction" aphasia) is rarely encountered. Verbal paraphasia is rare, while logorrhea and jargon do not occur. In fact, the latter are uncommon even in adults prior to 30 (p. 54).

Again the question arises: Can we make sense of such data within both a psychological process model of acquisition and within developmental neurophysiology?[25]

It is once more at this lowest level of realization in hardware that developmental information is most lacking. This is not, of course, to say that nothing is known about embryological growth and neuronal differentiation and connectivity (Gaze, 1970; Jacobson, 1970; Conel, 1939–1967). From genetic structure to protein synthesis and cell division through to the gross "hooking up" of the nervous system, data are available in abundance (Goodwin, 1976; Weiss, 1976). Rather the point is that developmental neuroanatomy and neurophysiology have provided few or no principles that have specific reference to the neuronal foundations of language acquisition.[26] No doubt some parts of the nervous system do mature earlier than others, and no doubt the degree of structural maturity is related to functional capacity. But the traditional correlational approach to such relationships has not (and perhaps cannot) support much theoretical weight. Let us see why.

The rate of development of axonal myelination in some fibers of the nervous system has often been regarded as a critical assay of structural maturity; myelin sheaths assist the effective propagation of nerve impulses, acting both as insulators and as aids to "jumping." The chronology of myelogenesis can be followed in parallel with the unfolding of speech and language skills (Yakovlev and Lecours, 1967). But such correlations do not license one to infer either the causes or necessary preconditions of language acquisition. The postthalamic pathways to auditory cortex typically show a relatively late onset of myelination and a long, slow progress to their "mature" adult values. Can we conclude from this fact that the child's auditory abilities must be severely limited? Certainly not, for we know from behavioral studies (Mehler and Bertoncini, 1979) that the very young infant is responsive to a variety of sophisticated acoustic cues that form the basis for the development of the phonological component of the infant's native language. Correlations do not carry their interpretation with them. The data are consistent with the claim that myelination is (relatively) unimportant for the effective conduction of impulses to auditory cortex or that thalamic nuclei can mediate subtle perceptual differences (Walker and Halas, 1972). But we discover what the system as a whole can do at particular ages by seeing what it can do; it is counterproductive to infer from physiological parameters that the system cannot, could not display behavior of a particular type. As Lipsitt (1969) has remarked in a related context, it was for many decades assumed that "myelination was insufficiently advanced to permit learning in the newborn, and this premature conclusion inhibited functional studies of learning processes."[27]

These same considerations apply to the study of any other parameter of brain growth, including such potentially interesting candidates as dendritic arborization, density of axodendritic synapses, and number of glial cells. We know that the mentally retarded have learning difficulties, including slow and incomplete language acquisition; they would not be classified as retarded were this not so. But synaptic density may be within the normal range, although brain weight (and thus by inference the number of structural elements) is typically lower than in control subjects (Cragg, 1975). The interpretation of such structural differences must, of course, be made in the light of our knowledge of function. As Marr and Poggio (1976) point out when discussing the relationship between levels of description, "reductionism does not imply constructionism."

The real problem, however, I have left until last. As Lashley (1950) remarked, despite all the evidence against it "learning does sometimes occur." However strong the "innate" constraints, language acquisition is still language learning. And there are, with one or two fascinating but limited exceptions, no theories of language learning. Just as what used to be called learning theory in the behaviorist era was really the study of what was learned and under what conditions, so is universal grammar the study of what can be acquired from and projected from exposure to primary linguistic input. In neither case is a learning mechanism specified.

There are, however, very encouraging signs within psycholinguistics. I have already mentioned the valuable work of Wexler and his colleagues (Wexler, Culicover, and Hamburger, 1975). Other work has been reported by Anderson (1977) on the "induction of augmented transition networks" as models for the emergence of sentence production and comprehension in the child. Believers in a rich innate base for language acquisition will note that Anderson's program takes as input to the learning device a grammatically structured semantic representation and thus can give no comfort to hardline empiricists. Anderson does not, of course, specify how the child acquires "the language of thought" (Fodor, 1975) that is incorporated in the input. A recent program of great interest has been presented by Power and Longuet-Higgins (1978). They display an effective procedure for the acquisition of number naming and—here lies the novelty and virtue of the program—test it across a variety of diverse natural languages.

All available computational models of any interest presuppose a strongly constrained hypothesis space and a well-defined input "language." But when we turn to the learning theories currently available in a (quasi-)physiological format, we find associative theories of the most classical kind. Neuronal networks become programmed by principles no more sophisticated than contiguity of stimulation in time and space. How right George Henry Lewes was to emphasize that physiological theory is simply outdated psychological theory.

However much importance one attaches to the role of the linguistic, social, and physical environment in which language learning takes place, it is not likely that such principles (plus the minimal and mysterious stimulus generalization of the behaviorists) will suffice to project the examples to which the child is exposed to the language that constitutes his final steady state.

The neuronal substrate for associative learning is frequently held to reside in modifiable synapses, and many scholars have speculated that environmental influences can lead to hypertrophy, branching, and atrophy of these dendritic synapses. But there is a well-known difficulty with such concepts.

The simplest concept of learning and forgetting is that excess usage of synapses leads to hypertrophy and enhanced function, whereas disuse leads to regression and diminished function. This theory can be criticized because it is now recognized that almost all cells at the highest levels of the nervous system are discharging impulses continuously. One can imagine therefore that there would be overall hypertrophy of all synapses under such conditions of continued activation, and hence but little possibility of any selectivity in the hypertrophic change. Evidently, frequent synaptic excitation alone could hardly provide a satisfactory explanation of synaptic changes involved in learning. Such "learned" synapses would be too ubiquitous (Eccles, 1977, p. 334).

Two basic approaches have been tried in response to this little problem. The first is the approach represented by the Marr-Szentagothai "conjunction" theory of learning (Marr, 1959 and 1971; Szentagothai, 1971). The aim here of this approach is to formulate a physiologically plausible mechanism to constrain learning by requiring the simultaneous activation of two independent systems to induce growth. The other proposal stands traditional accounts on their heads by suggesting that learning proceeds by synaptic decay, repression, or atrophy. One can see the point of this by reflecting that in mammalian cortex the number of synapses that terminate on

the average cell is of the order of fifty thousand synapses per cell
(Cragg, 1967). As Mark (1974) has noted, "Nerve cells act as inte-
grators but how could integrating units each with an average of
50,000 inputs and 50,000 outputs possibly work?" A useful account
of the functional complexity of individual nerve cells can be found
in Scott (1977). Like grammars (Wasow, 1978), these devices are if
anything too powerful.

In embryogenesis of topographically organized parts of the brain it
is common for synaptic growth to be initially more widespread
than the final functional pattern requires. Precision of connections
depends upon competitive mechanisms acting to select the synaptic
input best suited, on embryological grounds, to a given post-
synaptic cell (Mark, 1974, p. 125).

It is against such a background that ideas of functional validation
and selective stabilization of developing synapses arise (Changeux
and Danchin, 1977). Jacobson (1975) proposes the concept of specification of language-subserving neurons, where the specification
consists of "progressive, irreversible restriction of their possible
functional roles." Shades of the prisonhouse begin to close on the
growing neuron, as Wordsworth no doubt intended to write.

Of all scholars who have embraced this point of view, Jean-
Pierre Changeux has been the most forthright. With true Gallic logic
he writes,

one might say that the potentialities of learning all the human languages known are proposed by the genetic program of the human
species as "latent" structures, following Lenneberg's terminology
(1967). The transition from the latent to the "realized" structure
would correspond to a *selection* of pathways characteristic of a
given language among these potentialities. Such a selective mechanism contrasts with any kind of "instructive" effect of the environment on brain structure long postulated by behaviorists. It is interesting to mention, with respect to the evolution of ideas in biological
sciences, that instructive theories always seem to precede selective
theories. In the case of the evolution of species, the synthesis of an-
tibodies, and enzymatic adaptation, the selective theories were
finally demonstrated to be correct. Why not as well in the case of
storage of memory? (Changeux, 1974, p. 296).

This is fine, except, of course, for the difficulties involved in un-
packing the notion of latent. If latent means already there (even
if only as veins or faults in the block of marble), then the idea is
highly implausible. The world's languages are clearly not prewired
into the central nervous system, with French (and many thousands
of other languages) decaying if the child happens to be born in

Peking. The sense in which Mandarin is selected needs careful consideration if selective theories are not to look exactly like tabula rasa accounts in which exposure to a linguistic environment stamps the language into the nervous system.

As Chomsky has always stressed, the central observation of developmental psycholinguistics is that the child acquires more than he experiences. We are beginning to see ways in which psychological theory can respond to this fact; it would be a pity if physiological theory were never to advance beyond the study of Hebb synapses.[28] Let us hope that eventually we shall be able to falsify Antoine Arnauld's claim that "the mind knows least of that to which it is most closely united, namely the brain" (Smith, 1902).

ACKNOWLEDGMENTS

I am very grateful to all the participants in the MIT Interdisciplinary Workshop on Cognitive Science for the informed, stimulating, and friendly atmosphere in which our discussions took place. "The work is not yours to finish, but neither are you free to take no part in it."

NOTES

1. The subtitle for this section is taken from Bullock (1965): "The brain does not divide up its functions into categories that correspond to our concepts or vocabulary. We are like blind botanists examining an elephant they can reach only with long probes. Commonly we have only a few specific effects of stimulation or ablation and are channeled thereby, with the aid of our language, so that radically different or subtler tests for the more adequate characterization are delayed" (p. 473).

2. It would be valuable to have a comparative analysis of the notion of stages as used in, say, biology, diachronic linguistics, and developmental psychology.

3. Similar "maps" result when the interference effects provoked by electrical stimulation of the exposed brain are plotted (Whitaker and Ojemann, 1977).

4. With respect to the Bogens' point, Selnes and Whitaker (1977) note, correctly, that differing views on what constitutes Wernicke's area "may in part be explained in terms of different views of what constitutes Wernicke's aphasia." Ojemann's remark appears to be immune to this observation, however.

5. On one interpretation this is to ask again for a characterization of the transition rules between stages.

6. My favorite example is quoted by Young (1970): "It is reported that when Descartes' skull was found to be remarkably small in the anterior and

superior regions of the forehead, where the rational faculties were localized, Spurzheim replied that Descartes was not so great a thinker as he was held to be" (p. 43).

7. Lewes is not, however, a Platonist: "To suppose that these laws have an à priori independence, and render our feelings and knowledge possible, is equivalent to the supposition of planes of cleavage floating about in the cosmos, and when descending upon certain solutions fashioning them into crystals" (Lewes, 1879, p. 174). One suspects that neither Popper's third world (Popper, 1972) nor Katz's abstract entities (Katz, 1977) would hold much appeal to Lewes.

8. A very sensible discussion of the role of cognitive development in language acquisition will be found in Schlesinger (1977).

9. Peters (1977), however, has suggested that "two fundamentally different strategies may be employed by very young children learning their first language." And she wonders whether these gestalt and analytic approaches may be related to lateralization.

10. The classical observations of Ruth Weir (1962) suggest that even in the very early stages of learning to talk, a child may practice without the instant praise of proud parents.

11. No one denies that many mothers may be quite helpful. But the assumption of much of the motherese literature—that all mothers are perfect teaching machines—is odd, to say the least.

12. A recent example is provided by Moskowitz (1978): "It is not surprising that elaborate theories of innate language ability arose during the years when linguists examined the speech adults addressed to adults and assumed that the speech addressed to children was similar" (p. 94).

13. Cragg (1974) writes, "Deviations of brain size, cortical thickness and other gross variables are not necessary or sufficient to entail (mental) deficiency" (p. 144).

14. There are, however, many problems with any straightforward anatomical interpretation of dichotic listening studies. The chief difficulty concerns the extent to which dichotic listening is influenced by subjects' adopting strategies that are not under the experimenter's control. This raises awkward conceptual issues concerning the hardware-software distinction (Moor, 1978). Related problems with strategy effects arise also in EEG studies (Beaumont, Mayes, and Rugg, 1978). Some experiments have been reported that run counter to the usual finding of greater asymmetry in men than women (Gale et al., 1978).

15. Failure to replicate the results of Levy (1969) has been a major growth industry in neuropsychology in recent years.

16. Even right-handed men without familial sinistrality *can* have right-hemisphere language. Hutton et al. (1977) have reported on such a case.

This man showed no aphasic signs following surgical excision (for tumor) of the greater part of the left hemisphere. (Prior to surgery his only deficit was mild difficulty in object naming). A good review of putative sex differences in cerebral organization can be found in Bryden (1978). Waber (1977) gives an interesting maturational account of such differences.

17. The individual differences observed among commissurotomy patients provide a rich source of data highly relevant to these issues (Bogen, 1976b; Ledoux et al., 1977). Goldman (1972) gives an elegant account of the general problem of cortical plasticity. Jacobs (1977) cautions that "hemispherectomies" differ from one surgeon to another.

18. Zaidel (1977) has also noted the aphasiclike character of the right-hemisphere's language.

19. An interesting example of a neural model that does model something other than itself is to be found in Anderson et al., (1977).

20. Molfese (1978) has attempted to bring some order into electrophysiological studies of speech perception.

21. To further illustrate our lack of a common, agreed upon framework, I note that the absolute antithesis of Lenneberg's "brain view" is alive and well. Thus Konorski (1970) claims that "not only letters but also common words are represented by single units." And Wickelgren (1977) has even proposed a way whereby one might find a single grandmother cell in the haystack of the brain.

22. At artificial intelligence conferences, it is apparently permissible to make a virtue of having no theory of a natural language computation. Thus Shank (1978) wrote, "Suppose every domain we worked on required yet another ad hoc solution. This might well be the case after all. What would we lose if this happened? Nothing at all. That's what artificial intelligence is all about" (p. 9). If this is the methodology of artificial intelligence, would it not be easier to revert to the traditional biological technique for making a language acquisition device? The time-honored method could hardly be less rewarding intellectually, and it is far more enjoyable.

23. Von Eckardt Klein (1978) gives a very clear account of the logic of functional localization. Marin, Saffran, and Schwartz (1976) outline some crucial results.

24. Chapter 2 of Lenneberg (1967) summarizes some of the basic information.

25. Geschwind (1972) has some provocative remarks on this problem, although the psychology is rather crude.

26. We have, for instance, nothing as neat as Bard's model (1977) of zebra generation.

27. A further cautionary tale can be found in Lewis, Maurer, and Kay (1978).

28. I do not wish to suggest by this that the modeling of formal synapses for associative learning is either an uninteresting or an easy task. Some insightful results and conjectures are presented by Brindley (1969).

REFERENCES

Akesson, E. J., Dahlgren, W. J., and Hyde, J. B. 1975. Memory and growth in the superior temporal gyri. *Can. J. Neurol. Sci.* 7: 191–194.

Anderson, J. 1977. Induction of augmented transition networks. *Cognitive Science* 1: 125–157.

Anderson, J. A., Silverstein, J. W., Ritz, S. A., and Jones, R. S. 1977. Distinctive features, categorial perception, and probability learning: Some applications of a neural model. *Psychological Review* 84: 413–451.

Bard, J. 1977. A unity underlying the different zebra striping patterns. *Journal of Zoology, London* 183: 527–539.

Beaumont, J., Mayes, A. R., and Rugg, M. D. 1978. Asymmetry in EEG alpha coherence and power: Effects of task and sex. *Electroencephalography and Clinical Neurophysiology* 45: 393–401.

Bever, T. 1970. The influence of speech performance on linguistic structures. In *Advances in psycholinguistics*, ed. G. B. Flores d'Arcais and W. J. M. Levelt. Amsterdam: North-Holland.

Bogen, J. E. 1976. Hughlings Jackson's heterogram. In *BIS Conference Report* 42, ed. D. O. Walter, L. Rogers, and J. M. Finzi-Friied. Berkeley and Los Angeles: University of California Press.

———. 1976b. Linguistic performance in the short-term following cerebral commissurotomy. In *Studies in neurolinguistics, vol. 2*, ed. H. Whitaker and H. A. Whitaker. New York: Academic Press.

Bogen, J. E., and Bogen, G. M. 1976. Wernicke's region: Where is it? *Annals of the New York Academy of Sciences* 280: 834–843.

Brindley, G. S. 1969. Nerve net models of plausible size that perform many simple learning tasks. *Proc. Roy. Soc. Lond. B* 174: 173–191.

Broadbent, D. E. 1977. Levels, hierarchies, and the locus of control. *Quarterly Journal of Experimental Psychology* 29: 181–201.

Broadbent, W. B. 1878. A case of peculiar affection of speech, with commentary. *Brain* 1: 484–503.

Brown, J. 1977. *Mind, brain, and consciousness.* New York: Academic Press.

Brown, R., Cazden, C., and Bellugi, U. 1969. The child's grammar from I to III. In *Minnesota symposia on child psychology*, ed. J. P. Hill. Minneapolis: University of Minnesota Press.

Bruner, J. S. 1978. The role of dialogue in language acquisition. In *The child's conception of language,* ed. A. Sinclair, R. J. Jarvella, and W. J. M. Levelt. Berlin: Springer-Verlag.

Bryden, M. P. 1978. Evidence for sex differences in cerebral organization. In *Sex-related differences in cognitive functioning: Developmental issues,* ed. M. A. Wittig and A. C. Peterson. New York: Academic Press.

Bullock, T. H. 1965. Physiological bases of behavior. In *Ideas in modern biology,* ed. J. A. Moore. New York: Natural History Press.

Campain, R., and Minckler, J. 1976. A note on the gross configurations of the human auditory cortex. *Brain and Language* 3: 318–323.

Caplan, D., and Marshall, J. C. 1975. Review article: Generative grammar and aphasic disorders. A theory of language representation in the human brain. *Foundations of Language* 12: 583–596.

Carey, S. 1978. The child as word learner. In *Linguistic theory and psychological reality,* ed. M. Halle, J. Bresnan, and G. A. Miller. Cambridge, Mass.: MIT Press.

Cazden, C. 1965. Environmental assistance to the child's acquisition of grammar. Doctoral dissertation; Harvard University.

Changeux, J.-P. 1974. Some biological observations relevant to a theory of learning. In *Current problems in psycholinguistics,* ed. F. Bresson and J. Mehler. Paris: CNRS.

Changeux, J.-P., and Danchin, A. 1977. Biochemical models for the selective stabilization of developing synapses. In *Synapses,* ed. G. A. Cottrell and P. Underwood. London: Blackie.

Chi, J. G., Dooling, E. C., and Gilles, F. H. 1977. Left-right asymmetries of the temporal speech areas of the human fetus. *Archives of Neurology* 34: 346–348.

Chomsky, N. 1975. *The logical structure of linguistic theory.* New York: Plenum Press.

———. 1965. *Aspects of the theory of syntax.* Cambridge, Mass.: MIT Press.

———. 1976a. *Reflections on language.* New York: Pantheon.

———. 1976b. On the biological basis of language capacities. In *The neuropsychology of language,* ed. R. W. Rieber. New York: Plenum Press.

———. 1978. Language and unconscious knowledge. In *Psychoanalysis and language,* ed. J. H. Smith. New Haven, Conn.: Yale University Press.

Chomsky, N., and Lasnik, H. 1978. A remark on contraction. *Linguistic Inquiry* 9: 268–274.

Colby, K. M. 1978. Mind models: An overview of current work. *Mathematical Biosciences* 39: 159–185.

Conel, J. L. 1939–1967. *The postnatal development of the human cerebral cortex.* Cambridge, Mass.: Harvard University Press.

Cragg, B. G. 1967. The density of synapses and neurones in the motor and visual areas of the cerebral cortex. *Journal of Anatomy* 101: 639–654.

———. 1974. Plasticity of synapses. *British Medical Bulletin* 30: 141–144.

———. 1975. The density of synapses and neurons in normal, mentally defective, and aging human brains. *Brain* 98: 81–90.

Curtiss, S., Fromkin, V. A., and Krashen, S. D. 1978. Language development in the mature (minor) right hemisphere. *ITL: Review of Applied Linguistics* 39/40: 23–37.

Dennis, M. 1977. Cerebral dominance in three forms of early brain disorder. In *Child neurology,* ed. M. E. Blaw, I. Rapin, and M. Kinsbourne. New York: Spectrum Publications.

Dennis, M., and Kohn, B. 1975. Comprehension of syntax in infantile hemiplegics after cerebral hemidecortication: Left-hemisphere superiority. *Brain and Language* 2: 472–482.

Dennis, M., and Whitaker, H. A. 1976. Language acquisition following hemidecortication: Linguistic superiority of the left over the right hemisphere. *Brain and Language* 3: 404–433.

DePaulo, B., and Bonvillian, J. D. 1978. The effect on language development of the special characteristics of speech addressed to children. *Journal of Psycholinguistic Research* 7: 189–211.

Donchin, E., Kutas, M., and McCarthy, G. 1977. Electrocortical indices of hemispheric utilization. In *Lateralization in the nervous system,* ed. S. Harnad, R. Doty, L. Goldstein, J. Jaynes and G. Krauthamer. New York: Academic Press.

Eccles, J. C. 1977. An instruction-selection theory of learning in the cerebellar cortex. *Brain Research* 127: 327–352.

Eggert, G. H. 1977. *Wernicke's works on aphasia.* The Hague: Mouton.

Entus, A. K. 1977. Hemispheric asymmetry in processing of dichotically presented speech and nonspeech stimuli by infants. In *Language development and neurological theory,* ed. S. Segalowitz and F. Gruber. New York: Academic Press.

Fairweather, H. 1976. Sex differences in cognition. *Cognition* 4: 231–280.

Flechsig, P. 1901. Developmental (myelogenetic) localization of the cerebral cortex in the human subject. *Lancet* 2: 1027–1029.

Fodor, J. A. 1975. *The language of thought.* New York: Crowell.

Freud, S. 1891. *Zur Auffassung der Aphasien.* Vienna: Deuticke.

———. 1896. Letter 52. *The standard edition*, vol. 1. London: Hogarth Press.

———. 1913. The claims of psychoanalysis to scientific interest. *Scientia* 14: 240–250, 369–384.

Galaburda, A. M., LeMay, M., Kemper, T. L., and Geschwind, N. 1978. Right-left asymmetries in the brain. *Science* 199: 852–856.

Gale, A., Brown, A., Osborne, K., and Smallbone, A. 1978. Further evidence of sex differences in brain organization. *Biological Psychology* 6: 203–208.

Gall, F. J., with J. C. Spurzheim. 1835. *On the functions of the brain and of each of its parts.* Boston: Marsh, Capen, and Lyon.

Gardiner, M. F., and Walter, D. O. 1977. Evidence of hemispheric specialization from infant EEG. In *Lateralization in the nervous system*, ed. S. Harnad, R. Dotty, L. Goldstein, J. Jaynes, and G. Krauthamer. New York: Academic Press.

Gaze, R. M. 1970. *The formation of nerve connections.* New York: Academic Press.

Geschwind, N. 1972. Disorders of higher cortical function in children. *Clinical Proceedings Children's Hospital National Medical Center* 28: 261–272.

Geschwind, N., and Levitsky, W. 1968. Human brain: Left-right asymmetries in temporal speech region. *Science* 161: 186–187.

Glanville, B., Best, C., and Levenson, R. 1977. A cardiac measure of cerebral asymmetries in infant auditory perception. *Developmental Psychology* 13: 54–59.

Gloning, K. 1977. Handedness and aphasia. *Neuropsychologia* 15: 355–358.

Goldin-Meadow, S., and Feldman, H. 1977. The development of language-like communication without a language model. *Science* 197: 401–403.

Goldman, P. S. 1972. Developmental determinants of cortical plasticity. *Acta Neurobiologiae Experimentalis* 32: 495–511.

Goodwin, B. C. 1976. *Analytical physiology of cells and developing organisms.* New York: Academic Press.

Hansen, S., Perry, T. L., and Wada, J. A. 1972. Amino acid analysis of speech areas in human brain: Absence of left-right asymmetry. *Brain Research* 45: 318–320.

Hardyck, C., and Petrinovich, L. F. 1977. Left-handedness. *Psychological Bulletin* 84: 385–404.

Head, H. 1926. *Aphasia and kindred disorders of speech.* Cambridge: Cambridge University Press.

Hebb, D. O. 1942. The effect of early and late brain injury upon test scores, and the nature of normal adult intelligence. *Proceedings of the American Philosophical Society* 85: 275–292.

Hutton, J. T., Arsenina, N., Kotik, B., and Luria, A. R. 1977. On the problems of speech compensation and fluctuating intellectual performance. *Cortex* 13: 195–207.

Ingvar, D. H. 1976: Functional landscapes of the dominant hemisphere. *Brain Research* 107: 181–197.

Jackson, J. H. 1874. On the nature of the duality of the brain. *Medical Press and Circular* 1: 19–41.

——. 1876. Case of large cerebral tumour without optic neuritis and with left hemiplegia and imperception. *Royal London Opthalmic Hospital Reports* 8: 434–441.

——. 1884. Evolution and dissolution of the nervous system. *Popular Science Monthly* 25: 171–180.

Jacobs, J. 1977. An external view of neuropsychology and its working milieu. In *Language development and neurological theory*, ed. S. Segalowitz and F. Gruber. New York: Academic Press.

Jacobson, M. 1970. *Developmental neurobiology*. New York: Holt, Rinehart and Winston.

——. 1975. Brain development in relation to language. In *Foundations of language development*, vol. 1, ed. E. H. Lenneberg and E. Lenneberg. New York: Academic Press.

James, W. 1891. *The principles of psychology*. London: Macmillan.

Jerison, H. J. 1977. The theory of encephalization. *Annals of the New York Academy of Sciences* 299: 146–160.

Johnston, V. S., and Chesney, G. L. 1974. Electrophysiological correlates of meaning. *Science* 186: 944–946.

Katz, J. J. 1977. The real status of semantic representations. *Linguistic Inquiry* 8: 559–584.

Konorski, J. 1970. Pathophysiological mechanisms of speech on the basis of studies on aphasia. *Acta Neurobiologiae Experimentalis* 30: 189–210.

La Forge, L. de. 1677. *Remarques*. Paris.

Lashley, K. S. 1937. Functional determinants of cerebral localization. *Archives of Neurology and Psychiatry* 38: 371–387.

——. 1950. In search of the engram. *Symposia of the Society for Experimental Biology* 4: 454–482.

Ledoux, J., Risse, G., Springer, S., Wilson, D., and Gazzaniga, M. 1977. Cognition and commissurotomy. *Brain* 100: 87–104.

Lenneberg, E. H. 1967. *Biological foundations of language*. New York: Wiley.

———. 1973. The neurology of language. *Daedalus* 102: 115–133.

Levy, J. 1969. Possible basis for the evolution of lateral specialization of the human brain. *Nature* 224: 614–615.

Lewes, G. H. 1879. *The study of psychology*. Cambridge, Mass.: Riverside Press.

Lewis, T. L., Maurer, D., and Kay, D. 1978. Newborns' central vision: Whole or hole? *Journal of Experimental Child Psychology* 26: 193–203.

Lipsitt, L. P. 1969. Discussion. In *Brain and early behavior*, ed. R. J. Robinson. New York: Academic Press.

Lovaas, O. I., Varni, J. W., Koegel, R. L., and Lorsch, N. 1977. Some observations on the nonextinguishability of children's speech. *Child Development* 48: 1121–1127.

Marcus, M. P. 1977. A theory of syntactic recognition for natural language. Ph.D. thesis, Massachusetts Institute of Technology.

Marin, O. S. M., Saffran, E. M., and Schwartz, M. F. 1976. Dissociations of language in aphasia: Implications for normal function. *Annals of the New York Academy of Sciences* 280: 868–884.

Mark, R. 1974. *Memory and nerve cell connections*. Oxford: Clarendon Press.

Marr, D. 1969. A theory of cerebellar cortex. *Journal of Physiology* (London) 202: 437–470.

———. 1971. Simple memory: A theory for archicortex. *Phil. Trans. Roy. Soc. B* 252: 23–81.

———. 1976. Early processing of visual information. *Phil. Trans. Roy. Soc. B* 275: 483–524.

———. 1977. Artificial intelligence: A personal view. *Artificial Intelligence* 9: 37–48.

Marr, D., and Poggio, T. 1976. From understanding computation to understanding neural circuitry. *MIT A.I. Memo 357*, May 1976.

Marshall, J. C. 1973. Some problems and paradoxes associated with recent accounts of hemispheric specialization. *Neuropsychologia* 11: 463–470.

Marshall, J. C., and Wales, R. J. 1974. Pragmatics as biology or culture. In *Pragmatic aspects of human communication*, ed. C. Cherry. Dordrecht: D. Reidel.

McCulloch, W. S., and Pitts, W. 1943. A logical calculus of the ideas immanent in nervous activity. *Bulletin of Mathematical Biophysics* 5: 115–133.

McGlone, J. 1977. Sex differences in the cerebral organization of verbal functions in patients with unilateral brain lesions. *Brain* 100: 775–793.

————. 1978. Sex differences in functional brain asymmetry. *Cortex* 14: 122–128.

McNeill, D. 1971. Explaining linguistic universals. In *Biological and social factors in psycholinguistics*, ed. J. Morton. London: Logos Press.

Mehler, J., and Bertoncini, J. 1979. Infants' perception of speech and other acoustic stimuli. In *Psycholinguistics series, structures and processes*, vol. 2, ed. J. Morton and J. C. Marshall. London: Elek.

Molfese, D. 1978. Left and right hemisphere involvement in speech perception: Electrophysiological correlates. *Perception and Psychophysics* 23: 237–243.

Molfese, D., Freeman, R., and Palermo, D. 1975. The ontogeny of brain lateralization for speech and nonspeech stimuli. *Brain and Language* 2: 356–368.

Moor, J. H. 1978. Three myths of computer science. *Brit. J. Phil. Sci.* 29: 213–222.

Morton, J., and Smith, N. 1974. Some ideas concerning the acquisition of phonology. In *Current problems in psycholinguistics*, ed. F. Bresson and J. Mehler. Paris: CNRS.

Moskowitz, B. A. 1978. The acquisition of language. *Scientific American*, November 239: 92–106.

Munsinger, H., and Douglass, A. 1976. The syntactic abilities of identical twins, fraternal twins, and their siblings. *Child Development* 47: 40–50.

Nathan, P. W., and Smith, M. C. 1950. Normal mentality associated with maldeveloped "rhinencephalon." *Journal of Neurology, Neurosurgery, and Psychiatry* 13: 191–197.

Nelson, K. E. 1977. Facilitating children's syntax acquisition. *Developmental Psychology* 13: 101–107.

Nelson, K. E., Carskaddon, G., and Bonvillian, J. 1973. Syntax acquisition: Impact of experimental variation in adult verbal interaction with the child. *Child Development* 44: 497–504.

Newcombe, F. 1969. *Missile wounds of the brain.* London: Oxford University Press.

Ojemann, G. A. 1977. Comments. *Neurosurgery* 1: 14–15.

Oke, A., Keller, R., Metford, I., and Adams, R. N. 1978. Lateralization of norepinephrine in human thalamus. *Science* 200: 1411–1413.

Perkel, D. H., and Bullock, T. H. 1968. Neural coding. *Neurosciences Research Bulletin* 6: 221–348.

Peters, A. M. 1977. Language learning strategies: Does the whole equal the sum of the parts? *Language* 55: 560–573.

Pick, A. 1931. Aphasie. *Handbuch der normalen und pathologischen Physiologie* 15: 1416–1524.

Popper, K. R. 1972. *Objective knowledge.* Oxford: Clarendon Press.

Power, R. J. D., and Longuet-Higgins, H. C. 1978. Learning to count: A computational model of language acquisition. *Proc. R. Soc. Lond. B* 200: 391–417.

Roeper, T. 1978. Linguistic universals and the acquisition of gerunds. *Occasional Papers in Linguistics,* vol. 4. Linguistics Department, University of Massachusetts, Amherst.

Rubens, A. B. 1977. Anatomic asymmetries of human cerebral cortex. In *Lateralization in the nervous system,* ed. S. Harnad, R. Doty, L. Goldstein, J. Jaynes, and G. Krauthamer. New York: Academic Press.

Rubens, A. B., Mahowald, M. W., and Hutton, J. H. 1976. Asymmetry of the lateral (Sylvian) fissures in man. *Neurology* 26: 620–624.

Sankoff, G., and Laberge, S. 1974. On the acquisition of native speakers by a language. In *Pidgins and creoles: Current trends and prospects,* ed. D. DeCamp and I. F. Hancock. Washington, D. C.: Georgetown University Press.

Schlesinger, I. M. 1977. The role of cognitive development and linguistic input in language acquisition. *Journal of Child Language* 4: 153–169.

Scott, A. C. 1977. Neurodynamics: A critical survey. *Journal of Mathematical Psychology* 15: 1–45.

Selnes, O. A., and Whitaker, H. A. 1977. Neurological substrates of language and speech production. In *Sentence production,* ed. S. Rosenberg. Hillsdale, N.J.: L. Erlbaum.

Shank, R. C. 1978. What makes something "ad hoc"? *Theoretical Issues in Natural Language Processing* 2: 8–13.

Slobin, D. 1968. Imitation and grammatical development in children. In *Contemporary issues in developmental psychology,* ed. N. Endler, L. Boulter, and H. Osser. New York: Holt, Rinehart and Winston.

———. 1978. Universal and particular in the acquisition of language. Paper prepared for the workshop on language acquisition, University of Pennsylvania, May 19–22.

Smith, A., and Sugar, O. 1975. Development of above normal language and intelligence 21 years after left hemispherectomy. *Neurology.* 25: 813–818.

Smith, N. V. 1973. *The acquisition of phonology: A case study.* Cambridge: Cambridge University Press.

Smith, N. 1902. *Studies in the cartesian philosophy.* London: Macmillan.

Snow, C., and Ferguson, C. (eds.) 1977. *Talking to children.* Cambridge: Cambridge University Press.

Sperry, R. 1968. Plasticity of neural maturation. *Developmental Biology Supplement* 2: 306–327.

Stam, J. H. 1976. *Inquiries into the origin of language.* New York: Harper and Row.

Szentagothai, J. 1971. Memory functions and the structural organization of the brain. *Symposia Biologica Hungariea* 10: 21–35.

Teszner, D., Tzavaras, A., Gruner, J., and Hecaen, H. 1972. L'asymmetrie droite-gauche du *planum temporale:* Á propos de l'étude anatomique de 100 cerveaux. *Rev. Neurol.* 126: 444–449.

Teyler, T. J., Roemer, R. A., Harrison, T. F., and Thompson, R. F. 1973. Human scalp-recorded evoked-potential correlates of linguistic stimuli. *Bull. Psychon. Soc.* 1: 333–334.

Thorne, J. P. 1966. On hearing sentences. In *Psycholinguistics Papers,* ed. J. Lyons and R. J. Wales. Edinburgh: Edinburgh University Press.

———. 1968. A computer model for the perception of syntactic structure. *Proc. R. Soc. Lond. B* 171: 377–386.

Tyler, L. K., and Marslen-Wilson, W. 1978. Some developmental aspects of sentence processing and memory. *Journal of Child Language* 5: 113–129.

Von Eckardt Klein, B. 1978. Inferring functional localization from neurological evidence. In *Explorations in the biology of language,* ed. E. Walker. Montgomery, Vt.: Bradford Books.

Vygotsky, L. S. 1965. Psychology and localization of functions. *Neuropsychologia* 3: 381–386.

Waber, D. P. 1977. Sex differences in mental abilities, hemispheric lateralization, and rate of physical growth at adolescence. *Developmental Psychology* 13: 29–38.

Wada, J. A., Clarke, R., and Hamm, A. 1975. Cerebral hemispheric asymmetry in humans: Cortical speech zones in 100 adults and 100 infant brains. *Archives of Neurology* 32: 239–246.

Wada, J. A., and Davis, A. E. 1977. Fundamental nature of human infant's brain asymmetry. *Canadian Journal of Neurological Sciences* 4: 203–207.

Walker, J. L., and Halas, E. S. 1972. Neural coding at subcortical auditory nuclei. *Physiology and Behavior* 8: 1099–1106.

Wasow, T. 1978. On constraining the class of transformational languages. *Synthese* 39: 81–104.

Weir, R. 1962. *Language in the crib.* The Hague: Mouton.

Weiss, P. A. 1976. Neurobiology in statu nascendi. *Progress in Brain Research* 45: 7–38.

Wexler, K. 1978. Empirical questions about developmental psycholinguistics raised by a theory of language acquisition. In *Recent advances in the psychology of language,* ed. R. N. Campbell and P. T. Smith. New York: Plenum Press.

Wexler, K., Culicover, P., and Hamburger, H. 1975. Learning-theoretic foundations of linguistic universals. *Theoretical Linguistics* 2: 215–253.

Whitaker H. A., and Ojemann, G. A. 1977. Graded localization of naming from electrical stimulation mapping of the left cerebral cortex. *Nature* 270: 50–51.

Whitaker, H. A., and Selnes, O. A. 1976. Anatomic variations in the cortex: Individual differences and the problem of the localization of language functions. *Annals of the New York Academy of Sciences* 280: 844–854.

Wickelgren, W. 1977. Concept neurons: A proposed developmental study. *Bulletin of the Psychonomic Society* 10: 232–234.

Witelson, S. F. 1977. Anatomic asymmetry in the temporal lobes: Its documentation, phylogenesis, and relationship to functional asymmetry. *Annals of the New York Academy of Sciences* 299: 328–354.

Witelson, S. F., and Pallie, W. 1973. Left hemisphere specialization for language in the newborn: Neuroanatomical evidence of asymmetry. *Brain* 96: 641–647.

Yakolev, P. L., and Lecours, A. R. 1967. The myelogenetic cycles of regional maturation of the brain. In *Regional development of the brain in early life,* ed. A. Minkowski. Oxford: Blackwell.

Young, R. M. 1970. *Mind, brain and adaptation in the nineteenth century.* Oxford: Clarendon Press.

Zaidel, E. 1977. Unilateral auditory language comprehension on the token test following cerebral commissurotomy and hemispherectomy. *Neuropsychologia* 15: 1–18.

8

Observations on the
Neurological Basis
for Initial
Language Acquisition

Bryan T. Woods

For a long time research into the neurological basis of language and language development was based almost entirely on observation of the effects of brain lesions. A standard doctrine about the differences between the effects on language of childhood and adult lesions of one or the other cerebral hemisphere had already arisen before the end of the last century (Freud, 1897). In recent times these views were restated by Lenneberg with scant modification (1967). In brief, it was held that (1) acquired aphasia after right-hemisphere lesions is much more common in children than adults; (2) recovery from early-onset aphasia is rapid; (3) the pattern of aphasia seen with early lesions is of the motoric type (Broca-type; nonfluent); (4) there is a critical age for language recovery, with complete recovery the rule if the lesion occurs before that age.

These largely empirical principles have been used by Lenneberg (1967) and others to develop a model of the neurological basis of language acquisition. In outline the model holds, first, that both hemispheres initially play an active role in both comprehension and production of language, hence the frequency of aphasia after early lesions of either hemisphere. Second, the left hemisphere comes to assume a more and more predominant role in speech during the years of most active language acquisition, perhaps by an active inhibition of the right hemisphere. Third, during the period when both hemispheres are active in speech, either one may rapidly take over the whole role if the other is damaged, which is why rapid recovery is seen in childhood aphasia. Fourth, once the dominance of the left hemisphere is complete, about the end of the first decade, the other hemisphere can no longer take over the language function.

Since Lenneberg wrote, data that have emerged from a number of lines of research into hemispheric specialization for language suggest the contrary view, that the left hemisphere is (in almost all right-handers and the majority of left-handers) the predominant hemisphere for speech from the onset (Molfese, Freeman, and Palermo, 1975; Witelson and Pallie, 1973; Wada, Clark, and Hamm, 1975; LeMay and Culebras, 1972), but Lenneberg's model has remained influential, probably because of its apparently firm empirical basis. The results of a series of studies undertaken at the suggestion of and in collaboration with H.-L. Teuber led to different conclusions (Woods and Teuber, 1973, 1978). These studies, all involving a group of persons who had suffered lesions of one or the other hemisphere in either infancy (before age one) or childhood (from one to fifteen), have resulted in findings at variance with the empirical findings in acquired aphasia of childhood, and these findings led inevitably to dissatisfaction with the model.

The first observation arising from this study that did not fit the usual teaching on childhood aphasia is in table 8.1. In the patients studied, the incidence of aphasia after right-hemisphere lesions is far lower than that after left-hemisphere lesions, and half of those who were aphasic after the right-sided lesions were known left-handers. Since these data were contrary to the standard teaching, the next step was a review of the literature to look at the experience of others. The unexpected finding was that the results in reports before 1942 were quite different from those in more recent studies (figure 8.1). It appears that the more recent studies, with the exception of that of Basser (1962), have recorded very few cases of aphasia following right-hemisphere lesions. In fact, only 8 percent of the 270 cases of acquired aphasia reported in these studies followed right-hemisphere lesions; if one excludes known left-handers, that figure drops to 5 percent.

Table 8.1
Incidence of aphasia accompanying onset of hemiplegia in sixty-four children with previously acquired speech

Right hemiplegia	Left hemiplegia
20/33	4/31[a]
(61%)	(13%)

a. Two of these four patients were known to be left-handed before onset of their hemiplegia.

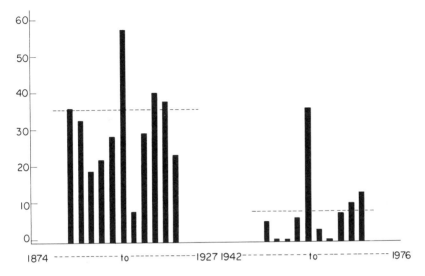

8.1
Percentage of aphasic children with right-hemisphere lesions in twenty-one
series reported from 1974 to 1976 (dashed lines represent mean percentage)

Our second observation, based on the same group of patients,
was that recovery from early-onset aphasia, although apparently
complete from the viewpoint of clinical observation, was very variable in terms of time required. One child of five required more than
thirty months for recovery, while others, older and younger, recovered in a few weeks. Similarly, type of aphasia was more variable
than expected. Records indicated that the same patient who was so
slow to recover had initially manifested a form of jargon aphasia;
that is, fluent but incomprehensible speech and a severe comprehension defect, while another showed loss of comprehension with preserved repetition.

The first stage of our study of these patients was restricted to his-
torical review and clinical neurological examination. At that point
the results still continued to support the "critical age" dictum, since
none of the children who had acquired their aphasia before age eight
was still aphasic when we first saw them several years later. However, when we tested all the children in the study on special tests of
language production and comprehension (Woods and Carey, in
press), contrasting them with age-similar controls, we found that the
patients with left-hemisphere lesions incurred after the first birthday
were significantly worse than controls on most of the tests. This

group contained almost all the "recovered" aphasics. One might have attributed the poor performance to the lower verbal IQ (since the special language tests were highly correlated with verbal IQ), but another group of patients with the same mean verbal IQ, those with left-sided lesions before the first birthday, were much less impaired relative to controls (table 8.2). Since these two patient groups both had had left-hemisphere lesions and differed, as far as we could tell, only in time of onset (before or after the first birthday), we concluded that the result was likely to be due to language difficulties in the later lesion group that were too subtle for detection by individual clinical observation alone. Further analysis of the left later lesion group supported this view, by showing that it was the recovered aphasic subgroup and not the never-aphasic patients whose performance was defective on the language tests (table 8.3).

This result indicates that the critical age concept may well be an artifact of the methods used to diagnose aphasia. If one relies on the neurological examination of single patients, one will not be able to detect with certitude abnormalities in performance that will clearly emerge when a group of patients is compared with appropriate controls using standardized tests. Our view is that the persistent effects of left-hemisphere lesions on language are more pronounced with increasing age at time of lesions, that this occurs in a gradated manner, and that even with early childhood lesions something of language function is permanently lost.

While our studies failed to support the hypothesis that the right hemisphere (of right-handers) has an early active role in speech, they have shown a time-of-lesion-dependent effect of right-hemisphere lesions on language to the extent that language functions are measured by verbal IQ scores (Woods, in press). When patients with right-hemisphere lesions and sibling controls were given the Wechsler Intelligence Scale for Children (WISC), the patients whose lesions had occurred before their first birthday were significantly below their siblings on verbal IQ (as well as performance IQ). In contrast, patients with right-hemisphere lesions after the first birthday had mean verbal IQ scores slightly higher than those of siblings, while performance IQ scores remained significantly lower. In patients with left-hemisphere lesions the verbal IQ scores were significantly below sibling scores with both earlier and later lesions.

Most studies of Wechsler scores in brain-damaged adults indicate that the verbal IQ (VIQ) score is relatively unaffected by well-

Table 8.2
Postrecovery language test performance of patients with early left hemisphere (LE) lesions (before age one) and later left-hemisphere (LL) lesions (ages one to fifteen) compared with age-similar controls, utilizing the Mann-Whitney test

Test	LE patients (N = 11; VIQ = 90.3) versus controls		Nonaphasic LL patients[a] (N = 14; VIQ = 93.6) versus controls	
	z-score	p	z-score	p
Picture naming	− 0.05	ns	2.41	.01
Spelling	0.98	ns	2.43	.01
That clause	0.96	ns	2.33	.01
Token test	1.42	.08	1.74	.05
Relations syntax	0.29	ns	1.43	.08
Sentence completion	− 0.08	ns	1.60	.05
Ask-tell	0.49	ns	0.94	ns
Rhyme-completion	− 0.29	ns	0.01	ns

a. Two other patients in this group were still clinically aphasic when examined and have not been included in this analysis.

Table 8.3
Results of comparison of language test performance of recovered aphasic and never-aphasic later left-hemisphere (LL) lesion patient to age-similar controls, utilizing the Mann-Whitney test

Test	Recovered aphasic (N = 7; VIQ = 88.4) versus controls		Never aphasic (N = 7; VIQ = 99.3) versus controls	
	z-score	p	z-score	p
Picture naming	2.80	.003	1.26	ns
Spelling	2.14	.02	1.50	.07
That clause	2.17	.02	1.54	.06
Token test	1.37	.09	1.25	ns
Relations syntax	0.80	ns	0.70	ns
Sentence completion	2.40	.01	0.09	ns
Ask-tell	0.59	ns	0.53	ns
Rhyme completion	1.36	.09	1.20	ns

localized right-hemisphere lesions (Woods, in press); thus VIQ measures primarily left-hemisphere functions. We therefore concluded from our WISC data that the very early right-hemisphere lesions could somehow interfere with the normal development of left-hemisphere functions, but similarly localized lesions later in childhood could not. Whether the effect of the very early lesions arises because of an actual shift of normally right-sided functions to the left, with a subsequent crowding effect, or rather because of the lack of some critical early facilitatory role of the right hemisphere (Holmes, personal communication) cannot be determined from our data.

If one attempts to use these and other recent observations to reformulate the theory of the neurological basis of language acquisition, it becomes clear that an adequate distinction has not always been made between hemispheric potential for language acquisition and an actual hemispheric role in ongoing language functions. The critical test of one hemisphere's potential for language acquisition is the ultimate outcome following loss of the speech areas of the other hemisphere, while the critical test of a hemisphere's actual role in language is the short-term effect of impairment of the language areas of that hemisphere itself.

The reality of the distinction between a hemisphere's capability for language production and its capability for language comprehension has also been brought out recently by studies in split-brain and left-hemispherectomy patients (Zaidel, 1976, 1977). It appears that the right hemisphere of left-dominant individuals may acquire a considerable amount of language comprehension while remaining unable to initiate any significant speech production. It remains an open question whether the right hemisphere in such individuals can utilize syntactic information or must rely on semantic-pragmatic knowledge to decode speech utterances (Zaidel, 1976, 1977; Caramazza and Berndt, 1978; Denis and Kohn, 1975; Dennis and Whitaker, 1976).

Using these distinctions and setting aside considerations of the minority of (mainly left-handed) individuals who have right-hemisphere or bilateral speech representation even in adult life, one can suggest a fairly simple formulation of the developmental history of language acquisition. At birth both hemispheres have the potential for language acquisition, and damage to either hemisphere does not prevent the development of apparently normal speech. However, the work of Dennis and Kohn (1975) indicates that even at this stage the greater potential already resides in the left hemisphere, particularly when the language tasks require adequate syntactic comprehension and cannot be mastered through heuristic strategies employing semantic or pragmatic knowledge.

During the years of most rapid development, the left-hemisphere plays the active role in speech production and comprehension, while the language potential of the right side gradually diminishes. These conclusions are based on the findings of infrequent aphasia following right-hemisphere lesions, even between ages two and five, and failure of completely normal recovery of language function following left-hemisphere lesions before age eight (Woods and Carey, in press).

During this same period between one and eight there is indirect evidence (based on the WISC results; Woods, in press), that the left hemisphere becomes firmly committed to language functions so that these functions can no longer be crowded by competing functions displaced from a damaged right-hemisphere. On the other hand, the remaining language potential of the right-hemisphere shows that side to be not so irrevocably committed to its proper functions.

By the end of the first decade, or soon thereafter, the potential of the right hemisphere for language acquisition has diminished to the point that clinically evident aphasia frequently persists after damage to the speech areas of the left hemisphere. This is not to say that the right hemisphere cannot take over the active role in speech for the first time during adolescence or adult life, because there is some evidence that it can (Kinsbourne, 1971); but it can no longer achieve an adequate level of language performance. Even here one must be cautious in suggesting that there is an absolute loss of language acquisition potential. Even in mature adults there appears to be an inverse relationship between age of aphasia onset and degree of ultimate recovery (Kertesz and McCabe, 1977).

The formulation I have outlined is of course excessively simple because it neglects the very real possibility that the decline in right-hemisphere potential for comprehension may have a different time course from the decline in potential for production or that the syntactic potential of the right side may never approach its semantic potential (Dennis and Whitaker, 1976). It also neglects the important variable of lesion location within the damaged hemisphere, since a childhood lesion limited to Broca's area alone may have very different consequences than one affecting Wernicke's area as well. Finally it neglects the potential role of handedness and inherited variability in degree of intrinsic language lateralization (Luria, 1970). Let me say by way of apology only that introduction of such considerations would go beyond the data now available on the neurology of language development. Let us hope that the deficiency will soon be remedied.

ACKNOWLEDGMENTS

Dr. Woods' work was supported in part by NINDS Special Fellowship Grant 2 F11 NS 2370-02 NSRB, National Institutes of Health; in part by Grant RR-88 from the General Clinical Research Center Program of the Division of Research Resources, National Institutes of Health; in part by Grant 72-4-1 from the Alfred P. Sloan Foundation; and in part by NIMH Grant NIH-5-R01-MH24433 to Dr. S. Corkin.

Presented in part at the 98th and 102nd Annual Meetings of the American Neurological Association; Montreal, Canada, June 12, 1973, and Chicago, Illinois, June, 1977.

I have a special debt of gratitude for inspiration and guidance to Professor Hans-Lukas Teuber, without whom this work would not have been possible.

REFERENCES

Basser, L. S. 1962. Hemiplegia of early onset and the faculty of speech with special reference to the effects of hemispherectomy. *Brain* 85: 427–460.

Caramazza, A., and Berndt, R. S. 1978. Semantic and syntactic processes in aphasia: A review of the literature. *Psychological Bulletin* 85: 898–918.

Dennis, M., and Kohn, B. 1975. Comprehension of syntax in infantile hemiplegia after cerebral hemidecortication: Left hemisphere superiority. *Brain and Language* 2: 472–482.

Dennis, M., and Whitaker, H. A. 1976. Language acquisition following hemidecortication: Linguistic superiority of the left over the right hemisphere. *Brain and Language* 3: 404–433.

Freud, S. 1897. *Infantile cerebral paralysis (Infantile Cerebrallähmung)*. Translated by L. A. Russin. 1968. Coral Gables, Fla.: University of Miami.

Holmes, J. (Personal communication).

Kertesz, A., and McCabe, P. 1977. Recovery patterns and prognosis in aphasia. *Brain* 100: 1–18.

Kinsbourne, M. 1971. The minor hemisphere as a source of aphasic speech. *Trans. Am. Neurol. Assoc.* 96: 141–145.

LeMay, M., and Culebras, A. 1972. Human brain: Morphologic differences in the hemispheres demonstrable by carotid angiography. *N. Engl. J. Med.* 287: 168–170.

Lenneberg, E. H. 1967. *Biological foundations of language.* New York: John Wiley.

Luria, A. R. 1970. *Traumatic aphasia.* Paris: Mouton.

Molfese, E. L., Freeman, R. B., and Palermo, D. S. 1975. The ontology of brain lateralization for speech and nonspeech stimuli. *Brain and Language* 2: 356–368.

Wada, J., Clark, R., and Hamm, A. 1975. Cerebral hemispheric asymmetry in humans. *Arch. Neurology* 32: 239–246.

Witelson, S. F., and Pallie, W. 1973. Left hemisphere specialization for language in the newborn: Neuroanatomical evidence of asymmetry. *Brain* 96: 641–646.

Woods, B. T. The restricted effects of right hemisphere lesions after age one; Wechsler test data. *Neuropsychologia* (in press).

Woods, B. T., and Carey, S. Language deficits after apparent clinical recovery from childhood aphasia. *Ann. Neurol.* (in press).

Woods, B. T., and Teuber, H.-L. 1973. Early onset of complementary specialization of the cerebral hemispheres in man. *Trans. Am. Neurol. Assoc.* 98: 113–117.

Woods, B. T., and Teuber, H.-L. 1978. Changing patterns of childhood aphasia. *Ann. Neurology* 3: 273–280.

Zaidel, E. 1976. Auditory vocabulary of the right hemisphere following brain bisection or hemidecortication. *Cortex* 12: 191–211.

Zaidel, E. 1977. Unilateral auditory language comprehension on the Token Test following cerebral commissurotomy and hemispherectomy. *Neuropsychologia* 15: 1–18.

9

Language Acquisition
in a Single Hemisphere:
Semantic Organization

Maureen Dennis

How does the left hemisphere mediate the acquisition of language? One type of answer would be a formalism for the linguistic operations it performs; another would be a description of how early lateralized brain damage fractions the language process into dissociable components.

In neither model nor description has the question been answered. The problem itself has been interpreted as one of time parameters rather than processing characteristics, and efforts to discover when the left hemisphere assumes a preeminent linguistic role have preempted study of the operations it performs. As a result, there is an extensive data base for the time course of left-hemisphere ascendancy over the right but almost no information about the processing features that enable the left hemisphere to develop the rich and flexible structures of mature language.

What kinds of language operations does the left hemisphere acquire that the right does not? It is proposed that certain physiological or structural features of the immature brain constrain language development to a range of potential realizations, with experience— including aberrant events like seizures (Kohn, 1979)—specifying what actually develops within the range (Chomsky, 1976; Grobstein and Chow, 1975). The empirical question is whether each hemisphere, as a language acquisition substrate, meets the requirements for a constrained functional system, and, if so, what kinds of linguistic operations such constraints allow.

This chapter considers how each isolated hemisphere acquires semantic structures. The data are the semantic capacities of three children with hemidecortication before five months of age. Early removal of one hemisphere fixes the onset of hemispheric asymmetry before the development of speech. The fact of early asymmetry, then, is a given; the issue is whether that given determines the nature and extent of semantic acquisition.

SUBJECTS

The three children studied are cases of Sturge-Weber syndrome. One hemisphere was surgically removed in each to control perinatal seizures which had proved resistant to anticonvulsant medication. A pathological examination of the resected brain tissues showed the changes of the Sturge-Weber syndrome: microscopic foci of calcification in the cortex itself and widespread angiomatoses of the meninges. After surgery, no child had seizures in the next five years, the period of primary language acquisition. Each child is of average intelligence and normal educational level. The medical history and IQ test results are summarized in table 9.1 and discussed in Dennis and Whitaker (1976, 1977).

Differences in language skill are apparent depending on the side of hemidecortication. The right hemidecorticate child has acquired language rapidly and well. The left operates show a pattern of language typical of adult hemidecorticate infantile hemiplegics; despite normal intelligence, syntactic discrimination is poor (Dennis and Kohn, 1975).

Two types of syntactic asymmetries are demonstrable in the hemidecorticate subjects. The first is a loss of efficiency in the left operates, who identify fewer syntactic forms and take longer to discriminate any type of sentence than right hemidecorticates (Dennis and Kohn, 1975; Dennis and Whitaker, 1976). The second is the application of different strategies for performing discrimination tests. Even when the outcome is the same, syntactic proficiency in left and right hemidecorticates is correlated with different operations (Dennis, 1979).

The suggestion that different processing mechanisms might produce the same behavioral result in the two hemispheres motivated a more detailed study of the Sturge-Weber children's semantic abilities. While receptive vocabulary, fluency, and naming had developed similarly in each hemisphere, the ability to identify entailment was better in the right hemidecorticate (Dennis and Whitaker, 1976). Such data suggested that the apparent dissociation between pro-

Table 9.1
Sturge-Weber children with hemidecortication in infancy

Subject (sex)	Onset of pathology	Signs	Neurosurgery	Pathology of resected tissue	Postoperative development	Verbal IQ	Performance IQ	Full-scale IQ
MW (male)	Birth	Left hemiparesis Left-sided seizures Facial naevus	Right hemispherectomy at age of 4½ months	Microscopic foci of calcification in cortex	Seizures in immediate postoperative period; seizure-free from then until present except for one seizure age 9½	96	92	93
SM (male)	Birth	Right hemiparesis Right-sided seizures Facial naevus	Left hemispherectomy at age of 4½ months	Areas of gliosis, calcification, and demyelinization in cortex	Seizures in immediate postoperative period; seizure-free from then until present except for staring spells age 9	94	87	90

Table 9.1 (continued)
Sturge-Weber children with hemidecortication in infancy

Subject (sex)	Onset of pathology	Signs	Neurosurgery	Pathology of resected tissue	Postoperative development	Verbal IQ	Performance IQ	Full-scale IQ
CA (female)	Birth	Right hemiparesis Right-sided seizures Facial naevus	Left hemispherectomy at age of 28 days	Calcification and gliosis of white and gray matter	Right-sided twitching for several days after surgery; seizure-free from then until present	91	108	99

ducing and understanding single words and the identification of the semantic function of words in sentence contexts should be explored further.

THE MEANING OF WORDS AND SENTENCES

Most discussions of lexical semantics, whichever words they use to capture the difference, distinguish between sense (intension, having a definition) and reference (extension, the set of instances, or, more properly, the rules that govern what an instance may be). The sense of a word is part of its formal description, while the referential component specifies the rules needed to identify members of a category (Russell, 1905; Fodor, Bever, and Garrett, 1974).

When words are placed in context, or combined in groups, their interrelationships may be traced by analyzing the dimensions that link their sense elements. One reason for considering this a separate component of meaning is empirical. The definition and referential meaning of individual words are dissociable from the relations that connect lexical concepts (Zurif et al., 1974). There are various techniques for establishing the dimensions (Clark and Clark, 1977), but some agreement exists that the conceptual relationships among words reveal an individual's subjective semantic organization.

The interpretation of a sentence is more than the sum of its individual words. Sentences exhibit a variety of semantic properties not shown by words, for example, questioning, promising, presupposing. To give the meaning of a word is to do more than show what things it names; it is to account for the effect of the word on the semantic features of sentences in which it occurs (Fodor, Bever, and Garrett, 1974).

One type of semantic information is derived from functional sentence forms. In the sentences, "Jane kisses Tarzan" and "Tarzan is kissed by Jane," for example, knowledge of the agent and patient roles is conveyed by functional structure. Other kinds of semantic features are in the surface form. In "Jane kisses Tarzan," it is presupposed that Jane kissed someone; in "Tarzan is kissed by Jane," it is assumed that someone kissed Tarzan. By manipulating such surface features as stress and word order, it is possible for a speaker to convey different emphases, intentions, or presuppositions. What is important here is the hypothesis (Jackendoff, 1972) that functional sentence structure does not wholly determine meaning; that some semantic information is available only after surface structures are created.

We will consider, in turn, how each isolated hemisphere has acquired the meaning and reference of single words, the lexical concepts joining words in groups, and the semantics of the surface structures of syntactically varied sentences.

LEXICAL SEMANTICS: THE MEANING OF INDIVIDUAL WORDS

Understanding and Producing Names

To assess how the hemidecorticate children processed single words, they were given tests of lexical comprehension and production (Dennis and Whitaker, 1976). The Peabody Picture Vocabulary Test requires a match of heard words to four-choice picture displays; the scores are in terms of test mental age and IQ. The Goodglass and Kaplan (1972) tests of word discrimination, visual confrontation naming, and responsive naming assess, respectively, word-picture matching, naming to pictures, and naming to oral questions; the scores are the percentage of the total possible score. The naming fluency test (Goodglass and Kaplan, 1972) measures the number of animal names produced in a sixty-second period.

There are no differences among the children in these lexical semantic tests (table 9.2). The Peabody scores are all within the normal range, and the difference between the right and left operates is small enough to occur by chance on repeated testing. Word discrimination and production are equally well developed in each hemisphere.

Lexical Access from Semantic, Rhyming, and Visual Cues

The previous tests tapped naming ability, although they were not systematic in the type of eliciting cues. In the Cued Word Retrieval Test (Wiegel-Crump and Dennis, 1979), the same words are retrieved in response to different cues. The child is told to use the cue provided to seek out the word in the experimenter's mind. The items are words in the categories of animals, food, clothing, household items, and actions, of three levels of word frequency. The retrieval cue is either a semantic description, a rhyme, or a picture. The semantic description uses the same type of cues within each category; for example, the cue for animals involves group membership, habi-

Table 9.2
Understanding and producing names

	Right hemidecorticate (MW)	Left hemidecorticate (SM)	Left hemidecorticate (CA)
Age at PPVT	9;5	7;11	7;11
Age at other tests	10;11	9;6	9;7
Peabody picture vocabulary (Dunn, 1965)			
PPVT mental age	9;10	7;3	7;5
PPVT IQ	106	93	95
Word discrimination (Goodglass and Kaplan, 1972)			
Percentage correct	94.4	98.6	98.6
Visual confrontation naming (Goodglass and Kaplan, 1972)			
Percentage correct	100.0	98.0	99.0
Responsive naming (Goodglass and Kaplan, 1972)			
Percentage correct	100.0	83.3	90.0
Naming fluency (Goodglass and Kaplan, 1972)			
Number of names in 60 sec	14	16	10

tat, mode of locomotion, and two characteristic features. The test allows comparison of different retrieval systems for the same words. "Lion," for example, is the response to the following cues.

1. "I'm thinking of an animal. It lives in the jungle. It walks on four legs. It has a mane. It roars."
2. "Tell me an animal that rhymes with /dzaɪən/."
3. "What is this a picture of?" (showing a picture of a lion).

The results are in table 9.3.

All three children retrieve words rapidly and well to visual and semantic cues, confirming the earlier observation that neither hemisphere has word-finding problems. The left hemidecorticates have considerable difficulty with the rhyming cues. They appear to possess limited access to a phonological retrieval system for common words, despite ready production of words to pictures or descriptions. Lexical access is a rapid and efficient operation for either hemisphere, although the left appears to possess an additional retrieval channel.

REFERENCE AND THE PROTOTYPICALITY OF NAMES

The hemidecorticate children proved similarly fluent in naming. To what extent do the names they produce resemble critical superordinate features of the referent? Grossman (1977, 1978) addressed this issue in applying Rosch's (1975) prototypicality model to the naming of adult aphasics. A prototypical name embodies the most important features of the superordinate. A name may be assigned a score, derived from the judgments of normal subjects, which represents how well it resembles the ideal referent of its category.

Grossman's technique was applied by asking the hemidecorticate children to name as many —— as possible in sixty seconds, using in the blank the five Rosch (1975) superordinates of fruit, furniture, clothing, birds, and sports. Names on Rosch's lists were given a rank and score from those lists; correct subordinates not on the lists were not included. Errors were classified according to Grossman's (1978) division: elaborations (boots, hard boots), simple repetitions, syntagmatic responses (swan, feathers), subset or wrong level responses, and out-of-set errors. The results are in table 9.4.

Table 9.3
Retrieving words to visual, semantic, and rhyming cues

	Right hemidecorticate (MW)	Left hemidecorticate (SM)	Left hemidecorticate (CA)
Visual cues (45)			
Target (N)	42	42	43
Target ($\bar{X}$ latency in sec)	1.15	1.21	1.28
Semantic cues (45)			
Target (N)	42	39	40
Target ($\bar{X}$ latency in sec)	1.17	1.36	1.33
Rhyming cues (45)			
Target (N)	31	17	9
Target ($\bar{X}$ latency in sec)	1.35	2.35	1.56

Note: Test ages: MW 11;10, SM 10;3, CA 10;3.

Table 9.4
Prototypicality of names

	Right hemidecorticate (MW)				
	Fruit	Furn-iture	Cloth-ing	Birds	Sports
Total responses (N)	13	11	17	9	14
Different subordinates (N)	11	11	16	8	12
Rosch responses (N)	11	8	9	7	7
Rank ($\bar{X}$)	10.55	23.19	19.22	21.42	11.14
Score	1.52	2.71	2.41	2.13	1.53
Errors (N)	2	0	1	1	2
Elaboration (N)	0	0	0	1	2
Repetition (N)	2	0	0	0	0
Syntagmatic (N)	0	0	0	0	0
Level/subset (N)	0	0	1	0	0
Out of set (N)	0	0	0	0	0

Note: Test ages: MW 14;5, SM 12;11, CA 12;11.

Table 9.4
Prototypicality of names, continued

| | Left hemidecorticate (SM) | | | | |
	Fruit	Furn-iture	Cloth-ing	Birds	Sports
Total responses (N)	9	8	14	11	9
Different subordinates (N)	9	7	13	10	9
Rosch responses (N)	9	7	12	7	8
Rank ($\bar{X}$)	15.56	23.93	32.58	22.14	9.38
Score	1.92	2.90	3.82	2.34	1.41
Errors (N)	0	1	1	1	0
Elaboration (N)	0	0	0	0	0
Repetition (N)	0	0	0	1	0
Syntagmatic (N)	0	0	0	0	0
Level/subset (N)	0	0	1	0	0
Out of set (N)	0	1	0	0	0

Table 9.4
Prototypicality of names, continued

| | Left hemidecorticate (CA) | | | | |
	Fruit	Furn-iture	Cloth-ing	Birds	Sports
Total responses (N)	12	14	13	10	16
Different subordinates (N)	11	9	9	8	9
Rosch responses (N)	10	8	5	6	6
Rank ($\bar{X}$)	13.35	18.31	15.0	16.67	7.25
Score	1.76	2.22	2.07	1.78	1.31
Errors (N)	1	5	4	2	7
Elaboration (N)	0	0	1	0	0
Repetition (N)	11	4	3	1	5
Syntagmatic (N)	0	0	0	1	0
Level/subset (N)	0	0	0	0	2
Out of set (N)	0	1	0	0	0

There are no differences between the children in naming fluency, the number of correct subordinates, or the rank and score of the Rosch list names. Nor does the pattern of errors reveal any asymmetry. These data should be interpreted with the reservation that the cognitive categories of Canadian schoolchildren may not be measured best by the prototypicality scores of U.S. college students; nevertheless, there is no evidence that the similar naming in the hemidecorticate children represents a different kind of mechanism for retrieving instances of superordinate categories.

Definite and Indefinite Reference

One aspect of reference concerns whether the object denoted is a member of a limited or of an indefinite set. As part of a study of the subjective organization that left and right hemidecorticates impose on grammatical forms, the children made similarity judgments of the words in six active sentences. Their judgments served as an input matrix to a hierarchical clustering procedure, which generated a description in the form of a phrase structure tree (see Zurif, Caramazza, and Myerson, 1972, and Dennis, 1979, for procedural details). Each sentence (the dog chases a cat, the train hits a car, the teacher sees a child, the girl rides a horse, the woman eats an apple, the bird builds a nest) contained one noun phrase with a definite referent and another with an indefinite referent. The issue is whether the children differ in the way that they connect the definite and indefinite articles to their respective noun phrases. The minimum-distance solutions to the phrase structure trees from these clusters are in figure 9.1.

The two left hemidecorticates show a tighter link between definite article and noun for both reversible and nonreversible active forms. They do not associate the second noun phrase and definite article. Since the definite article was tied to the first noun in the sentence, it is not clear that this reflects anything more than a tendency to perceive the first two words in the sentence as most related. The right hemidecorticate child perceives the agent-verb relationship as being the most important in the active reversible sentences. In neither form does he judge the article-noun relationship as primary.

While these data are not perhaps the ideal test context for a study of definite and indefinite reference—the object of the study was

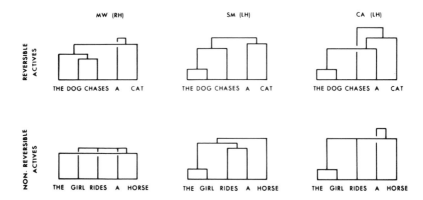

9.1
Minimum-distance solutions for relatedness judgments of words in active
sentences (RH: right hemidecorticate, LH, left hemidecorticate. Test
ages:MW 9;4, SM 7;11, CA 8;0)

otherwise—they nevertheless serve to extend the complex of findings
showing that different components of linguistic reference are not
selectively acquired by a left hemisphere.

ESTABLISHING "MEANING" FOR NONSENSE WORDS:
THE SOUND-SYMBOL HOOKUP

Experience with the lexical items of English has established, in each
child, the meaning and reference relationships of single words;
however, it is possible that the learning process was protracted in
some manner for some of the children. It is thus of interest to mimic
one type of word learning by teaching the children an arbitrary set
of words to name random visual symbols. The sound-symbol subtest of the Sound-Symbol Test (Goldman, Fristoe, and Woodcock,
1974) requires the subject to learn, over fifty-five trials, the nonsense
names for a set of designs. The test was given to the hemidecorticate
children as part of a longitudinal study of reading (Dennis, Lovett,
and Weigel-Crump, 1979), and the results are in table 9.5.
    The two left hemidecorticates have higher percentile ranks for
learning the names of nonsense designs than the right operate. The
result is a stable one, replicable over three years. Evidently, the process by which words become attached to visual arrays is mediated
equally well by each hemisphere, perhaps even more efficiently by
the right. The absence of a selective left-hemisphere superiority in a

Table 9.5
Sound-symbol association: Establishing names for nonsense designs

	Right hemi-decorticate (MW)		Left hemi-decorticate (SM)		Left hemi-decorticate (CA)	
	First test	Second test	First test	Second test	First test	Second test
Sound-symbol association (Percentile rank)	25	18	53	58	63	76

Note: Test ages: MW 11;10 and 14; 11, SM 10;3 and 13;4, CA 10;3 and 13;6.

test using individual nonsense words is consistent with previous results showing that the children perform similarly on processing single lexical items. What requires an explanation, however, is the superior performance of the left hemidecorticates—those missing the left angular gyrus—on this cross-modal task. The greater proficiency of the isolated right hemisphere for certain types of visuospatial processing (Kohn and Dennis, 1974) may contribute to the ease with which the left hemidecorticate children form associations to visual arrays. The finding of an atypical asymmetry, rather than the absence of asymmetry found on other lexical tests, raises the question whether cross-modal learning is the paradigmatic naming relationship. Perhaps this is not how names are learned.

WORDS IN CLUSTERS: THE SENSE RELATIONS THAT LINK SEMANTIC STRUCTURES

The next experiment studied the dimensions of a conceptual system binding words. The assumption is that word meanings can be separated into elements that represent the relations among words (Caramazza and Berndt, 1978). The senses of groups of words are represented as locations in a semantic space.

Four sets, each of five words, were chosen to have the following properties:

Word pair	*Relationship*	
1, 2	Synonyms	Having similar (if not identical) meaning but different pronunciation

2, 3	Homophones	Having different meaning and spelling but similar pronunciation
3, 4	Antonyms, associates	Contrasting on one semantic component, either as a binary taxonomy (male/female) or differing in one component with a switch in argument (here/there, to/from)
5, others	Unrelated	Unrelated in meaning but visually similar to two others

Each set of words was presented as ten triads of all the words in a set. For each triad the children were asked to judge the most and least related words. The list of words was in view throughout the test. The children, as part of a pretest, had been asked to read the list and say whether they know the words on it. They easily managed this screening test, as the words were well within their reading vocabularies. The instructions stressed that there were no right or wrong answers in the test, that the examiner wanted to see how the children thought the words were related.

The judgments served as an input matrix to a clustering procedure, which generated a description in the form of a phrase structure tree, and also as data for a multidimensional scaling procedure. Only the latter results will be described.

Multidimensional scaling brings out the associative structure in a set of similarity measures by plotting the items represented by these measures in an n-dimensional space, in such a way that the distance between a pair of items is a monotonic function of their similarity measures. The fewer the dimensions extracted, the poorer the fit of the distances between points to the interpoint similarity measures; the stress measure indicates the poorness of fit (Kruskal, 1964). The scaling is performed by iteratively adjusting the location of the points (in a first, randomly chosen, configuration) in the direction of the sharpest decrease in stress until the configuration that minimizes stress is found.

The data were submitted to the scaling procedure M-D-SCAL (Kruskal and Carmone, 1973) to find a semantic space in which the more similar the average rating of two words, the closer they are in the semantic space. The objective of the technique is to show the optimal spatial representation that fits all the pairs simultaneously.

The results of the scaling procedure are presented as both dimen-

sion loadings and as a spatial solution. The results for the two-
dimensional solutions are in table 9.6 and figure 9.2.

The hemidecorticate children are different in three ways. MW is
better able to apply a consistent organizing principle to a semantic
space, because his judgments have a better fit to dimensional structure (his stress value is considerably lower than that of SM and CA).
In addition, MW extracts a greater number of similarity dimensions.
Third, his dimensions are orthogonal and independent, whereas
those of SM and CA are either not clearly separated in two dimensions or else are poorly factored.

MW has a clear synonymity factor. Words 1 and 2 have the same
polarity and load to an almost identical extent on the two factors.
Words 3 and 4 also form a tight grouping. Word 5 is seen as unrelated to the other two clusters. No homophone relationship is extracted in his scaling solutions; he appears to reject, as a semantic
dimension, the sound properties of words (at least in this particular
context). What is of considerable interest is that the property of
synonymity is perceived as orthogonal, on two dimensions (both the

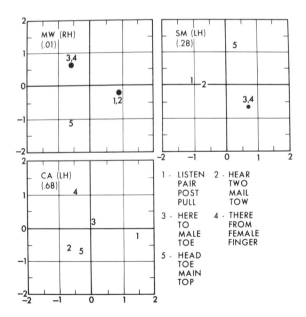

9.2
Two dimensional scaling solution for combined word clusters. The stress
measure is in brackets (RH = right hemidecorticate; LH = left hemidecorticate. Test ages: MW 11;10, SM 7, CA 10;9)

Table. 9.6
Scaling of semantic properties: All word clusters (two dimensions)

Words	Right hemidecorticate (MW)		Left hemidecorticate (SM)		Left hemidecorticate (CA)	
	Dimension 1	Dimension 2	Dimension 1	Dimension 2	Dimension 1	Dimension 2
1. (Listen, pair, post, pull)	0.906	−0.187	−1.071	0.095	1.433	−0.167
2. (Hear, two, mail, tow)	0.925	−0.177	−0.688	−0.055	−0.731	−0.530
3. (Here, to, male, toe)	−0.620	0.710	0.708	−0.624	0.097	0.243
4. (There, from, female, finger)	−0.618	0.715	0.730	−0.623	−0.482	1.121
5. (Head, toe, main, top)	−0.593	−1.061	0.321	1.206	−0.318	−0.667

Note: Test ages: MW 11;10, SM 10;7, CA 10;9.

polarity and the weighting are different), to that of antonymity/associativeness.

The main principle in SM's clusters is that of antonymity/associativeness. Words 3 and 4 are tightly clustered and load on the same dimensions. Words 1 and 2 are related, but SM is different from MW in the manner of the relationship. For SM, words 1 and 2 have a similar polarity but only roughly comparable weight on dimension 1, and there is a small but definite switch in polarity on the second dimension. As with MW, word 5 is separated from the others.

CA's clusters are not easy to interpret, largely because she did not extract a similar set of components from each group of words. She treated the individual sets as if they represented different judgment problems, with the result that the scaling procedure gave a high stress factor in finding a combined solution for the clustering judgments. The first point about CA's clusters is that word 1 is separated from all others by the strength of its loading on dimension 1. The main cluster, and it is not a tight one, is between word 1 and all the others. This may represent such nonsemantic properties of word 1 as visual difference from the others.

The hypothesis that CA organizes words on a more visual basis than the other children is confirmed in two ways. First, her strongest single two-dimensional cluster is that between words 2 and 5, which differ only in a single letter. The second evidence is stronger. Corcoran (1966) observed that subjects scanning prose to cross out E's would overlook unsounded letters more than sounded ones, that is, they performed some semantic analysis in what might have been a simple visual matching task. The hemidecorticate children were asked to cross out all the E's in two prose passages taken from an elementary reader, one in English and one in Portuguese. Their results are in table 9.7. Of the three children, CA is both better (she made fewer errors) and less prone to the sounded-unsounded effect (ratio 3:4). Most errors for MW and SM are on unsounded letters; MW never missed a sounded E. The children do not differ in the miss rate on the Portuguese text, showing that it is the semantic processing induced by a familiar language, not the matching task itself, that produces the results. CA, it appears, is sparing of her semantic processing when a task can be treated as a visual one.

Yet she must perform sufficient processing to determine that the particular configuration of letters does or does not form an English word. The children were given a lexical decision task, in which they

Table 9.7
Number and type of misses in crossing out E's in prose

	Right hemidecorticate (MW)	Left hemidecorticate (SM)	Left hemidecorticate (CA)
English text			
Misses	17	26	7
Sounded misses	0	5	3
Unsounded misses	17	21	4
Latency (min and sec)	3′ 55″	5′ 3″	5′ 11′
Portuguese text			
Misses	22	28	24
Latency (min and sec)	4′ 44″	5′ 48″	5′ 20″

Note: Test ages: MW 11;10, SM 10;3, CA 10;3.

judged whether eighty of the following were words: homophonic words (bear, sail, paws, pair), homophonic nonwords (bote, nife, nale, yorn), nonhomophonic words (post, snow, lion, talk), and nonhomophonic nonwords (cale, lote, geez, vone). All the words obeyed the common grapheme rules of English and were readily pronounceable. The results are in table 9.8.

All the children succeeded in identifying the words from the nonwords. Latency was not timed, although it would be of interest to determine whether it took longer to reject as words the homophonic nonwords than the nonhomophonic nonwords. Nevertheless, the data suggest that CA does not treat strings of letters simply as visual arrays.

The described data reveal something of the relations between lexical concepts. The scaling solutions suggest that the semantic space is both more lawful and more tightly organized in the right hemidecorticate. Even when dimensions like synonymity are extracted by the left hemicorticates, they are less well structured and less separable from other components of meaning.

THE SEMANTICS OF SURFACE STRUCTURES: WHICH NOUN IS THE TOPIC?

How is the meaning of a lexical item part of the meaning of a sentence? Certain semantic features of a sentence are represented in

Table 9.8
Lexical decision task (N correct)

	Right hemi-decorticate (MW)	Left hemi-decorticate (SM)	Left hemi-decorticate (CA)
Words (40)			
Homophonic (20)	20	18	18
Nonhomophonic (20)	20	20	19
Nonwords (40)			
Homophonic (20)	20	20	19
Nonhomophonic (20)	20	19	20

Note: Test ages: MW 12;8, SM 11;2, CA 11;3.

functional structure, and there is no doubt that each child uses some parts of this semantic system. When confronted with two tokens and a sentence requiring the use of each as either instrument or object, for example, the children use tokens in the two roles, even though the left hemidecorticates make errors in noncanonical sentence forms (Dennis, 1979). What is now considered is a component of semantic representation not present in functional form, the thematic structure, focus, or topic. How does each child understand the role of topic or focus, and is this determined by the syntax of the sentence?

The Subjective Subject Test
There is general agreement that a sentence can convey to a listener something of the speaker's intention, emphasis, or focus. Whether this information is carried by the surface structure or intonational contours of the sentence or by both is in dispute.

The theme or psychological subject is conveyed by the surface structure. Halliday (1967) asserts that the speaker assigns a theme-rheme structure to a sentence. The theme is what the speaker is talking about; the rheme what is being said about it. The theme, because it almost always precedes the rheme, will correspond to surface structure subject in declarative sentences. Hornby (1971, 1972) identifies the psychological subject in terms of new (introduced for the first time) and given (available from preceding context) information. The psychological subject refers to the given content, the comment to the new information. In this view the superficial subject is the same as the topic or psychological subject because of the typical order of words in English. The two authors make different predictions about the topic in cleft and pseudocleft constructions. For Halliday, the theme is the first noun phrase, regardless of the particular syntactic construction; Hornby predicts a different noun phrase depending on the syntactic form. In a cleft sentence, for example, the psychological predicate is the element in the first clause, so that the new information occurs before the given. The clefted-patient construction, by contrast, presents the old before the new information. The pseudocleft sentence is similar to the cleft in that the psychological predicate is stated as the grammatical object, or predicate nominal, of the sentence.

The focus, indicated by intonation (Chomsky, 1965; Jackendoff, 1972), is the item in the sentence receiving the heaviest stress, whether as a result of normal intonational contours, contrastive or emphatic stress, or else some component (actually of surface structure) of the phrase in which the maximal stress falls. Thus in the sentence "The giraffe kisses the elephant with the blue eyes," the stress at the end of *eyes* would enable any of the following components of the phrase to be the focus: eyes, the blue eyes, the elephant with the blue eyes. In normal active sentences, stress usually falls on the last item, although it may not always be that stress is unambiguous between surface structure subjects and the last word. A second feature of this approach is that overt surface structure reorderings such as clefting, pseudoclefting, and topicalization alter the focus by putting it in cleft, pseudocleft, or topicalized positions.

However they are characterized and whichever sentence properties convey them, the focus, theme, psychological subject, and topic are separable from both the logical and grammatical sentence subjects. The logical subject does interact, however, with thematic relations; for example, the animate logical subject of an active verb is the agent of the sentence. In Chomsky's (1965) formalism for recovering logical subjects from underlying (deep structure) phrase markers, the superficial subject of a sentence is the leftmost noun phrase immediately dominated by the sentence node in the surface structure. The surface structure or grammatical subject interacts with the predicate to determine properties such as agreement of the main verb. Neither surface nor deep subjects need be the focus of the sentence in the analyses of focus presented here.

Do the hemidecorticate children derive a focus or topic in a sentence, and which aspects of the sentence form might they use to mark this distinction? The subjective subject test was designed to assess how they assigned focus or topic in sentences of varying syntactic structure. The ninety-six sentences were of six types: active (the lion chases the tiger), cleft agent (it's the giraffe who leads the elephant), pseudocleft patient (what the zebra pulls is the horse), passive (the chicken is pushed by the duck), cleft patient (it's the lion that the tiger chases), and pseudocleft agent (the one who pushes the chicken is the duck). The sentences used common, high-frequency animals, with logically reversible semantic relationships; each sentence was read to the child with a natural intonation. The child's task was to select the animal he or she thought the sentence was about.

The frequency with which each noun phrase was chosen as topic, and the mean response latency, are in table 9.9.

The children do not differ in response latency, but they diverge in how they assign the topic or focus of the sentences. Consider first MW, the right hemidecorticate. Surface structure reorderings altered his choice of topic, in accordance with the Chomsky (1965), Jackendoff (1972), and Halliday (1967) proposals, although not with the specific predictions of Hornby (1972). Were MW to have chosen focus or topic on the basis of the old-new distinction, for example, there would have been a significant choice of logical patient in the cleft agent construction, and this was not the case. The lack of preference for either animal in the pseudocleft patient and pseudocleft agent constructions is also consistent with the theme and focus analyses. The true topic, in these sentences, would be "What" and "The one who," respectively. His selection of the surface subject in both active and passive forms of the same sentence indicates the importance of surface structure syntactic groupings. Evidently, surface structure is one determinant of MW's assignment of topic (Clark and Begun, 1968).

What is uncertain is whether surface syntax interacts with intonation contours to cue focus or topic for MW. Stress contours in declarative sentences are subtle and may be ambiguous between surface subjects and the last word. The particular test conditions used could have allowed focus to be assigned to the surface structure subjects by the mechanisms that Chomsky (1965) and Jackendoff (1972) describe. Studies of topic and focus identification using contrastive stress will clarify how surface structure and intonation produced the described results.

Table 9.9
Determining the sentence topic: The subjective subject sentences (N=96)

	Right hemidecorticate (MW)			Left hemidecorticate (SM)			Left hemidecorticate (CA)		
	Logical agent choices (%)	Logical patient choices (%)	(X̄) Response latency (sec)	Logical agent choices (%)	Logical patient choices (%)	(X̄) Response latency (sec)	Logical agent choices (%)	Logical patient choices (%)	(X̄) Response latency (sec)
Agent-patient sentences									
Active	87.50[a]	12.50[a]	1.69	43.75	56.25	1.56	43.75	56.25	1.63
Cleft agent	81.25[a]	18.75[a]	1.38	37.50	62.50	1.31	31.25	68.75	1.19
Pseudocleft patient	50.00	50.00	1.56	31.25	68.75	1.50	31.25	68.75	1.31
Patient-agent sentences									
Passive	25.00[a]	75.00[a]	1.38	62.50	37.50	1.56	75.00[a]	25.00[a]	1.25
Cleft patient	0.00[a]	100.00[a]	1.56	37.50	62.50	2.88	50.00	50.00	1.56
Pseudocleft agent	62.50	37.50	1.44	81.25[a]	18.75[a]	1.50	62.50	37.50	1.50

Note: Test ages: MW 14;11, SM 13;5, CA 13;6.

a. Significantly different from chance on binomial test (Siegel, 1956).

Two features of the left hemidecorticate performance are striking: first, the absence of focus choices in most syntactic forms and, second, the tendency to select the logical agent in patient-agent sentences. Overall these children show no consistent rule for this focus identification task.

Perhaps the left hemidecorticates assign a focus or topic to the sentence after the logical relationships have been derived, but because they do not accurately find these relationships (Dennis and Kohn, 1975; Dennis and Whitaker, 1976; Dennis, 1979), no consistent preference for focus emerges in discrimination tasks such as the subjective subject test. Whether this is the case or whether they do not possess any manner of marking this semantic relationship, the result is a failure to assign conceptual focus to the sentence. The isolated right hemisphere does not capture the semantic information conveyed by the surface structure and/or stress patterns of particular syntactic forms.

SEMANTIC ACQUISITION IN THE LEFT AND RIGHT HEMISPHERES

Either hemisphere acquires the sense and reference of common words. The loss of 50 percent of the cortical mass need not prevent the development of a rich system for these types of lexical knowledge. But finding meaning for individual words does not seem to be the unique contribution of the left hemisphere to semantic acquisition.

The matrix of interrelationships among words appears less well integrated in the right hemisphere than in the left, suggesting that learning about new words, not by visual associational processes, but by exposure to the lexical concept (Grossman and Carey, 1978) might be different in the two hemispheres. When the meaning of a word is defined by its role in sentence contexts, the isolated left hemisphere is the more efficient processor. Semantic information about conceptual focus is available to the left hemisphere from the surface structure or intonation of the sentence but is not accessed by the right hemispheres in any consistent manner.

The described results form part of a data base for a model of semantic processing in the isolated left and right hemispheres. Beyond revealing empirically based dissociations of semantic capacities, the data may be used to assess the adequacy of semantic theories as they

apply to hemispheric asymmetry. If particular semantic capacities
are separable by early brain damage, they should be treated independently in any theory dealing with the acquisition of meaning by
the two halves of the brain. It is important to note the sense in
which the data are tests of a theory. To say, for example, that a particular model does not allow for the observed dissociation between
focus and lexical meaning is to indicate that such a theory has a con-
stricted data range but not to judge how well it defines a class of
grammars.

The pattern of data obtained can be accommodated by some theoretical positions but not others. In this sense the results separate
theories that account for the observed functional dissociations from
those that do not.

The operations involved in identifying and retrieving a lexical
item are at least partly dissociable from the ability to understand the
conceptual role of the item in determining the meaning of an utterance. Word-based theories of semantics, or theories of intermodal
learning as the paradigmatic semantic relationship, do not capture
this dissociation.

Relationships in sentence structure (agent) do not seem to be the
sole source of semantic information. The focus or topic of a sentence
depends on its surface properties. As a result, transformations that
do not change the logical relationships of the sentence alter its meaning. In the two sentences "The giraffe chases the elephant" and "The
elephant is chased by the giraffe," the focus is the giraffe in the first
but the elephant in the second, although in both the giraffe is doing
the chasing. Such findings are hard to explain if base rules work
directly on deep structures to generate a semantic reading (Katz and
Postal, 1964). Some semantic information comes from the surface
features of a sentence, at least in the left hemisphere, with the result that all semantic information is not represented in underlying
structure.

Meaning must be a generative process rather than a set of associative operations (see also Katz and Fodor, 1963; Jackendoff, 1972).
To conceive of meaning as the establishment of word-image or
word-object hookups is to obliterate the distinctive contribution of
the left hemisphere to language acquisition. In this context the idea
that primary language development involves the association of
words with objects in the environment is not as plausible a model of
early left-hemisphere acquisition as a theory that stresses that single

words are shorthand devices for predicating properties of situations and making assertions about the world (Preyer, 1889).

Although the data reflect on the descriptive adequacy of some semantic theories as accounts of single-hemisphere acquisition, they do not themselves constitute a model. Several other language functions remain to be analyzed in the hemidecorticate children before any formalism can be attempted; for example, how coreference rules are applied, how new words are learned in sentence contexts. The relation between the contextual semantic problems and the previously reported syntactic impairments in the right hemisphere, in addition, is yet to be established. While the failure to derive a sentence focus from certain surface features might be a consequence of the inability to represent syntactically varied relations in surface form, it is less apparent whether the poor syntax and ill-structured semantic relations should be considered separate right-hemisphere deficits.

The left hemisphere allows for the development of a set of semantic abilities not available to the right. Even without a processing model to incorporate them, then, the data show that the perinatal brain mediates functionally constrained semantic acquisition.

ACKNOWLEDGMENTS

This research was supported by Ontario Mental Health Foundation Individual Award Grant No. 704 and by an Ontario Mental Health Research Scholarship to the author. I am grateful to E. Bruce Hendrick for access to his patients, to Sally Kuehn and Connie Taras for help in collecting the data, and to Judith Sugar for data analysis. For their prompt and helpful comments on the various drafts of the manuscript, I thank David Caplan, Bruno Kohn, and Maureen Lovett.

REFERENCES

Caramazza, A., and Berndt, R. S. 1978. Semantic and syntactic processes in aphasia: A review of the literature. *Psychological Bulletin* 85: 898–918.

Chomsky, N. 1965. *Aspects of the theory of syntax.* Cambridge, Mass.: MIT Press.

———. 1976. On the biological basis of language capacities. In *The neuropsychology of language,* ed. R. W. Rieber, pp. 1–24. New York: Plenum Press.

Clark, H. H., and Begun, J. S. 1968. The use of syntax in understanding sentences. *British Journal of Psychology* 59: 219–229.

Clark, H. H., and Clark, E. V. 1977. *Psychology and language.* New York: Harcourt Brace Jovanovich.

Corcoran, D. W. J. 1966. An acoustic factor in letter cancellation. *Nature* 210: 658.

Dennis, M. 1979. Correlates of syntactic comprehension in hemidecorticate infantile hemiplegics: Hemispheric asymmetry for language strategy? *Brain and Language* (in press).

Dennis, M., and Kohn, B. 1975. Comprehension of syntax in infantile hemiplegics after cerebral hemidecortication: Left hemisphere superiority. *Brain and Language* 2: 472–482.

Dennis, M., and Whitaker, H. A. 1977. Hemispheric equipotentiality and language acquisition. In *Language development and neurological theory,* ed. S. Segalowitz and F. Gruber, pp. 93–106. New York: Academic Press.

———. 1976. Language acquisition following hemidecortication: Linguistic superiority of the left over the right hemisphere. *Brain and Language* 3: 404–433.

Dennis, M., Lovett, M. W., and Wiegel-Crump, C. A. 1979. Acquisition of written language skills after left or right hemidecortication in infancy (in preparation).

Dunn, L. M. 1965. *Expanded manual for the Peabody picture vocabulary test.* Circle Pines, Minn.: American Guidance Service.

Fodor, J. A., Bever, T. G., and Garrett, M. F. 1974. *The psychology of language.* New York: McGraw Hill.

Goldman, R., Fristoe, M., and Woodcock, R. W. 1974. *Manual for Goldman-Fristoe-Woodcock sound-symbol tests.* Circle Pines, Minn.: American Guidance Service.

Goodglass, H., and Kaplan, E. 1972. *The assessment of aphasia and related disorders.* Philadelphia: Lea and Febiger.

Grobstein, P., and Chow, K. L. 1975. Receptive field development and individual experience. *Science* 190: 352–358.

Grossman, M. 1977. Category naming and semantic organization after brain damage. Paper presented at the Academy of Aphasia Fifteenth Annual Meeting, October 9–11, 1977, Montreal.

———. 1978. The game of the name: An examination of linguistic reference after brain damage. *Brain and Language* 6: 112–119.

Grossman, M., and Carey, S. 1978. Word learning after brain damage. Paper presented at the Academy of Aphasia Sixteenth Annual Meeting, October 15–17, 1978, Chicago.

Halliday, M. A. K. 1967. Notes on transitivity and theme in English, part 2. *Journal of Linguistics* 3: 177–204.

Hornby, P. A. 1971. Surface structure and the topic-comment distinction: A developmental study. *Child Development* 42: 1975–1988.
———. 1972. The psychological subject and predicate. *Cognitive Psychology* 3: 632–642.

Jackendoff, R. 1972. *Semantic interpretation in generative grammar.* Cambridge, Mass.: MIT Press.

Katz, J. J., and Fodor, J. A. 1963. The structure of a semantic theory. *Language* 39: 170–210.

Katz, J. J., and Postal, P. M. 1964. *An integrated theory of linguistic descriptions.* Cambridge, Mass.: MIT Press.

Kohn, B. 1979. Right hemisphere speech representation and comprehension of syntax after left cerebral lesions. *Brain and Language* (in press).

Kohn, B., and Dennis, M. 1974. Selective impairments of visuo-spatial abilities in infantile hemiplegics after right cerebral hemidecortication. *Neuropsychologia* 12: 505–512.

Kruskal, J. B. 1964. Multidimensional scaling by optimizing goodness of fit to a nonmetric hypothesis. *Psychometrica* 29: 1–27.

Kruskal, J. B. and Carmone, F. 1973. How to use M-D-SCAL (version 5M) and other useful information. Bell Telephone Laboratories, Murray Hill, N.J., 1973.

Preyer, W. 1889. *The Mind of the child. Part II: The development of the intellect.* New York: D. Appleton and Company.

Rosch, E. 1975. Cognitive representations of semantic categories. *Journal of Experimental Psychology: General* 104: 192–233.

Russell, B. 1905. On denoting. Mind 14: 479–493.

Wiegel-Crump, C. A., and Dennis, M. 1979. Processes of word retrieval in normal children (in preparation).

Zurif, E. B., Caramazza, A., and Myerson, R. 1972. Grammatical judgments of agrammatic aphasics. *Neuropsychologia.* 10: 405–417.

Zurif, E. B., Caramazza, A., Myerson, R., and Galvin, J. 1974. Semantic feature representations for normal and aphasic language. *Brain and Language* 1: 167–187.

10

Broca and Lashley
Were Right:
Cerebral Dominance
Is an Accident
of Growth

Thomas G. Bever

The more precocious development of the left hemisphere predisposes
us in our first gropings to execute the more complicated material
and intellectual acts with that half of the brain. . . . this specialization of function does not imply the existence of a functional distinction between the two halves of the brain.
Broca, 1865

On anatomical grounds alone there is no assurance that cerebral
dominance is anything other than an accident of growth.
Lashley, 1937

Clinical and experimental evidence suggests that the left hemisphere of the brain is specialized for speech activity and the right hemisphere is specialized for many nonlinguistic functions.[1] The characteristic association of language with the left hemisphere raises two
questions.

• Is cerebral asymmetry specific to each skill or to a general difference in processing style? Is the left hemisphere uniquely predisposed
for language, or does language itself have certain properties that are
always more easily processed by the left hemisphere?
• How specific must the evolutionary development be that could
provide a mechanistic basis for the observed hemispheric differences? Is relational processing qualitatively "innate" to the left hemisphere, or does the left hemisphere assume relational processing because of a general quantitative difference between the hemispheres?

I shall agree with those who claim that there is a general difference in processing style between the hemispheres in adults; the left is
dominant for relational processing, the right for holistic processing.
Language is left-hemisphered because it typically requires relational
processing. This claim has received some acceptance in the field.

Moreover, I also demonstrate that the available data are consistent with the view that at birth the only difference between the
hemispheres is that the left hemisphere has more computational
power. This implies that the evolution of asymmetries could be the
direct result of the evolution of a general physical asymmetry (in
size at birth, oxygenization, metabolic rate, perinatal maturation
rate). As the quotations from Broca and Lashley show, this view is
not novel. My present goal is to show that all the highly specific and
intricate facts about linguistic and nonlinguistic asymmetries that
have been recently documented can follow from such a relatively
simple evolutionary development.

A CAUTIONARY NOTE ON AN EASY MISTAKE

Humans are the only organisms we know of that characteristically
have both language and processing-related cerebral asymmetries.
Reasoning of the post hoc ergo propter hoc variety can lead to the
easy assumption that language capacity and cerebral asymmetries
are directly related. An intuitive and strong version of this claim is
the following: The critical mechanism underlying language is structurally innate in the left hemisphere. This claim can be turned
around: If we can prove that the left hemisphere is innately structured for language, we have added evidence that language itself is
innate. This interpretation could stimulate interest among linguists
in the innate basis for cerebral asymmetries. But the innateness of
language and of cerebral asymmetries are logically independent.
Language could be learned and asymmetries innate, asymmetries acquired and language innate, both acquired, or both innate. At most,
any unique evolutionary relation between cerebral asymmetries and
linguistic capacity is a matter for empirical discovery: One cannot
conclude anything about the (non)innateness of one from the
(non)innateness of the other.

Why then, should we be concerned about cerebral asymmetries at
all, if our main concern is with language? There are two reasons.
First, despite their logical independence, there is a plausible empirical connection between language and asymmetries. We must determine whether this connection is causal or coincidental, if we are to
see clearly into the biological mechanisms for the knowledge of
language. Second, cerebral asymmetry is a robust instance of localization of brain function in humans. It is relatively easy to study

in normal and clinical populations. Accordingly, it serves as an empirically fruitful example of how functional localization can develop.

THE NATURE OF ASYMMETRIES IN ADULTS

Two interpretations of asymmetries have emerged in recent years. In one view each hemisphere is adapted to different skills—for example, language and mathematics in the left hemisphere, form perception and music in the right (Kimura, 1973). The alternative view was proposed a century ago by the neurophysician, Hughlings Jackson (1932). He related the hemispheric linguistic differences to differences in cognitive activity, suggesting that the left hemisphere is specialized for "propositional" organization while the right hemisphere is adapted for "direct associations" among stimuli and responses. Modern researchers have substantially generalized this differentiation to encompass a wide range of behaviors in normal subjects.

Many experimental and clinical investigators of hemispheric asymmetry agree on the fundamental nature of the processing differences between the two sides of the brain: The left hemisphere is supposed to be specialized for propositional, relational, and serial processing of incoming information, while the right hemisphere is more adapted for the perception of appositional, holistic, and synthetic relations. However, there is also a body of evidence suggesting that form perception and music perception are dominant in the right hemisphere.[2] How could such a skill-specific difference be consistent with the differentiation of hemispheric processing in terms of two kinds of processing? I shall show that studies of music and visual form that bring out right-hemisphere superiority are holistic tasks, either by virtue of the subjects' processing strategies (music) or by virtue of the simplicity of the stimuli (vision). Crucial experiments that bring out relational processing also bring out left-hemispheric dominance for music and form perception.

RELATIONAL AND HOLISTIC PROCESSING

We can make our discussions more precise if we have a formal definition of the difference between holistic and relational processing. Of course, we could treat each kind of processing as a primitive concept, but this would not leave us any way to decide a priori whether a particular task or behavioral strategy is itself holistic or relational.

Pretheoretically, the difference is intuitively clear. Holistic processing involves the direct association of a mental representation with a stimulus and response; relational processing involves at least two such associations, and the manipulation of a relation between the two mental representations. We can give a formal account of this difference in the following way: A holistic task involves the activation of one mental representation one or more times; a relational task involves the activation of at least two distinct mental representations and of a (nonidentity) relation between them.[3] It remains in part an empirical question whether this distinction is the behaviorally relevant one. The following sections demonstrate its adequacy, at least to a first order of approximation. These sections are organized according to predictions about types of processing rather than about types of skilled behavior.

Prediction 1. The kind of processing that subjects are asked to perform can determine which hemisphere is dominant in processing a stimulus.

SPEECH

Varying the task within a modality is a strong way of testing the claim that indeed it is the kind of processing that determines behavioral asymmetry, not the modality (language, music, vision). To show this, Richard Hurtig, Ann Handel, and I ran monaurally an initial-phoneme versus syllable-recognition experiment (Bever et al., 1976). We found that the time taken to recognize a syllable beginning with *b* is shortest when the materials are presented to the right ear and the subject responds with the right hand compared with other hand-ear configurations. There was no difference in amount of time to recognize an entire syllable, for example, *bik*. We verified this result in two paradigms; in one paradigm we alternated whether listeners were listening for an entire syllable target or an initial phoneme target; in a second paradigm we held the task constant but alternated the ear to which the stimulus was presented (see table 10.1).

The two tasks exemplify the formal distinction between the two types of processing. Recognizing a syllable (in a sequence of syllables) in terms of its first /b–/ sound requires perception of an initial part of the whole syllable and a decision that the first compo-

Table 10.1

Mean reaction time (msec) to identify a syllable in terms of the initial phone or whole syllable

	Left ear	Right ear	Right-ear advantage
Initial phone	369	348	+21
Syllable	259	258	+1
Phone-syllable	110	90	

Source: Bever, Hurtig, and Handel (1976), combining experiments 1 and 2, and right- and left-hand responses.

nent phoneme of that part is indeed /b–/. That is, this task is relational. The corresponding task of recognizing the syllable from a syllable target is holistic, involving only matching an initial part of the whole syllable against the expected "template."

Accordingly, this investigation shows that the same stimulus can be differentiated according to the kind of processing that the subject must carry out on the stimulus. If the subject must analyze the stimulus internally, then the condition in which only the left hemisphere is involved (right ear, right hand) is more facilitating than the other conditions. The syllable task, in which the subject listens holistically, shows no overall differences in this case. (It remains to be seen whether one can show a statistically reliable favoring of left-ear input with a linguistic stimulus.)

VISION

Recently, Hurtig (in preparation) ran a visual analog of the preceding experiment. Subjects saw brief presentations of nonsense figures. In critical cases these figures were followed by the same figure or by a more complex figure of which they were a part. Subjects were to say yes as quickly as possible in either of these cases and no in control negative cases. Hurtig found that correct responses were faster and more frequent in the left visual field (right hemisphere), when the second figure was the same figure. Correct responses were faster and more accurate in the right visual field (left hemisphere) when the second figure included the first. That is, the holistic visual task stimulated left-field superiority, while the relational visual task stimulated right-visual-field superiority.[4]

Hurtig's experiment is a direct investigation of the holistic/relational distinction in vision. It demonstrates that the dominant side for form perception can be reversed from left to right if the kind of visual processing is shifted from holistic to relational. If this is so, why do the overwhelming majority of studies claim to show a left-field superiority? The explanation is methodological.

Visual stimuli must be presented outside of the fovea to be completely lateralized neuroanatomically. Consequently, such experiments characteristically use visual stimuli simple enough to be differentiated in the visual periphery (for example, recognition of the angle of line, recognition of a simple geometric figure). Overall performance on complex stimuli in the periphery can be so low that observed laterality differences might not be statistically meaningful. The methodological requirement that the visual discrimination task must be simple when stimuli are in the visual periphery may account for the apparent right-hemisphere dominance for vision that is claimed in the literature; the simple recognition tasks are characteristically holistic. This leads to the prediction that complex figures might be better recognized in the right visual field.

To test this, Victor Krynicki (1975) used a figure-recognition task with brief presentations of irregular eight- and sixteen-sided geometric figures.[5] In one situation the subjects had to recognize rapidly presented stimulus figures from a target set of twenty. While the success rate was low, the sixteen-sided figures (but not the eight-sided figures) were identified better in the right visual field. Krynicki suggested that the subjects recognize the complex figures in terms of isolated visual features (such as a jagged edge or a particular angle), thus requiring relational processing and a consequent left-hemisphere superiority. The basis for this assumption is that a large number of complex and similar figures would be easiest to differentiate, identify, and recognize in terms of some criterial visual feature that distinguishes it from the others in the target set.

In a second task subjects made same-difference judgments on pairs of figures. On positive trials the second stimulus was a rotation of the first. There was a left-visual-field superiority for both eight- and sixteen-sided figures. This result was predicted by the view that holistic processing is relegated to the right hemisphere and the assumption that recognizing a figural rotation is a holistic task that can operate on the gross contour of the stimulus. In this condition both eight- and sixteen-sided figures showed a left-visual-field superiority, suggesting that figure complexity was not an effective variable. Also the rotation task was more difficult than the direct recognition task. This shows that task difficulty per se is not the relevant variable, only that complex stimuli usually are more likely to be perceived relationally.

If such results hold up in other paradigms, they will show that the frequent claim that vision (of nonlinguistic stimuli) is dominant in the right hemisphere was based on research involving simple holistic processing tasks; relational processing can stimulate left-hemisphere dominance in visual recognition of nonlinguistic stimuli.

The critical experimental demonstrations of this claim are cases of right-field superiority in usual tasks. Goldberg et al. (1978) found such an effect for the recognition of irregular many-sided figures (roughly, replicating Krynicki's results). Their interpretation is that right-field superiority emerges because such complex shapes are "codable in a discrete set of features" and the left hemisphere is adapted to such codes. (Their proposal is similar to the one in this paper, except that it incorrectly predicts that simple geometric figures would be better perceived in the right visual field.)

Krynicki had also monitored the average evoked response (AER) activity at the right and left parietal scalp positions. Subjects in the rotation task showed greater electrical activity in the right hemisphere than the left (regardless of the original stimulus visual field). The same subjects in the complex-figure-recognition task showed greater AER activity in the left hemisphere (also regardless of the input stimulus field).

The study of patients with unilateral brain lesions can provide a "converging methodology" to confirm the results of such neurophysiological asymmetries in normals (although patients with such lesions present self-compensating bilateral systems with unilateral damage, rather than isolated unilateral systems). In this case one would predict that patients with left-hemisphere lesions will be selectively impaired on a relational visual task while patients with right-hemisphere lesions will be relationally impaired on a holistic visual task. Veroff (1978) found exactly such a difference. She had patients place in correct order a randomized sequence of cartoons depicting a common change in category (for example, a tadpole becoming a frog). She found that changes of location are more impaired in right-hemisphere patients, while changes of category are more impaired in left-hemisphere cases. She concludes, "Patients with right hemisphere damage [were] impaired on . . . [configurational] processing and patients with left-hemisphere damage were . . . impaired on . . . [categorical] processing" (p. 139). Veroff's task is a nonstandard experimental task adapted to the special needs of working with patients. However, we can distinguish her "configurational" task as holistic, since the object in each picture of a sequence remains the same; the "categorical" task is relational, since the object in each picture is different, yet related to the previous one. In this sense her results provide independent clinical confirmation of the behavioral difference found in normals.

The overall result of these studies is that that the left hemisphere can be dominant for visual processing, if the task is relational.

Prediction 2. If one shifts ontogenetically from holistic to relational ways of perceiving a stimulus, one should also shift from being right-hemisphere dominant to being left-hemisphere dominant for that stimulus.

The perception of music has so far been a well-documented exception to the differentiation of the hemispheres according to relational versus holistic processing. Melodies are composed of an ordered series of pitches and hence should be processed relationally, and be dominant in the left hemisphere rather than the right. Yet until recently the recognition of simple melodies was usually reported to be better in the left ear than in the right.[6] This finding is prima facie evidence against the functional differentiation of the hemispheres; rather, it seems to support the view that the hemispheres are specialized according to stimulus-response modality. Such conclusions, however, are simplistic; they do not consider the different kind of processing strategies that listeners use as a function of their musical experience.

It has long been recognized that the perception of melodies can be a gestalt phenomenon. That is, that a melody is composed of a series of isolated tones is not relevant for naive listeners; they focus instead on the overall melodic contour. The view that musically experienced listeners have learned to perceive a melody as an articulated set of relations among components rather than as a whole is suggested directly by Werner (1948). "In advanced musical apprehension a melody is understood to be made up of single tonal motifs and tones which are distinct elements of the whole construction." This is consistent with Meyer's (1956) view that recognition of "meaning" in music is a function not only of perception of whole melodic forms but also of concurrent appreciation of the way in which the analyzable components of the whole forms are combined. If musically naive listeners normally treat a melody as a holistic gestalt, then the processing account of the difference between the two hemispheres predicts that melodies will be processed better in the right hemisphere for such subjects. If experienced listeners normally treat a melody as a relational sequence, then they should show a corresponding right-ear superiority. It is significant that Gordon (1970), the first recent investigator who failed to find a superiority of the left ear for melody recognition, used "college musicians" as subjects; the subjects in other studies were musically naive (or unclassified).

If music perception is dominant in the right hemisphere only insofar as musical form is treated holistically by naive listeners, then the generalization of Jackson's proposals about the differential functioning of the two hemispheres can be maintained. To establish this we conducted a study with subjects of varied levels of musical sophistication that required them to attend to both the internal structure of a tone sequence and its overall melodic contour. The listener's task is sketched as follows:

| hear melody | 2 sec pause | hear excerpt | say if excerpt was from melody | say if melody was heard before in the experiment |

We found that musically sophisticated listeners could accurately recognize isolated excerpts from a tone sequence whereas musically naive listeners could not. However, musically naive people could recognize the entire tone sequences and did so better when the stimuli were presented in the left ear; musically experienced people recognized the entire sequence better in the right ear (table 10.2). This

Table 10.2
Recognition of whole melodies (percentage correct)

	Left ear	Right ear	Right-ear advantage
Musicians	44	57	+13
Nonmusicians	54	36	−18
Musicians' advantage	−10	21	

Note: Percentages are corrected for guessing.

demonstration of the superiority of the right ear for music shows that it depends on the listener's musical experience; it demonstrates that the previously reported superiority of the left ear was due to the use of musically naive subjects, who treat simple melodies as unanalyzed wholes.

We also compared the performance of a group of choir boys with nonmusical boys from the same school on a similar task.[7] The choir boys performed more effectively on stimuli presented to the right ear, while the musically naive boys performed better on the left-ear stimuli. Since half the choir boys cannot read music (they memorize their parts), this could not be due to mapping the music onto a score or note names. It is also possible in principle that developing musical ability is not the cause of left-hemisphere dominance but its result: It might be that those boys who are *already* left-hemisphered for music are thereby more musical and that is why they join the choir. This possibility is inconsistent with several facts. First, the boys join the choir for a mixture of social and financial reasons (choir boys received a scholarship to their school). Second, the longer a boy was in the choir the more pronounced his right-ear dominance (compared with nonchoir boys in the same age and grade).

Our interpretation is that musically sophisticated subjects can organize a melodic sequence in terms of the internal relation of its components. This is supported by the fact that only the experienced listeners could accurately recognize the two-note excerpts as part of the complete stimuli. Dominance of the left hemisphere for such analytic functions would explain dominance of the right ear for melody recognition in experienced listeners; as their capacity for musical analysis increases, the left hemisphere becomes increasingly involved in the processing of music.

These studies have received considerable attention and some replication. (Specific issues raised by these studies are discussed in the appendix to this chapter.) First, Gordon (1975), who had run the study with "college musicians," reanalyzed his data. He found that subjects who performed better on his melody-recognition task tended to perform relatively well on right-ear stimuli while this was not true of the subjects who did not do well overall. P. R. Johnson (1977) reported a replication of our melody-recognition results with dichotic stimuli. R. C. Johnson et al. (1977) examined the effects of whether the musicians could transcribe music or not; they found a significant right-ear advantage on a melody-excerpt-recognition task only for subjects who could transcribe music. However, combining the results of Johnson et al. for the two groups of musicians who can read music (which embraces our original definition of musician) and comparing the Johnson et al. musicians with the nonmusicians yields a pattern of results similar to Johnson's and ours.

Three other recent studies on melody perception have used experimental paradigms that bring out right-ear superiority in both musicians and nonmusicians (see the appendix for a discussion of the reasons for this result). These results give support to our underlying original claim that music is not uniquely processed in the right hemisphere. Furthermore, in each of these three experiments the musicians were relatively more right-eared than the nonmusicians (table 10.3). For this comparative analysis I considered only tasks that came reasonably close to replicating our original paradigm; the melodies were presented only a few times at most and were tonal (see the appendix).

Finally, a startling fact about EEG activity gives independent validity to our claim that musicians process melodies in the left hemisphere, nonmusicians in the right. Hirshkowitz, Earle, and Paley (1978) showed that electrical activity at the scalp is greater on the left side for musicians listening to melodic sequences, while it is greater on the right site for nonmusicians.

Prediction 3. Variation in the complexity of syntactic structure should stimulate greater correlations with behavioral difficulty when heard in the right ear than in the left.

Language is an intrinsically relational task. The cognizance of a sentence characteristically requires both isolation of the phrases and an intuitive understanding of their relations to each other in the whole sentence. If the left hemisphere carries out relational processing, then the perceptual strategies that listeners use to analyze relations among the words in sentences must be indigenous to the left hemisphere. This is reflected in an overall superiority of the right ear for sentence recognition, compared with sequences of random words. In one experiment subjects heard ten monaural seven-word sentences (for example, "They in fact did seem very nice") constructed by splicing from a randomly recorded list. After each sentence, there was a two-second silence, followed by a number from which subjects counted backwards by threes for five seconds and then recalled the sentence. Subjects performed better on recall of

Table 10.3

Summaries of studies on melody perception by musicians and nonmusicians

Study	Left ear	Right ear	Right-ear advantage
Johnson[a]			
Musicians	16.0	19.8	+3.8
Nonmusicians	15.7	13.7	–2.0
Musicians' advantage	0.3	6.1	
Johnson et al.[b]			
Musicians	4.9	4.5	+0.4
Nonmusicians	6.5	6.7	–0.2
Musicians' advantage	1.6	2.2	
Gaede et al.[c]			
Musicians	10.87	10.00	+0.88
Nonmusicians	12.19	11.48	+0.71
Musicians' advantage	1.32	1.48	
Gates and Bradshaw[d]			
Musicians	0.83	1.10	+0.27
Nonmusicians	0.14	0.35	+0.21
Musicians' advantage	0.69	0.75	
Gordon[e]			
Musicians	15.3	17.6	+2.3
Nonmusicians	14.7	16.7	+2.0
Musicians' advantage	0.6	0.9	

Sources: Johnson (1977, table 1); Johnson et al. (1977, table 1); Gaede et al. (1978, table 1); Gates and Bradshaw (1977, table 2); Gordon (1978, table 1). Note: Advantage scores compensate for whether the raw scores are based on correct responses or errors.
a. Scores are the mean number of correct positive responses.
b. Musicians are their groups 1 and 2; nonmusicians are their group 4. Scores are the mean number of errors.
c. Groups the means of their high-aptitude and low-aptitude subjects. Scores are the mean number of errors.
d. Groups the means of male and female subjects, responding to long and short excerpts, from their unfamiliar melodies. The scores are means of presented d's.
e. Excludes subjects performing at chance level. Scores are number correct (out of possible 24) on dichotic melodies differing in rhythm.

sentences heard in the right ear; however, there was no difference in recall of the same word sets reordered into random sequences ("nice in seem did fact very they") (table 10.4). The syntactic organization of the sequence is critical to bringing out the asymmetry.[8]

I also examined performance in this immediate verbal task with sentences that varied according to the negative, passive, and question constructions, and their combinations.

The bug bit the dog.
The dog was bitten by the bug.
The bug did not bite the dog.
Did the bug bite the dog?
The dog wasn't bitten by the bug.
Was the dog bitten by the bug?
Didn't the bug bite the dog?
Wasn't the dog bitten by the bug?

Sentences heard in the left ear generated about the same number of meaning-preserving errors as in the right ear (passive to active, question to negative question). However, sentences in the right ear were recalled with far fewer meaning-changing errors (passive to negative, question to active) (table 10.5). This kind of result was confirmed by a separate study using the same paradigm and varying only the position of an adverb and verb particle.

The waiter quickly sent back the order.
The waiter quickly sent the order back.
Quickly the waiter sent back the order.
Quickly the waiter sent the order back.

Table 10.4
Immediate recall of sequences arranged in sentence order and random order (percentage correct)

	Left ear	Right ear	Right-ear advantage
Sentence order	54	65	+11
Random order	4	4	0
Sentence advantage	50	61	

Source: Bever (1971, table 2).

Table 10.5
Errors to sentences in immediate recall

	Left ear	Right ear	Right-ear advantage
Meaning-preserving errors	16	19	–3
Meaning-changing errors	16	5	+11

Source: Bever (1971, table 3).

In this paradigm subjects made more syntactic recall errors (incorrect adverb or particle placement) to sentences presented to the right ear (table 10.6).

All these studies demonstrate the same principle: The right ear processed sentences more immediately for meaning. I have argued elsewhere that comprehension proceeds in part by the application of perceptual strategies, which map surface sequences onto underlying representations (Bever, 1970). A basic strategy of speech comprehension is one that maps a noun-verb-noun (NVN) sequence onto the grammatical relations "actor, action, object." This strategy accounts for the fact that the first sentence is easier to compare with a picture than the second sentence.

1. They are fixing benches. (progressive construction)
2. They are performing monkeys. (participial construction)

In the first sentence the NVN pattern conforms to the expectation expressed by the strategy, while in the second it does not. Jacques Mehler, Peter Carey, and I tested the comprehension of these sentences monaurally to see if the comprehension time between sentences like 1 and 2 would differ more in the right ear than in the left. Listeners heard five sentences structurally like the first or five sentences like the second and matched each one to a picture; the sentences were always presented to the same ear for a particular subject (Carey et al., 1970). The results are summarized in table 10.7. The predicted differences occurred for sentences heard in the right ear, but the results were actually the reverse numerically for those heard in the left ear. The average comprehension time for the two constructions together was similar in the two ears. However, the right-ear presentation differentiated the constructions according to their conformity with the perceptual strategy while the left-ear presentation did not.

Table 10.6
Syntactic errors in sentences with adverbs and particles

	Left ear	Right ear	Right-ear advantage
Percentage of syntactic errors	52	77	25

Source: Bever (1971, table 4).

Table 10.7
Mean latency (seconds) to match pictures to progressive and participial sentences

	Left ear	Right ear	Right-ear advantage
Participial	0.98	1.29	−0.31
Progressive	0.96	0.79	+0.17
Difference	0.02	0.50	

Source: Bever (1971, figure 3).
Note: Subjects without experience.

The preceding experiment is devoted to a perceptual strategy that applies within a single clause. David Townsend and I have also examined sentences with different kinds of relations between main and subordinate clauses. In this experiment we probed for subjects' coding of the meaning of a clause by interrupting a monaural presentation of it with a potential paraphrase on a slide (subjects were to say yes when the paraphrase was appropriate). In both ear presentations subjects recognized such meaning-related material from main clauses faster than from subordinate clauses—suggesting that the meaning of a main clause is more immediately processed regardless of ear presentation (Townsend and Bever, 1978).

The main-subordinate difference bears an orderly relation to the strength of the causal link between the main and subordinate clause set up by each subordinating conjunction. For example, a causal "if" or "since" clause can be an explicit cause of what follows, while an "although" or "while" adversative clause must be explicitly not the cause of what follows; a "when" clause is neutral. In a sense the causal subordinate clauses do not depend on their main clause for interpretation, while adversative clauses do, since the information in the main clause clarifies which part of the subordinate clause is adversative. This formal difference is reflected behaviorally among sentences presented to the right ear (see figure 10.1). The

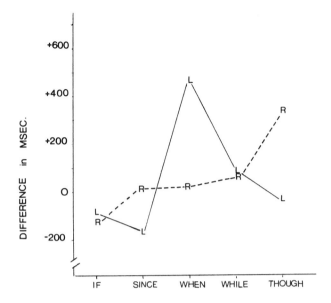

10.1
Response time differences between initial main clauses and subordinate clauses with different conjunctions (subordinate time – main time) in recognizing a subsequent paraphrase. (L = left ear; R = right ear)

main-subordinate difference is large for adversative subordinates and slightly reversed for causal subordinates, with temporal clauses intermediate.

We interpreted this and related results as showing that an interclausal comprehension strategy involves recoding an initial subordinate clause semantically, insofar as it can be a clause independent of a following main clause. This strategy does not characterize the responses to sentences presented to the left ear; there is no orderly relation (at least to do with causality). Rather, all the main-subordinate differences are similar to one another, except "when" clauses, which occasion much longer subordinate clause response times. This result may be of interest in relation to the occasional claim that the right hemisphere has a special difficulty with temporal order (but see Veroff, 1978). In any case it shows that biclausal sentences presented to the left ear are not subjected to the semantically systematic initial comprehension strategies that apply to right-ear input.

If the left-ear presentation does not show evidence of perceptual strategies, how are sentences understood at all in that condition?

One possibility is that the information is transmitted to the left hemisphere by way of the corpus callosum, thus circumventing the application of the strategies but leaving intact other mechanisms of perception. A second possibility is that the monotony of the task of hearing the same kind of construction type repeatedly in these experiments allows for the formation of a holistic schema in the right hemisphere.

Prediction 4. People who are relatively skilled in a modality are more left-hemisphered for relational tasks and more right-hemisphered for holistic tasks.

It would be easy to think of the general situation I have been outlining as one in which the two hemispheres share certain capacities but the left hemisphere takes on the development of special, or "complex," knowledge. This falsely predicts that relational skills are relatively more lateralized to the left hemisphere in highly skilled subjects, while there is no subject difference in the lateralization of holistic tasks. Rather the data suggest that being skilled at a modality involves being more left-hemisphered for relational tasks in that modality and more right-hemisphered for holistic tasks in that modality. This implies that holistic processes have certain independent properties, rather than simply being the mental chaff left behind by the relational processes.

RELATIONAL STRATEGIES

We can examine the behavioral asymmetry differences between musicians and nonmusicians to verify the independent lateralization of relational and holistic processes. Processing music can involve certain relational tasks (novel melody recognition) in which musicians are more right-eared than nonmusicians; it also involves holistic tasks (chord recognition or familiar melody recognition). The first question is, Why do musicians perform better on melody tasks presented to the right ear than on those presented to the left? Is it because their right-ear performance improves, or because the left-ear performance decreases, or both? We found no significant difference in the left-ear performance between musicians and nonmusicians; the musicians performed better than nonmusicians in the right ear, but the left-ear performances were the same (table 10.2). The same was found by Johnson. The same relative results were found by all the other studies summarized in table 10.3. In every study of unfamiliar melody perception, musicians are better than nonmusicians in the right ear to a greater degree than in the left ear. This suggests that the left hemisphere of musicians is particularly better at this task, while the right hemisphere is not worse.

It is possible that musicians are genetically left-hemisphered for music before they study it; that is, they do not become left-hemisphered as a function of learning relational melodic strategies. Final proof of this genetic hypothesis will require longitudinal investigation of children who are and are not studying music. However, we can examine musicians' performance on holistic musical tasks, to see whether such tasks are left-hemisphered as well.

HOLISTIC TEMPLATES

Music also offers holistic tasks that, unlike melody recognition, remain holistic regardless of one's musical skill. Chord perception (for people without perfect pitch) is one example; the independent notes of a chord cannot be identified by normal listeners, except by virtue of their contribution to the "color" of the chord. This makes chord perception a strong test of the formal explication of the relational-holistic differentiation. The notes of a chord are "related" to each other; indeed, the chord depends for its character on such a relation. But perceiving a chord is not a relational act in the technical sense of the term. While the perception involves a relation between two notes, it does not require separate identifications of the two notes independently *and* in relation to each other. This may clarify what should have bothered the acute reader in my discussion of visual asymmetries. For example, why is recognizing a rotated or displaced figure a holistic task; such recognition presupposes a relation just as a chord presupposes separate notes (physical movement). The answer is that the object is set only in relation to its (identical) self; therefore the rotation task does not meet the "found" criteria of relational processing.

What occurs in highly skilled musicians? Do they become less left-hemisphered for chords (because of a "migration" of music to the left hemisphere?), or do they become more right-hemisphered? The answer is the latter. Gaede et al. (1978) and Gordon (1978) tested chord recognition in musicians and nonmusicians. They both found that musicians are more left-eared on chord tasks than nonmusicians (table 10.8).

Why should this be so? One possibility is that holistic processing strategies can be learned. I shall call such strategies *templates* because they are processes that do not require any internal analysis. In this view musicians develop (or "have") chordal templates which they apply to chord tasks, heightening the superiority of left-ear performance on such tasks. If the template interpretation is appropriate, then even short or frequently repeated melodies might be holistically processed by musicians. (All the studies that show a significant right-ear superiority in musicians use relatively long melodies or melodies that occur only once or twice in the experiment.)

It should be possible to construct a holistic melody-recognition task. For example, if melodies are very short, listeners may be able to apprehend them holistically without internal analysis. In any case their brevity precludes the application of musically sophisticated strategies. Short atonal melodies might also resist the application of usual melodic strategies (in Western-trained amateur musicians). Finally, very familiar melodies or ones that are repeated many times during an experiment could be perceived holistically by way of constructed templates. Gates and Bradshaw (1977) presented subjects monaurally with ten- to fifteen-note familiar tonal melodies (melodies chosen to be familiar, repeated fifteen times during the course of the experiment). They found that recognition of excerpts from such melodies was numerically better in the left ear than the right for musicians (with no difference for nonmusicians). Johnson et al. (1977) found a similar asymmetry for the recognition of monaurally presented short, nontonal, random sequences of pitches. Finally, Zatorre (1978) found a similar effect by combining these stimulus parameters. He presented short (six-note) melodies a minimum of seventeen times and found that musicians performed better on stimuli in the left ear, and did so to a greater extent than nonmusicians.

The previous studies demonstrate that musicians are more left-eared for holistic tasks while being more right-eared for relational tasks; that is, the right hemisphere "learns" (or if musicians are genetically preformed, "has") templates that increase the efficacy of holistic processing.

If performance improves by way of acquired templates in the right

Table 10.8
Summaries of studies of holistic musical tasks in musicians and nonmusicians

Study	Left ear	Right ear	Right-ear advantage
Gordon[a]			
Musicians	16.9	14.6	–2.3
Nonmusicians	15.1	14.3	–0.8
Musicians' advantage	1.8	0.3	
Gaede et al.[b]			
Musicians	8.21	9.00	–0.79
Nonmusicians	9.94	10.08	–0.14
Musicians' advantage	1.73	1.08	
Gates and Bradshaw[c]			
Musicians	1.88	1.56	–0.32
Nonmusicians	0.61	0.65	+0.04
Musicians' advantage	1.27	0.91	
Johnson et al.[d]			
Musicians	4.6	5.7	–1.1
Nonmusicians	6.7	7.0	–0.3
Musicians' advantage	2.1	1.3	
Zatorre[e]			
Musicians	73	67	–6
Nonmusicians	63	59	–4
Musicians' advantage	10	8	

Sources: Gordon (1978, table 3); Gaede et al. (1978, table 1); Gates and Brad-shaw (1977, table 2); Johnson et al. (1977, table 1); Zatorre (1978, figure 2).
Note: Studies and subjects are the same as in the corresponding studies in table 10.3, except where noted.
a. Scores are number correct on chord recognition.
b. Scores are mean errors on note discrimination in chords.
c. Scores on familiar melodies.
d. Errors on short random-pitch sequences.
e. Scores are the percentage correct recognition of short, repeatedly presented dichotic melodies. See the appendix to this chapter.

hemisphere, the difference between musicians and nonmusicians should reside mostly in an improvement in the left-ear performance rather than a decrease in right-ear performance. This is numerically the case in each of the five recent studies that bring out an overall left-ear superiority (table 10.8).

In brief, being musically sophisticated is associated with an advantage in the left hemisphere for relational processes applied to music and in the right hemisphere for holistic musical tasks. Musicians are not more left-hemisphered for music; rather they are more differentiated hemispherically. The hypothesis that complex holistic templates can be learned from experience raises the possibility of a developmental pattern in which people oscillate between first treating a skill holistically, then relationally as experience with it increases, and then holistically again (with higher-order holistic templates the second time). The next section explores face recognition as potentially such as skill.

FACE RECOGNITION: A DEVELOPMENTAL CASE STUDY

A general point of this chapter is that language is characteristically a left-hemisphered skill because most language behaviors involve relational processing. Language is of more interest than many other skills, such as long division or skiing, because it is an indigenous part of all cultures, shared by all "normal" individuals. The ability to recognize faces also seems to be a likely candidate for a culturally universal skill (though it would be less surprising to find a culture in which individuals are not recognized by their faces than to find a culture in which nobody speaks a language). The recognition of familiar faces is important to consider because it is generally viewed as a function of the right hemisphere. This would be a prima facie counterexample to the proposal in this paper that a distinct processing style, not skill, is associated with the hemispheres. Of course, it is possible that faces are always recognized holistically, and that is why face recognition is right-hemisphered. However, I will argue that the generally accepted facts about face recognition are best understood as involving both right and left hemispheres, depending on the way a face is recognized. This variability is a function of such factors as the developmental stage of normal children or neurological state of brain-damaged adults. A full review of the face-recognition literature is beyond the scope of this paper. The reader should consult Carey (1978) for a recent review of most of the facts that I shall discuss.[9]

Typical specific phenomena are the following:

1. The bilateral recognition of photographs of acquaintances is good with little change, starting at age five years (Carey and Diamond, 1977).

2a. Inverted photographs of acquaintences are poorly recognized in children and adults, except

2b. At ages twelve to fourteen (Carey and Diamond, 1977).

3a. By age eight years, people recognize photographs of familiar people better in the left visual field except

3b. Famous faces (movie stars, and so forth) are better recognized in the right visual field (Marzi et al., 1974).

4a. The recognition of recently presented faces is based on para-phernalia (hats, glasses) until age ten, when each face becomes a perceptual constant. The overall ability to recognize recently presented faces increases with age up to age fourteen except

4b. At ages twelve to fourteen there is a decrease.

5a. Recently presented faces are recognized equally well in the visual fields between ages seven and ten; at ten they are better recognized in the left visual field. This asymmetry continues throughout life except

5b. At ages twelve to fourteen, the left and right visual fields perform equally well (Leehey, 1976).

6. The recognition of upside-down presentations of recently presented faces is poor throughout life.

7a. With (posterior) right-hemisphere lesions, adults cannot recognize recently presented faces, but

7b. Right-hemisphere-damaged adults can recognize familiar faces, and

7c. In certain cases, characteristically with bilateral (posterior) lesions, adults cannot recognize familiar faces but can recognize recently presented ones.

Carey argues that facts such as these (except 3b, which appeared after Carey, 1978, was written) suggest that there is, in effect, an organ of face recognition, which inhibits (and is facilitated by) a particular region of the right hemisphere. A hypothesis is that this organ has two related physiological substructures in the right hemisphere, an early maturing one for familiar faces and a later maturing one for unfamiliar faces.

   This hypothesis is certainly possible. If true, it would serve as a clear example of a maturationally based sociopsychological skill. However it is a very strong position and it cannot explain any of the exceptions noted in 2b, 3b, 4b, 5b, 7b. There is, moreover, a weaker hypothesis that would account for all the stipulated facts. The principles are the following.

A. Recognition of a small number of frequently presented family members and caretakers is important for the child.
B. The face offers a relatively constant and distinctive configuration for each person.
C. There are several ages when the number of individuals to be distinguished increases rapidly (in the social selection of subjects discussed in the literature): (1) at ages five to seven (when a child enters grammar school); (2) at ages twelve to thirteen when a child enters high school).
D. The left hemisphere emerges developmentally as dominant for relational processing, and the right hemisphere for holistic processing.
E. Holistic templates of increasing complexity are constructed developmentally as a result of being repeated in relational analysis.

Principles A–C are obviously true, at least at a nontechnical level; D and E have been postulated earlier in this paper to account for other data. It remains to show how A–E describe facts 1–7 (I take the nonexceptional facts first).

1. Principles A and B combine to predict the early emergence of family (and friend) face recognition.
2. Upside-down familiar faces are of no special import (and rarely experienced).
3. Principles A, B, and D together predict that familiar face recognition will emerge as a special right-hemisphere skill in childhood. Repeated presentation of the same small number of faces could build up a multiple representation of each that could be represented holistically.
4. To recognize discriminatively a recently and briefly presented face requires the ability to quickly form a discriminative representation of it. In children this should be reflected in a range of set cues (eyeglasses, beard, total shape). With development, practice, and an in-

creasing number of faces (implied by principle C1) an overall holistic framework could develop.

5. Some of the distinct facial cues may bear a relation to the whole face, at first being an initial approximation of a facial configuration. Accordingly, the recognition is sometimes relational sometimes holistic, leading to no overall asymmetɪy until age ten, when an overall holistic facial configuration is accumulated.

6. Recently presented upside-down faces should not show any interaction with ordinary face recognition and no developmental change related to face recognition.

7. If the right hemisphere is the repository for the overall face schema, then damage to it should damage new face recognition.

These facts are all related to the role of the right hemisphere in the emergence of particular holistic template patterns, first for family members and friends and then a more general all-purpose configuration for the rapid representation of new faces. These facts are also the nonexceptional ones. Consider now an exceptional fact (3b), that famous faces are better recognized in the right visual field. Famous persons are characteristically known for a particular facial attribute, usually through photographs alone (for example, Yul Brynner, Howdy Doody, Will Rogers, Santa Claus, Bugs Bunny, Richard Nixon). In fact, many such personages are facially defined by their main characteristic (Brynner by baldness, Doody by freckles, Claus by a beard, Bunny by teeth and ears, Nixon by jowls). A photograph of such personages can vary widely except for that characteristic and still be recognized, which is also why professional comics can do effective imitations of famous people. Thus famous faces might well be recognized by recourse to such isolated features in relation to the whole face; such processing would by definition be better carried out by the left hemisphere.

This kind of interpretation can also explain fact 7b, that right-brain-damaged people can recognize familiar faces; ex hypothesi they do so by reference to certain isolable features of their friends' and relatives' faces (in the traumatic absence of being able to rely on their right hemisphere). They remember that grandpa is bald, grandma wears glasses, junior has freckles. Accordingly these patients can rely on metonymous relational processing for recognition of familiar faces.

These interpretations suggest that adults can recognize faces relationally. This offers an explanation for a nexus of exceptions to the developmental pattern. At about age thirteen children temporarily lose the right-hemisphere dominance for recognizing new faces (5b). Principles C and E explain this as a function of the reorganization of facial templates, based on the many new faces that a child undertakes to recognize at that age. During this period there is greater interaction between relational and holistic processing as new configurations are being formed. This would also explain the compound perception of upside-down faces (based on isolated features processed in the left hemisphere). In this view the decrease in recognition of familiar faces occurs because of the unaccustomed (and less efficient) left-hemisphere processing.

Finally, we can explain the most bizarre fact of all—that certain patients, with bilateral lesions, can recognize new faces but not old (7c). To explain this we must first recall that reciprocal inhibition of function governs the interrelation of the hemispheres. When a particular function is being carried out in one hemisphere, the same function is inhibited in the corresponding area of the other hemisphere. This mechanism explains why a skill that is overlearned in one hemisphere cannot be easily transferred to the other if the first is damaged. The healthy hemisphere inhibits the damaged one but cannot itself carry out the skill. Complementary inhibition also explains why recovery of a trained function in a damaged hemisphere can occur if the opposite untrained hemisphere is damaged. The damage to the untrained hemisphere releases the trained one from its inhibition, since both hemispheres are now damaged and neither inhibits the other. The originally trained hemisphere can now carry out some of the skill (albeit less well than an undamaged hemisphere), leading to a partial recovery of function.

Suppose, as Carey argues, that the rapid encoding of a new face depends on a highly overlearned facial configuration that is multiply interpreted in adulthood more than any single face (since every normal face implies the configuration). If only the right hemisphere is damaged, access to the general configuration is lost because of the inhibitory action of the left hemisphere. If the left hemisphere is damaged as well, the right hemisphere is released from inhibition and can carry out some of its original functions, especially the one that was most overtrained, the encoding of a new face.

In brief, if one takes the position that face recognition is a highly valued activity potentially carried out by each hemisphere in the manner appropriate to that hemisphere, then all the stipulated facts can be explained, including those that are exceptional on the previous view that perception is an "organ" with two intrahemispheric sites[10].

We can also make predictions about new facts. One of the easiest to test would be the developmental prediction following from principle C2. Some time between two and seven children should become temporarily worse at face recognition and should also become relatively more left-hemisphered for it. This follows from the hypothesized shift from holistic to relational face processing that occurs under the impact of abruptly having to learn many new faces. Mehler (personal communication) has found some evidence related to the former prediction. Children do temporarily become less able to identify recently presented visual shapes between the ages two and seven. It remains to be seen whether this is true of face recognition in the same kind of paradigms used with adults.

The data on face recognition is consistent with the view that faces can be recognized relationally or holistically, depending on the developmental stage and neurological state of the subject. Such consistency does not disprove the view that normal adult face recognition is a right-hemisphere "organ," nor does it deny the importance of maturational factors in the development of this capacity. It does demonstrate that face recognition is not a counterexample to the main thesis of this chapter.

HOW DOES CEREBRAL ASYMMETRY COME TO EXIST?

The previous review documents the claim that the left hemisphere is dominant for relational processing and the right for holistic processing. What is the basis for this difference? The simplest answer would be the claim that it is innate in an interesting sense (as opposed to the sense in which everything about the hemispheres assumes a physiological representation). A substantive proposal is that the hemispheres process information in different ways at birth due to a direct genetically determined asymmetry that governs some physical aspect of neurological functioning. I shall call this the innate structure theory (IST).

Grosso modo IST is the only choice. How can a processing asymmetry exist without some genetically preconditioned physiological basis? The more interesting question is, What is the simplest physiological difference between the hemispheres at birth that could account for the functional asymmetries of adulthood?

The ontogenetic formation of regular relations between brain and behavior is a dynamic process of growth. The source of cerebral asymmetries must exert its influence during at least a decade while brain structures and behavioral systems emerge. Suppose the only difference between the hemispheres is that the left hemisphere is more capable during early childhood. That is, suppose that the two hemispheres function identically at birth but that the processing capacity of the left hemisphere is larger. This substantive claim, together with several other independently justified premises, is sufficient to account for the early appearance of cerebral asymmetries and their continuous development.[11] There are various models of how a quantitative asymmetry could result in the commonly observed qualitative asymmetries. The essential premises are the following.

1. Learning a relational skill involves more processing than learning a holistic skill.
2. Each hemisphere has anatomically specified cortical zones; each zone is physically predisposed to carry out certain functions, (due to its direct sensorimotor connections, functionally available cortical connections, or internal organization).
3. Any given hemispheric zone has a finite learning capacity.
4. When a skill is learned by one hemisphere the corresponding anatomical area of the opposite hemisphere is inhibited from expressing (or acquiring) that skill.
5. The left hemisphere is more powerful computationally than the right (at least during the years two to six), in the sense that it can simultaneously process a greater number of mental representations at a given maturational stage.

The first premise is a tautology and the next three premises are widely accepted.

The formal definition of the two kinds of processing automatically guarantees, *ceteris paribus*, that relational processing is more demanding than holistic. Since the formal definition of relational processing presupposes two simultaneous independent mental representations, it must be more complex than holistic processing which involves only one such representation. It is a commonplace view that intrahemispheric localization of function can be influenced by anatomical connections to other cortical areas and to particular peripheral organs. It is not controversial to suggest that, like the brain as a whole, each part of it can account for the learning of so much and no more. Contralateral hemispheric suppression of attentional processes and learning functions has received systematic experimental investigation in animals and is generally accepted for humans.[12]

The last premise is not as commonly assumed, though some arguments are plausibly consistent with it. First, systematic investigations of infant brains have brought out specific zones in which the left hemisphere is larger or more convoluted than the right at birth Recently, Corballis and Morgan (1978) have argued that a maturational gradient in favor of the left hemisphere would explain the left-hemisphere priority for language and complex motor behavior (on the assumption that they are the highest-priority skills to the exclusion of spatial organization, for example). However, they offer no independent evidence from human development. (But Brown and Jaffe (1975) and Whitaker (1978) argue that the left hemisphere matures more *slowly*.) Notice that principle 5a does not directly specify the physiological basis for the computational superiority of the left hemisphere; the left hemisphere could mature more quickly (and therefore can compute more at a time) or less quickly (and therefore is more adaptable to learning new kinds of computations).

Let us stipulate that principles 1–5 are true. Why would they lead to the observed asymmetric specialization of the left hemisphere for relational processing and the right hemisphere for holistic processing? The basic concept is that zones in the more powerful hemisphere (the left) end up carrying out the more demanding mental processes (relational). It is intuitively clear that this would occur reliably only if the acquisition of different kinds of skills is allocated to distinct brain zones (premise 2), each of which has limited capacity (premise 3). If each hemisphere had an arbitrarily large capacity, the computational superiority of the left and the relative difficulty of relational processing would be moot. Also, if there were no complementary inhibition between corresponding zones in the two hemispheres, multiple exposure of tasks would ultimately lead to bilateral representation and expression of every skill.

Still to be demonstrated is why a quantitative superiority of the left hemisphere does not predict dominance for all processing. For purposes of this discussion, the relevant feature of the quantitative model is that a hemispheric asymmetry of size $f(n)$ for learning an n-step skill is $(f(n))^2$ for learning a $2n$-step skill. If holistic tasks involve processing one mental representation and relational tasks involve processing two or more mental representations, then the hemisphere asymmetry will always be larger for relational than holistic tasks.

By hypothesis the left hemisphere learns all skills more efficiently. However, the stronger asymmetry for relational tasks automatically leads to a greater initial relational superiority in the left hemisphere during early childhood than holistic superiority. Each left-hemisphere zone will tend to become relatively specialized at an early age more often for relational tasks than for holistic tasks. After that, all new kinds of operations must be learned by the right hemisphere. If these operations are themselves roughly evenly distributed between relational and holistic ones, then the end result will be that the right hemisphere becomes relatively dominant for the elaborated holistic operations.[13]

This model would allow us to argue that the marked qualitative difference in the hemispheres results from a small quantitative difference in computational power, interacting with the dynamics of mental growth and the formal differences in complexity of the different kinds of operations. In brief, there is a class of models in which language, the quintessential relational skill, is acquired by the left hemisphere, because of a modest quantitative superiority of the left hemisphere.

SOME APPARENT EMPIRICAL COUNTEREXAMPLES

The preceding model is based on assumptions about normal growth of brain-behavior interrelations. The most obvious counterproposal is that the left hemisphere is dominant for language and relational tasks because of a unique structural attribute that makes language possible in that hemisphere. Two kinds of human populations offer evidence bearing on this proposal. First, prelinguistic infants might show a behavioral asymmetry in favor of language. Second, people with one hemisphere removed might exhibit the normal capacity of the other hemisphere in isolation.

Systematic research on infants is scant, since most methods have only recently been developed. A few experiments have found asymmetries in evoked response, measured on infants' skulls, stimulated by language versus music or flash versus speech.[14] This research is consistent with the following generalization: Complex stimuli (natural speech sounds) are more often processed in the left hemisphere. But that is what one would expect after a few months from the dynamic developmental model I have suggested. The finding that speech sounds evoke left-hemisphere response and music tones or white noise evokes right-hemisphere response is consistent with the fact that speech is a more complex waveform than music or undifferentiated noise. Furthermore, research during the last year has demonstrated that the left-hemisphere-evoked response in infants differentiates acoustic-voicing-onset variants of the same consonants (as categorized by adults) while the right hemisphere does not. The right hemisphere does, however, differentiate different consonants. Only the left hemisphere differentiates consonants that differ in place of articulation, an acoustically complex property. Both the right and the left hemisphere differentiate relatively steady tonal properties. Even in the infant only certain, complex characteristics of speech, *not* speech as a whole, are lateralized to the left hemisphere (Molfese, 1978).

This volume contains recent findings relating to the behavioral limitations of the surgically isolated right and left hemispheres (Dennis, chapter 9, this volume). Such cases are interesting and well worth pursuing. The linguistic capacity of the derelict right hemisphere at first seems impressive. However, the precise experimental results with such patients are also consistent with the following summary. The surgically isolated right hemisphere processes language less well than the surgically isolated left hemisphere. This finding does not invalidate the dynamic model of asymmetries in favor of IST for several reasons. First, according to the quantitative hypothesis, the right hemisphere is slower at multirepresentational tasks. Since language behavior is normally based on the intact left hemisphere, many language processes considered normal may themselves be predicated on an active short-term memory of a certain size and a perceptual mechanism of a certain speed. If the lone right hemisphere operates more slowly than the left (as it does, by my hypothesis) then it might appear to be relatively impaired on normal language tasks. (This point is like that raised against using

IQ tests to measure the intellectual capacity of minority groups; that is, the lone talking right hemisphere is a minority that is not taken into account in the majority measures of linguistic capacity.)

A second, more baffling, but potentially devastating point is that these subjects started out life with one extremely abnormal hemisphere. This must lead to some abnormality in the initial wiring of the normal hemisphere, thereby rendering abnormal the performance of the remaining hemisphere after surgery. (I am indebted to N. Geschwind for bringing this point to my attention.)

The most impressive fact is that the lone right hemisphere learns language at all. Surely, the strong structural theory of the usual dominance of the left hemisphere would not allow for that.

CONCLUSION

I have shown that language could be left-hemisphered because it characteristically involves relational activity and because the left hemisphere is dominant for all relational processing. I have shown further that the left hemisphere could become dominant for relational processing if there were a slight quantitative superiority in processing during childhood. In this view we must yet account for the evolution of a quantitative increase in the number of mental representations and relations that can be processed simultaneously and the emergence of a quantitative hemispheric asymmetry in functioning. Such evolutionary developments are prodigious. But at least we are relieved of the burden of accounting for the specific qualitative facts of hemispheric asymmetry.

Of course one could argue that it is easier to comprehend these asymmetries if one assumes an innate structural qualitative difference in the hemispheres. One could argue that asymmetries in other species give precedence to such innate structural differences. One could argue that the early appearance of phonetic asymmetries demonstrates an innate qualitative peculiarity of the left hemisphere.

Of course, one could. But first we must demonstrate that the prima facie simpler and more generally motivated explanation of the same facts is inadequate.

Broca had a hunch that qualitative asymmetries are the normal outcome of a quantitative perinatal asymmetry. Lashley supplemented this with the view that general laws of growth account for the emergence and localization of brain function. I have argued that these old suggestions can explain all the currently known facts about asymmetries.

APPENDIX: Five replications of relative right-ear superiority among musicians for processing melodies and one methodologically based failure to find this

Bever and Chiarello (1974) reported that melody recognition was better in the right ear than the left for musicians but the reverse for nonmusicians. Their theoretical position was that musicians have a set of melody-processing strategies that reflect the music they have heard and played. These strategies facilitate the mental description of a melody in terms of its component motifs and the relations between the motifs and the whole melody. Accordingly, musicians process melodies relationally, in the technical sense defined earlier (and thus better in the left hemisphere). Nonmusicians do not have such motif strategies and, insofar as they deal with them at all, must process melodies holistically (and thus better in the right hemisphere).

Bever and Chiarello's theoretical position motivates a number of design parameters in studying this phenomenon.

SUBJECTS

They excluded subjects with known hearing loss in either ear, self-reported tone-deaf subjects, and those with self-reported perfect pitch. Such subjects are incapable of or could avoid classifying a melody as a melody. They are not appropriate. All subjects were right-handed.

Musicians included only currently active amateur musicians. Nonmusicians included only those who never had more than a few years of training, not less than six years before the experiment.

Bever and Chiarello used these definitions as selection criteria to ensure a clear differentiation of subject groups. The musicians could all read music (usually they could sight-read with proficiency). Most

could take simple musical dictation (being an active amateur musician often involves making minor corrections on a score, copying
brief passages of another part). Bever and Chiarello did not test
for musicality, either among the musicians or nonmusicians. They
avoided using musicologists and composers as subjects because their
pilot research had indicated that such listeners treat the experiment
as an intellectual puzzle, apparently suspending normal listening
strategies.

MATERIALS

Bever and Chiarello used eight-note to twenty-note tonal melodies.
They reasoned that melodies must be long enough so that short-term
memory limitations are exceeded; only then do listeners need to apply recoding strategies. (Of course, this leaves open the possibility
that musicians use such strategies anyway.) The melodies were
tonal;that is, they were in the same key, began and ended on the
tonic, or implied a harmonic modulation, following standard laws
of tonal melody formation (no major leaps with a melodic phrase,
preparation or filling-in of leaps that do occur). This constraint en-
sured that the stimuli would be susceptible to standard occidental
music-recoding strategies.

PROCEDURE

Ear Presentation
The stimuli were presented monaurally and in blocks to the same
ear. Bever and Chiarello were concerned with the characteristic performance of each ear alone, not with the ear performance when the
ears compete actively (as in dichotic listening) or in anticipation
(when the listener does not know which ear to attend most).
Dichotic presentation of music involves a special problem that does
not arise for speech: the tendency to fuse the competing stimuli into
one musical whole. Charles Ives aside, simultaneous presentation of
different melodies is a common integrative task for music listeners;
the normal listener may integrate the two separate melodies in a
dichotic task, producing a third stimulus.[15] This problem is ecologically distinct from that of speech. Disentanglement of competing
speech messages is a listening problem (the so-called cocktail party
problem). Luciano Berio aside, several simultaneous speech messages

must ordinarily be kept distinct, not integrated. Accordingly, it may be an ecologically acceptable technique to use dichotic listening with speech, but it is not acceptable with music.

TASK

Bever and Chiarello required listeners both to recognize whether a melody was repeated and to recognize an excerpt from each melody. The effect of this double task was to reduce the possibility that listeners would encode the stimuli in an arbitrary or task-specific memory code. While listening to each melody they had to process it for immediate recognition of the following excerpt.

Each melody was presented only once (except for the positive repeated melody trials). Repeated presentation of a complex melody could allow both musicians and nonmusicians to build up a relational representation; repeated presentations of a simple melody, ex hypothesi, could allow all subjects to build up a holistic template. Single presentation follows the usual practice in psycholinguistic research on normal sentence comprehension—consider the absurdity of an experiment on normal speech comprehension involving the presentation of the same sentence fifty times.

Five recent experiments, each by different researchers in different laboratories, have included studies related to the main finding of Bever and Chiarello. They all report superior performance in the right ear for musicians, a finding generally unexpected before Bever and Chiarello. They all appear to report a numerically greater right-ear superiority for musicians than for nonmusicians. However, the differences among the experiments are worthy of comment and may be useful as a guide for further experimentation.

Two experiments replicate Bever and Chiarello fully. Not only do musicians show a right-ear superiority, but nonmusicians show a left-ear superiority. These experiments differ from the other three in that they present each stimulus to a given subject only once.

Johnson (1977) used two-second violin melodies differing in pitch and rhythm, presented in dichotic pairs with a following binaural probe. On half the trials the probe was not one of the stimulus melodies; on the other half it was. The subjects' main task was to say whether the probe was one of the just-heard dichotic melodies. The musicians were people with at least four years of music training, who were "currently [playing] . . . for . . . at least one hour daily." He also tested the subjects for normal hearing. He contrasted right-handed and left-handed subjects. The results for right-handers conformed to Bever and Chiarello exactly (table 10.3). The results for left-handers are much less extreme. Johnson concludes that "this result supports . . . they hypothesis that musical stimuli are processed mainly in the left hemisphere of musicians and the right hemisphere of nonmusicians."

Johnson et al. (1977) used short tonal, conventional melodies each presented once monaurally, followed by four binaural melodies. The task of the subjects on each trial was to identify which of the binaurally presented melodies they had just heard. They also used random pitch and rhythm sequences and random pitch sequences. Their subjects included nonmusicians, musicians who play instruments without being able to read and transcribe music, musicians with reading ability, and musicians with reading and transcribing ability. Only the last two groups are likely to correspond to Bever and Chiarello's musicians. (Almost no active amateur musician cannot read music; indeed most can also transcribe it. On the other hand musicians who play without reading music may not be similar to Bever and Chiarello's nonmusicians.) The last two groups of musicians in Johnson's study perform similarly to musicians in the previous studies, in comparison with the (nonsignificant) tendency of nonmusicians to perform better in the right ear (table 10.3) They conclude that "comparisons of error scores by ear and by types of musical stimuli confirm the findings of Bever and Chiarello" (p. 296).

Johnson and Johnson et al. show a reversal of ear superiority between proficient musicians and others. Three other paradigms have brought out right-ear superiority in all subjects, in contrast to the traditional claim that music is univocally right-hemisphered. Furthermore, each study brings out numerically more right-earedness among musicians than among nonmusicians.

Gates and Bradshaw (1977b) used a complicated stimulus paradigm varying familiarity of melodies, tonality, and the length of excerpts used in a recognition task. Their experiment VI contrasted musicians (defined as potential professionals) and self-classified nonmusicians. Subjects were required to decide whether a long (five-note) or short (two-note) excerpt was contained in a preceding melody. The false trials were transpositions of a correct sequence (five-note false probes) or a pair of notes from the melody with a missing intervening note (two-note false probes). The unfamiliar melodies were retrograde and retrograde inversion transformations of the equal-duration familiar tonal melodies.

They derived δ' analyses for each melody condition using hit and miss rates as well as confidence ratings. They found an overall superiority of the right ear for both kinds of probes in musicians and nonmusicians. Table 10.3 presents the averages of the δ's presented in their table II, for illustrative purposes. (Note that averaging δ' across groups does not necessarily produce the exact δ' that would be produced by analyzing all the data in a single group.) Overall the right-ear effect is numerically stronger among musicians, although this is strongly true of males and weakly reversed among females. They conclude (inter alia) that "in opposition to the widely-held views of right hemisphere 'dominance' for music, this result supports the claim of Bever and Chiarello (1974) for left-hemisphere involvement: however, contrary to their suggestion that musical training determines hemispheric specialization, the present findings indicate differential processing within, as well as between, musically selected groups of subjects" (p. 403).

The problem for them and us is to explain why all the subjects appear to have processed the unfamiliar stimuli better in the left hemispheres. Their unfamiliar melodies may have had peculiar nonmelodic properties, since they were created by transformations of standard melodies. They were also presented four times, perhaps enough to stimulate analysis of each into component phrases, but not enough to provide the basis for a total gestalt of each. Finally, the false probes were extremely similar to correct probes, perhaps accounting for the need to listen analytically, and also accounting for the fairly low overall detection rate. Gates and Bradshaw do not report the true and false-positive rates separately; it is possible that all the δ' differences are the result of different rates of false-positive responses.

Gaede et al. (1978) examined the effect of the subject variable *musical aptitude*. They reasoned that aptitude would ordinarily correlate with proficiency and that the previous research on musicians might demonstrate an effect, not of musical training, but of musical talent. They used a standard binaural test of melodic aptitude, which they describe as requiring subjects to report how each of a number of melodies differs from a presented standard melody. They used this test to segregate high- and low-aptitude nonmusicians and musicians (the musicians had at least five years of instrumental lessons, within the most recent five years). They then presented another melody memory test monaurally; on each trial a second melody was either identical to the first or differed by one note. The melodies were four to ten notes long.

All subject groups performed better in the right ear than in the left ear. (Table 10.3 groups the data across aptitude to demonstrate the consonance of their results with those of Bever and Chiarello.) They showed that the right-ear advantage is greater among musically experienced subjects. This difference is mostly due to subjects with high aptitude. Contrasting their results with those on a chord-perception task (which shows a left-ear advantage overall), Gaede et al. conclude that "the kind of processing applied to a musical stimulus (or in an experiment, required by the task) can determine which hemisphere is dominant." They also report a significant effect of musical aptitude on overall performance and argue that their significant effect of experience shows that aptitude is the relevant variable.

This conclusion is explicitly consistent with the view that there are different modes of melody analysis, relational and holistic. Furthermore Gaede et al. found no significant ear difference effects as a function of either experience or aptitude, so the experiment could simply be viewed as a failure in that regard. Their results can be interpreted as showing that musically untrained people may nevertheless possess musical skill. The binaural test of aptitude is very similar to the later experimental test. It is also ambiguous; it may be a test of raw aptitude (whatever that is) or a test of musical experience incorporated without instrumental training. After all, there are many people who are avid musical auditors without being recently trained performers.

Conversely, Gaede et al. have also shown that if a trained musician is poor at one musical task (the binaural aptitude test) he or she is poor at another musical task (the monaural memory test). That there are unmusical musicians and musical nonmusicians is important to have documented, but their results suggest that this is not an important variable in ear superiority.

Gordon (1978) was concerned with exploring whether it is the rhythmic pattern or pitch sequence that can be dominant in the left hemisphere. This was a curious goal, for several previous experiments that had revealed right-ear superiority used melodies lacking any internal rhythmic variation (Bever and Chiarello, 1974). However, Gordon presented two-second melodies dichotically that differed in either rhythm pattern (same note sequence) or note sequence (same rhythmic pattern). Subjects then had to choose among four binaural probe melodies, noting which they had just heard. Subjects were right-handed musicians and nonmusicians discriminated by the same criteria used by Gaede et al.

Gordon did not find any ear effects for melodies differing in notes. However, rhythmic differences did bring out an overall right-ear superiority, which is numerically larger among musicians than nonmusicians. (Table 10.3 presents the mean time positions, excluding subjects performing at chance levels, as does Gordon.)

Gordon's results join the ranks of those recent studies that elicit a right-ear advantage for melody processing. It remains for us (and Gordon) to understand why this different pitch task did not bring out any asymmetry, regardless of subjects, despite the previous reports of asymmetries in the processing of nonrhythmic melodies.

One possible interpretation is the difficulty of separating two dichotic melodies on the same instrument, which maintain strict parallel rhythm. The listener's tendency may be to hear such sequences as two-note chord sequences, rather than two separate melodies. (For this reason, identical rhythm among voices is forbidden, even in standard counterpoint.) Thus the task may have been a mixture of melodic-sequence processing and chord processing, eliciting no overall ear asymmetry effects. (The separate rhythm stimuli approximate an accepted occidental music form, the canon, in which one voice alternately follows and leads another voice in a sequence.)

Finally, I would like to consider a possible nonreplication of the result (Zatorre, 1978). In the text I interpret Zatorre's method as an example of a holistic musical task. However, since he takes his results to be a disconfirmation of Bever and Chiarello's results, I include his study in this review. Zatorre contrasted musician and nonmusician performance in a carefully constructed experimental design. All subjects were right-handed with no reported sinistrality in their immediate family. Subjects listened to eighteen six-note "melodies" produced by a tone generator. On each trial one of the eighteen melodies was paired dichotically with one of the others; following the dichotic presentation, subjects heard four melodies binaurally and had to choose which two they had heard. Table 10.4 shows an overall left-ear superiority on this task which is numerically stronger for musicians than for nonmusicians (the numbers in this table are read from Zatorre's figure 1 and so are approximate). Accordingly, Zatorre concludes, "These findings imply that melodies are processed by the right hemisphere regardless of training."

It is useful to understand why Zatorre's method did not replicate the previous findings. First, like Gaede et al.'s familiar melodies, Zatorre's melodies were each repeated at least seventeen times as a stimulus and an unclear (to me) number of times as a possible recognition foil. The repetition alone might account for the holistic processing of the melodies with constructed perceptual templates. Second, the method of presentation and probing was identical to that of Gordon's different-pitch task, although Gordon used larger and rhythmically varying melodies, again raising the possibility that subjects fused the dichotic sequences into sequences of two-note chords. Finally, melodies of only six notes might be processed holistically, especially in conjunction with the frequent repetition. They certainly would not ordinarily exceed short-term memory limits and therefore would not require relational processing. For these reasons, Zatorre's method would be expected to bring out holistic processing of melodies, if anything can. Accordingly, Zatorre is best viewed as a replication of Kimura (1964), not a nonreplication of the studies reviewed here.

CONCLUSION

These studies demonstrate that melody processing is not univocally superior in the left ear. Variations in stimuli, tasks, and subjects can each bring out a right-ear superiority. What these variables have in common is a differentiation of the kind of processing the subjects apply. When the processing is relational, right-ear superiority emerges.

ACKNOWLEDGMENTS

This research was supported by a grant from the Spencer Foundation. I also wish to express thanks for the critical advice of C. Daiute and the assistance of J. Robbart in the preparation of this manuscript.

NOTES

1. The literature on cerebral asymmetries has grown so fast in recent years that it is pointless to list the relevant publications. Recent comprehensive collections of articles are in Harnad et al. (1977), Segalowitz and Gruber (1977), and Kinsbourne and Smith (1974).

2. D. Shankweiler, *Journal of Comparative Physiological Psychology* 62 (1966): 115; M. S. Gazzaniga and R. W. Sperry, *Brain* 90 (1967): 131; J. E. Bogen, *Bulletin of the Los Angeles Neurological Society* 34 (1969): 135; J. Levy-Agresti and R. W. Sperry, *Proceedings of the National Academy of Science, USA* 61 (1968): 1151; B. Milner and L. Taylor, *Neuropsychologia* 10 (1972): 1; J. Bogen, in *Drugs and Cerebral Function*, ed. W. L. Smith. Springfield, Ill.: Thomas, 1972, pp. 36–37; B. Milner, in *Interhemispheric Relations and Cerebral Dominance*, ed. V. B. Mountcastle, Baltimore, Md.: Johns Hopkins University Press, 1961.

3. This formal analysis includes the unanalyzed pretheoretic terms *representation, activation, relation,* and *task.* Ultimately these terms themselves must be specified within a theory of cognitive action. For the present discussion the main role of the formal statement is to demonstrate that whatever the ultimate cognitive theory turns out to be, relational and holistic processing can be reduced to the same theoretical primitives, and it will always be the case that relational processing is more complex than holistic processing, at least because relational processing involves the activation of more mental representations. Thus whether the processing of a particular relation is complex or cost-free, relational processing is always more computationally demanding than holistic processing. (See premises 1 and 5.)

4. A full report can be obtained from R. Hurtig, Department of Psychology, Iowa University, Iowa City, Iowa. Hurtig monitored EOG to ensure proper eye fixation.

5. Krynicki also monitored EOG for proper eye fixation, as well as having an ancillary nonsense fixation task. Subjects responded immediately after seeing a brief presentation of the complex figures. Dee and Fontenot (1973) have reported that as the interstimulus interval of complex figures increases, recognition becomes relatively better in the left visual field. (They also report a superiority—nonsignificant in their results—in the right visual field for immediate recognition.) Birkett (1978) reports no asymmetry for twelve-sided figures, midway in complexity between Krynicki's eight- and sixteen-sided figures.

6. The basic reference is Kimura (1964). Others include F. J. Spellacy and S. Blumstein, *Journal of the Acoustical Society of America* 49 (1971): 87; O. Spreen, F. Spellacy, and J. Reid, *Neuropsychologia* 8 (1970): 243; D. Kimura, *Cortex* 3 (1967): 163. See also J. Bogen and H. Gordon, *Nature* (Lond.), 230 (1971): 524, for clinical evidence for the involvement of right-hemisphere functioning in singing.

7. More details of this experiment can be obtained from me. We used a yoked design; for every choir boy there corresponded a nonchoir boy of the same age, grade, and handedness.

8. This experiment was first reported in Bever (1971). In all the experiments reported from our laboratory, subjects were right-handed, native speakers of English with no known hearing defects. See also Frankfurter and Honek (1973) for a replication.

9. A modified view of Carey's 1978 position is presented by Carey and Diamond, chapter 5, in this volume. Face recognition asymmetries are now at least as well studied as music perception asymmetries and therefore warrant as much detailed review as is presented in the appendix to this paper. I limit myself primarily to Carey (1978) because, unlike most, she presents a coherent theory of the phenomenon as well as a representative review of relevant facts.

10. Of course face recognition can still be viewed as a mental organ despite its hemispheric diaspora.

11. An earlier version of this theory was presented in Bever (1975).

12. See, for example, Kinsbourne, (1975).

13. There are a number of specific models of how this works out. A simple one is based on the assumption that the mean time for a single mental representation to be processed by time t is r for the right hemisphere and $r-k$ for the left hemisphere. Suppose that each mean has the same normal distribution with a standard deviation d and with overlap. The proportion of times that the left hemisphere will complete its processing first (and inhibit the right from further processing or learning on that occasion) is a direct function of d. However, if the skill has two representations that must be processed serially, then the proportional advantage of the left hemisphere is greater than for a skill involving one mental representation. Characteristically for a skill involving n mental representations, the disparity between the two hemispheres is $f(n/\sqrt{n})$ because the standard distribution increases as the root of the mean). Since the expression increases as n increases, the more complex the skill, the greater the asymmetry in favor of the left hemisphere.

An alternative view allowing functional equality of the hemispheres is that the left hemisphere is more powerful just during the period when language is being learned and for that maturationally accidental reason, language is left-hemphered. (Such a view is consistent with the proposals of Corballis and Morgan, 1978.) That view is not tenable for number of reasons. First, language learning extends over a long period, roughly from ages two to ten years. If that is the period when the left hemisphere is more powerful, then that theory is virtually the same as the one in this paper. Furthermore, the maturational coincidence theory cannot explain why all relational tasks are left-hemisphered, even those that may be learned much later in life (music). To explain that would require a mechanism like generalization to explain nonlinguistic relational processing in the left hemisphere as a generalization of the basically linguistic relational processing.

14. See Entus (1977), Davis and Wada (1977). The latter is particularly interesting because the authors propose that the left hemisphere of infants produces a more coherent evoked response, which may reflect its greater computational capacity.

15. Fusion of dichotic notes into central chords is reported in Efron, Bogen, and Yund (1977).

BIBLIOGRAPHY

Bartholomeus, B. N. Effect of task requirements on ear superiority for sung speech. *Cortex* 10 (1974): 215–22.3

Bartholomeus, B. N., Doehring, D. G., and Freygood, S. D. Absence of stimuli effects in dichotic singing. *Bulletin of the Psychonomic Society* 1 (1973): 171–172.

Bever, T. G. The cognitive basis for linguistic structures. In *Cognition and the development of language*, ed. J. R. Hayes. New York: Wiley, 1970.

———. The nature of cerebral dominance in speech behavior of the child and adult. In *Language acquisition: Models and methods*, ed. R. Huxley and E. Ingram. New York: Academic Press, 1971.

———. Cerebral asymmetries in humans are due to the differentiation of two incompatable processes: Holistic and analytic. In *Developmental psycholinguistics and communication*, ed. D. Aaronson and R. Rieber. New York: Academy of Sciences, 1975.

Bever, T. G., and Chiarello, R. J. Cerebral dominance in musicians and nonmusicians. *Science* 185 (1974): 137–139.

Bever, T. G., Hurtig, R. R., and Handel, A. Analytic processing elicits right ear superiority in monaurally presented speech. *Neuropsychologia* 14 (1976):175–181.

Birkett, P. Hemisphere differences in the recognition of nonsense shapes: Cerebral dominance or strategy effects? *Cortex* 14, no. 2 (1978): 245–249.

Bogen, J. E., and Gordon, H. W. Musical tests for functional lateralization with intracarotid amobarbitol. *Nature* 230 (1970): 524–525.

Broca, P. Sur la faculté du langage articulé. *Bulletin of Social Anthropology* 6 (1865): 493–494.

Brown, J. W., and Jaffe, J. Note: Hypothesis on cerebral dominance. *Neuropsychologia* 13 (1975): 107–110.

Carey, S. Face recognition: A case study. In *Explorations in the biology of language*, ed. E. Walker. Montgomery, Vt.: Bradford Books, 1978.

Carey, S., and Diamond, R. From piecemeal to configurational representation of faces. *Science* 195 (1977): 312–314

Carey, S., Diamond, R., and Woods, B. The development of face perception: A maturational component? *Neuropsychologia* (in press).

Carey, P., Mehler, J., and Bever, T. G. Judging the veracity of ambiguous sentences. *Journal of verbal learning and verbal behavior 9*, no. 2 (1970):243–254.

Corbalis, M. C., and Morgan, M. J. On the biological basis of human laterality. *Behavioral and Brain Sciences* 1, no. 2 (1978):261–336.

Darwin, C. J. Ear differences in the recall of fricatives and vowels. *Quarterly Journal of Experimental Psychology* 23 (1971): 46–62.

Davis, A. E., and Wada, J. A. Hemispheric asymmetries of visual and auditory information processing. *Neuropsychologia* 15, no. 6 (1977): 799–806.

Dee, H. L., and Fontenot, D. J. Cerebral dominance and lateralization differences in perception and memory. *Neuropsychologia* 11 (1973): 167–173.

Efron, R., Bogen, J. E., and Yund, F. W. Perception of dichotic chords by normal and commissurotized human subjects. *Cortex* 13, no. 2 (1977): 137–149.

Entus, A. K. Hemispheric asymmetry in processing of dichotically presented speech and nonspeech stimuli by infants. In *Language development and neurological theory*, ed. S. Segalowitz and F. Gruber. New York: Academic Press, 1977.

Frankfurter, A., and Honek, R. P. Ear difference in the recall of monaurally presented sentences. *Quarterly Journal of Experimental Psychology* 25, no. 1 (1973): 138–146.

Gaede, S. E., Parsons, O. A., and Bertera, J. H. Note: Hemispheric differences in music perception: Aptitude vs. experience. *Neuropsychologia* 3 (1978): 369–373.

Gates, A., and Bradshaw, J. L. The role of the cerebral hemisphere in music. *Brain and Language* 4 (1977): 403–431.

———. Music perception and cerebral asymmetries. *Cortex* 13, no. 4 (1977): 390–401.

Goldberg, E., Vaughan, H. G., and Gerstman, L. J. Nonverbal description systems and hemispheric asymmetry: Shape versus texture discrimination. *Brain and Language* 5, no. 2 (1978): 249–257.

Gordon, H. Hemispheric asymmetries in the perception of musical chords. *Cortex* 6 (1970): 387–398.

———. Hemispheric asymmetry and musicial performance. *Science* 189 (1975):68–69.

————. Left hemisphere dominance for rhythmic elements in dichotically-presented melodies. *Cortex* 14, no. 1 (1978): 58–70.

Halperin, Y., Nachson, I., and Carmon, A. Shift of ear superiority in dichotic listening to temporally patterned nonverbal stimuli. *Journal of the Acoustic Society of America* 53 (1973): 46–50.

Harnad, S. R., Dotty, R. W., Goldstein, L., Jaynes, J., and Krauthamer, G. (eds.), *Lateralization in the nervous system.* New York: Academic Press, 1977.

Harnad, S. R., and Steklis, H. D. (eds.), Origins and evolution of language and speech. *Annals of the New York Academy of Sciences* (1976): 280.

Hirshkowitz, M., Earle, J., and Paley, B. EEG alpha asymmetry in musicians and nonmusicians: A Study of hemispheric specialization. *Neuropsychologia* 16 (1978): 125–128.

Hurtig, R. Visual asymmetries in holistic and analytic processing (in preparation).

Jackson, Hughlings. *Selected writings of John Hughlings Jackson,* vol. 2, London: Hodder and Stoughton, 1932.

Johnson, P. R. Dichotically-stimulated ear differences in musicians and non-musicians. *Cortex* 13 (1977): 385–389.

Johnson, R. C., Bowers, J. K., Gamble, M., Lyons, F. W. Presbrey, T. W.,and Vetter, R. R. Ability to transcribe music and ear superiority for tone sequences. *Cortex* 13 (1977): 295–299.

Kimura, D. Left-right differences in the perception of melodies. *Quarterly Journal of Experimental Psychology* 16 (1964): 355–358.

————. The asymmetry of the human brain. *Scientific American* 228 (1973): 70–78.

Kinsbourne, M. The cerebral basis of lateral asymmetries in attention. *Acta Psychologica* 33 (1970): 193–201.

————. The minor cerebral hemisphere as a source of aphasic speech. *Archives of Neurology* 25 (1971): 302–306.

————. The ontogeny of cerebral dominance. *Annals of the New York Academy of Sciences* 263 (1975): 244–250.

Kinsbourne, M., and Smith, W. L. (eds.) *Hemispheric disconnection and cerebral function.* Springfield, Ill.: Charles C. Thomas, 1974.

Krynicki, V. Asymmetries in perception of complex figures. Ph.D. dissertation, Columbia University, 1975.

Lashley, K. S. Functional determinants of cerebral localization. *Archives of Neuropsychiatry* 38 (1937): 371–387.

Leehey, S. C. Face recognition in children: Evidence for the development of right hemisphere specialization. Ph.D. dissertation, Massachusetts Institute of Technology, 1976

Leehey, S., Carey, S., Diamond, R., and Cahn, A. Upright and inverted faces: The right hemisphere knows the difference. *Cortex* 14, no. 3 (1978): 411–419.

Marzi, C. A., Brizzara, D., Rizzolatti, G., Umilta, C., and Berlucchi, G. Left hemispheric superiority for the recognition of well-known faces. *Brain Res.* 66 (1974): 358–359.

Meyer, L. B. *Emotion and meaning in music.* Chicago: University of Chicago Press, 1956.

Segalowitz, S. J., and Gruber, F. A. , *Language Development and Neurological Theory.* New York: Academic Press, 1977.

Spreen, O., Spellacy, F. J., and Reid, J. R. The effect of interstimulus interval and intensity on ear asymmetry for nonverbal stimuli in dichotic listening. *Neuropsychologia* 8 (1970): 245–250

Townsend, D. J., and Bever, T. G. Interclause relations and clausal processing. *Journal of Verbal Learning and Verbal Behavior* 17 (1978): 509–521.

Umilta, C., Baguara, S., and Simion, F. Laterality effects for simple and complex geometrical figures and nonsense patterns. *Neuropsychologia* 16,no. 1 (1978): 43–49.

Veroff, A. A structural determinant of hemispheric processing of pictoral material. *Brain and Language* 5 (1978): 139–148.

Werner, H. *Comparative psychology of mental development.* New York: International Universities Press, 1948.

Whitaker, H. Is the right leftover? *Behavioral and Brain Sciences* 1, no. 2 (1978): 323–324.

Zatorre, R. J. Recognition of dichotic melodies by musicians and nonmusicians. *Proceedings of the Acoustical Society of America,* 1978.

III

**Studies of Neural
Mechanisms Underlying
Language in the Adult**

11

Changing Models of the Neuropsychology of Language

David Caplan

The third section of this volume deals with mechanisms in the mature brain for the representation and utilization of language. The chapters all draw on material derived from the study of aphasic patients. Much of our information regarding brain mechanisms underlying language now comes from new techniques that allow limited observation of neurophysiological events during normal language use (Desmedt, 1977), experimental electrical stimulation of surface and deep structures in the brain (Penfield and Roberts, 1959; Schaltenbrand, 1975), pharmacological inhibition of parts of the brain (Wada and Rasmussen, 1960), and other less direct psycholinguistic methods. While adding immensely to our knowledge of the neural loci and processes related to language, these approaches have not supplanted detailed psycholinguistic analysis of aphasic symptoms and correlation of these analyses with lesion type and site. Indeed our basic neuropsychological model of the mechanisms involved in language is derived from such correlations and dates from models proposed in the nineteenth century. The studies reported here use this classical approach and present new solutions and considerations regarding several problems in this area.

The first two chapters in this section deal with linguistic and psycholinguistic analyses of Broca's aphasia. Broca's 1861 paper is recognized as the first scientific approach to the neurology of language. He described patients without bucco-oral paralysis, with almost total loss of expressive language, who retained one or two words and sounds and could communicate by means of intonational contours, repetition of these sounds, gestures, and other means. He argued that the deficit in the performance of these patients consisted of a loss of the faculty of articulate language, to be distinguished from communicative abilities in a larger sense, from general control of movements of the vocal tract, and from the ability to comprehend language.

Subsequent clinical studies demonstrated that this formulation of the deficit was too narrow. Of particular interest in light of the chapters by Kean and by Bradley, Garrett, and Zurif was the widespread appreciation that comprehension problems occur in Broca's aphasics. This was known very soon after Broca's paper, and Broca himself seems to have accepted it as a feature of the syndrome. The comprehension deficits were not accounted for by Broca's original formulation and proved difficult for all neuropsychological theories of the times.

The most popular nineteenth-century method of explanation of co-occurrence of different symptoms within an aphasic syndrome was derived from Wernicke's approach to the aphasia that bears his name (Wernicke, 1874). This symptom complex consists, in its essentials, of difficulty in comprehension of spoken language and fluent paraphasic speech. The lesion has its center in the second temporal gyrus near the primary cortical auditory receptor cortex. Wernicke argued that this area served as a storehouse for auditory memories for words and that the lesion thus led to difficulty in comprehending speech. He postulated that the difficulty in speech production was not due to disruption of a second center but to the pattern of what we might call information flow in speaking; that is, prior to initiation of motor programs for speech, auditory memories for words are evoked and passed from Wernicke's area to Broca's area. A lesion in Wernicke's area would thereby result in the joint occurrence of comprehension and production difficulties. The postulation of this information flow was considered justified because it was consistent with both the neurophysiological notions of reflex action of the day and the assumed importance of mimicry in language development. This mode of explanation could not be applied to the problem of a comprehension deficit in Broca's aphasia without adding an unjustified loop from Broca's area to Wernicke's area (or from motor representations to perceptual representations) in language comprehension, which had no basis in the normative psychology or physiology of the nineteenth century. The failure of this form of explanation to account for exactly this constellation of deficits led many thinkers away from various aspects of the connectionist approach to other models, none generally accepted.

The chapters by Kean and by Bradley, Garrett, and Zurif extend recent work directed specifically at this question. In complementary studies they describe a linguistic and psycholinguistic deficit that accounts for the grouping of these symptoms. Kean characterizes the particular class of linguistic elements affected in Broca's aphasia; Bradley, Garrett, and Zurif explore the psycholinguistic deficits relating to these items. The analysis begins with consideration of the items omitted in the speech of Broca's aphasics and proceeds to show that particular psycholinguistic processes involving these elements are disturbed in speech comprehension and in other tasks. It is premature to conclude that only one psycholinguistic function is disturbed in this syndrome, but these studies suggest that a limited number of functions centered on particular aspects of utilization of a specific class of language elements are involved.

The mode of explanation is similar to that of the classical connectionist work which postulates normal functions and views abnormal outputs of the system as results of damage to one functional component. It differs in several respects. It explains conjunctions of symptoms by virtue of the nature of componential functional analysis, not information flow, but this is an incidental feature of the model. More important, it utilizes psycholinguistic and linguistic constructs derived from scientific studies of language structure and processing rather than intuitive taxonomies and analyses. As a result, it achieves a degree of specificity in the description of the linguistic and psychological deficits not present in earlier accounts. That this more detailed analysis is consistent with a combination of functional deficits heretofore unaccounted for is evidence in favor of this formulation and encouraging to investigators working on integration of studies of normal and disordered language.

The most significant achievement of Broca's paper was not the psycholinguistic but the anatomical analysis of the syndrome. Broca asserted that the convolutional pattern of the forebrain was relatively constant from individual to individual and that gyri, or parts thereof, were possible loci for physiological mechanisms underlying particular psychological functions. Before this, "it was thought that the convolutions of the brain were as inconsistent as those of the intestine" (Moutier, 1908), and localization of psychological function was couched in terms of distances from major fissures, features of the skull, and other landmarks now appreciated as inconstantly and tangentially related to anatomically stable and functionally relevant partitions of the brain.

Broca's localization of the center of the lesions in his cases at the foot of the third frontal convolution, later appreciated to be on the left in right-handers, constituted a specific and testable hypothesis regarding localization of function. Numerous positive counterexamples to the general claim were documented, and it became apparent that there is more variation in the lesions producing Broca's aphasia than predicted by the hypothesis. The remaining chapters in this section deal, in general terms, with some of the sources of variation in neural representation of linguistic and other functions.

The best documented source of variation in neural loci where lesions produce particular aphasias is genetic and relates to handedness (Zangwill, 1960). Left-handers do not develop aphasias as severe or as long-lasting as those of dextrals, nor do the syndromes seen in sinistrals fall clearly into the classes of aphasias seen in right-handers. To a lesser extent the same is true for right-handers with left-handed family members. Other differences are documented for familial and nonfamilial left-handers. The neuroanatomical organization of language in these populations is grossly different from the pure right-hander's. To various extents in the different populations, right-hemisphere lesions produce aphasias and right-hemisphere mechanisms are largely involved in language. It is clear that the left-hander is not, on average, the mirror image, neurolinguistically or neuropsychologically, of the right-hander; but he differs in ways not entirely understood.

Neural mechanisms that might account for these differences are beginning to come to light. Geschwind discusses the lateral asymmetries in human neocortical areas related to language (and other functions) whose exploration he has pioneered. The direction and the degree of lateral asymmetries vary in dextral and sinistral populations, on the whole in the direction such that larger areas are more frequently found on the left in right-handers, at least in the posterior language zone for which most data are available. A reasonable working hypothesis is that this variation in size constitutes an important anatomical feature determining lateralization and localization of language functions, as well as other cognitive and emotional faculties.

Brown emphasizes the danger of regarding only neocortex as related to language. We know that the dominant peri-Sylvian area is not the only area involved in language; in addition to the linguistic capacities of the nondominant hemisphere, thalamus and supplementary motor areas are involved in some forms of language function, as manifested by the appearance of transient aphasias following lesions in these areas (Mohr, Watters, and Duncan, 1975; Masden, Schoene, and Frankenstein, 1978) and by the production and interruption of linguistic performance by their direct stimulation. Brown develops part of his theory of microgenesis of language, taking specific account of the role of subcortical structures in speech. Incorporation of these structures into theories of language function may also account for some of the variation in aphasic syndromes.

In addition to factors leading to variation in the anatomy of language-related mechanisms in the normal brain, inferences derived from pathology must take into account the differences between lesions. This is another major focus of Geschwind's remarks. The biology of lesions producing aphasia varies enormously. Infarction and neoplasia, to cite just two examples, share some but differ in many biological effects on neural tissue. We do not know all the relevant biological mechanisms resulting in disturbance of language, but some are beginning to be appreciated. Geschwind's emphasis on temporal aspects of lesions is borne out by the work of Mohr (1976) in this area, which suggests that Broca's aphasia is not the result of acute infarction, but occurs in the subacute and chronic stages of relatively large left frontal opercular strokes. The relevant physiological differences between the early and late stages of such lesions are not known, but the observations point to lesion taxonomy as a critical variable in producing aphasic syndromes and hence in the construction of neurolinguistic theories based on pathological material.

Our knowledge of the neuroanatomy of language is much advanced in relation to that of neurophysiological and other organic processes. Is there a temporal or spatial pattern of neural firing underlying information transfer from one area of the language zone to another? Do language systems depend on some neurotransmitters and not others? What is the chemistry and physiology of long-term storage of linguistic knowledge? These types of questions are unanswered, in part because of the limits on empirical observation set by existing experimental techniques, magnified by the lack of animal models, and in part because of the incompleteness of current theoretical formulations. These areas represent challenges for future investigation. The new conceptual approaches from psychology, linguistics, and neuroanatomy characterizing the papers in this section will, we hope, be combined with work in related areas to yield a more general theory of the neurology of language.

REFERENCES

Broca, P. 1861. Remarques sur le siège de faculté de langage articulé, suivies d'une observation d'aphémie (perte de parole). *Bulletin de la Société d'Anatomie*, 330–357.

Desmedt, J. E. (ed.) 1977. *Language and hemispheric specialization in Man: Cerebral event-related potentials.* Basel: S. Karger.

Masden, J. C., Schoene, W. C., and Frankenstein, H. 1978. Aphasia following infarction of left supplementary motor area: A clinical-pathological study. *Neurology* 28: 1220–1223.

Mohr, J. P. 1976. Broca's area and Broca's aphasia. In *Current trends in neurolinguistics*, ed. H. Whitaker. New York: Academic Press.

Mohr, J. P., Watters, W. C., and Duncan, L. W. 1975. Thalamic hemorrhage and aphasia. *Brain and Language* 2: 3–17.

Moutier, F. 1908. *L'aphasie de Broca.* Paris: Steinhaul.

Penfield, W., and Roberts, L. 1959. *Speech and brain mechanisms.* Princeton, N.J.: Princeton University Press.

Schaltenbrand, G. 1975. The effects on speech and language of stereotactical stimulation in thalamus and corpus callosum. *Brain and Language* 2: 70–77.

Wada, J., and Rasmussen, T. 1960. Intracartoid injection of sodium amytal for the lateralization of cerebral speech dominance. *Journal of Neurosurgery* 17: 266–282.

Wernicke, K. 1874. *Der aphasische Symptomen complex: Eine psychologissche Studie auf anatomischer Basis.* Cohn and Wiegert.

Zangwill, O. L. 1960. *Cerebral dominance and its relation to psychological function.* Edinburgh: Oliver and Boyt.

12

Grammatical Representations and the Description of Language Processing

Mary-Louise Kean

In a recent paper on Broca's aphasia I argued that from a *grammatical* point of view agrammatism was best understood as a phonological deficit (Kean, 1977). The purpose of this paper is to clarify some of the issues raised in that paper and relate that line of research to the very interesting work on sentence processing by Edgar Zurif (Bradley, Garrett, and Zurif, chapter 13, this volume). My remarks are divided into three sections. In the first section the characteristics of agrammatism are recapitulated and some previous linguistic analyses are discussed. In the second section I review the analysis presented in Kean (1977) in the hopes of clarifying what that position entails. Finally, the question of the relation between grammatical analyses and processing analyses of deficits is considered.

SOME PLAUSIBLE ANALYSES OF AGRAMMATISM

What one takes to be a possible analysis of any deficit on any level of description is determined by what one assumes to be the form of possible analyses. Therefore, before turning to a direct discussion of some proposed grammatical analyses of agrammatism, I want to outline my assumptions about the structure of analyses of deficits. I assume that the linguistic description of any deficit must have two components. First, there must be a characterization of the impairment to normal linguistic capacity. Second, there must be a characterization of how, given such an impairment, the otherwise intact linguistic capacity gives rise to the actual observed linguistic behavior. That is, the capacity for language use of any otherwise normal adult with a language deficit is a function of the interaction of some impaired component of his linguistic capacity with the intact components of that capacity. To accept this assumption is to accept what seems to me the completely plausible assumption that normal linguistic behavior arises as a consequence of the functioning of a complex system of components.

A further assumption is that language is to be conceptualized in terms of a grammar and a processing mechanism. I take a theory of grammar to be an empirical hypothesis about the structure of the tacit knowledge that a child brings to bear on the task of acquiring his language, and I take the grammar of a language to be a characterization of what a native speaker knows about his language. The grammar of a language characterizes the structural descriptions of the well-formed sentences of a language. Any sentence in a language is assigned a set of representations by the grammar—a deep structure, a surface structure, a phonological representation, a phonetic representation, a morphological representation, a logical form, and a semantic representation.

A normal individual not only knows his language but can also exploit that knowledge in use. In particular, he can both produce and comprehend sentences of his language whether or not he has spoken or heard any given sentence previously. The mechanism for this exploitation will be called the processor. I assume that the processor, like the grammar, consists of a series of autonomous components including, for example, mechanisms for lexical accessing in both production and comprehension, parsing routines, and so on. Crucial to my view is the further assumption that the representations of sentences characterized by the grammar are realized by the processor in language use. This assumption does not entail the further assumption that the processor simply applies the rules of grammar "forward" in production and "backward" in comprehension; such an assumption would render the distinction between grammar and processor effectively meaningless for all domains of language structure characterized by the grammar. I assume that a theory of sentence processing, when developed, will include computational mechanisms distinct in kind from the rules of grammar. What role the rules of grammar will have in a theory of processing mechanisms is an open question. Thus one cannot (at this time, at least) provide a grammatical description of ordinary language data such as that encountered in deficit research in terms of grammatical rules. Rather, if one accepts these assumptions, the only available grammatical analyses of such data are those made in terms of levels of representation.

This picture of the grammar and processor is, of course, an idealization of the speaker-hearer. Our actual language use no doubt involves various heuristic strategies as well, and our abilities to process sentences are constrained by memory load and the like. In talking about a language deficit as a deficit to normal linguistic capacity, we must abstract from factors such as these, for they are not components of the language faculty per se. The research of deVilliers (1974) on agrammatism, in which she argued that the likelihood of omission of some forms was in part a function of pragmatic considerations, is an example of work on language deficits that is not concerned with the language faculty. Variation in production may or may not in any given instance be due to linguistic factors or nonlinguistic factors. The importance of deVilliers work is twofold. On one hand, it is a proposal to account for some degree of the observed variation in production found in agrammatism; on the other hand, it more closely circumscribes the body of data that must be addressed by any analysis of agrammatism in terms of the language faculty. The remainder of my remarks are addressed to considerations of the analysis of agrammatism in terms of the structure of the language faculty just outlined.

Agrammatism generally refers to the tendency of Broca's aphasics to omit function words and certain bound morphemes in their speech. Among the class of items designated as "function words" are prepositions and determiners. The set of bound morphemes that are often omitted includes inflectional morphemes (e.g., the genitive marker, the plural marker). The tendency to "ignore" these items is not limited to speech production; the agrammatic aphasic appears to show a parallel deficit in virtually every modality of language use (for example, Goodenough et al. (1977) show that this deficit is realized in comprehension).

Descriptions of the deficit that gives rise to agrammatism have often implicated virtually every level of grammatical description above the phonological level. Agrammatism has frequently been characterized as a syntactic deficit (Goodglass, 1973; Goodglass et al. 1972). The reasoning behind this position is that function words are syntactic elements and that many of the omitted bound morphemes are syntactically derivable. Because of the omission of bound morphemes it has also been suggested that agrammatism involves a morphological compromise (Goodglass and Berko, 1960; Gleason et al., 1975). Here the issue rests on the assumption that the properties of some bound morphemes are to be characterized by the morphological component of the grammar. Finally, it has been proposed that agrammatism involves a semantic deficit (Goodenough et al., 1977) on the basis of the observation that agrammatic aphasics cannot retrieve the semantic information conveyed by determiners, in particular, the *a/the* contrast. Each of these proposals characterizes some aspect of the deficit of agrammatism in terms of grammatical structure. I do not, however, think that any of them can be accepted as grammatical characterizations of the deficit of agrammatism.

In light of the assumptions I put forward here, there are three fundamental problems with most of the literature on the analysis of aphasic syndromes, problems typified by the works cited. First, they typically do not consider or even acknowledge the assumption that deviant linguistic behavior arises as a consequence of an interaction between impaired and intact components of the language faculty. The functioning of the intact components of the system has no implicit role in the analysis of a deficit, that is, there is a tacit analytic assumption that the intact components of the language faculty make no significant or interesting contribution to the observed deficit. Second, seldom are analyses based on explicitly stated assumptions about the structure of the language faculty. Rather they have tended to be made on the basis of a "neutral" position—not distinguishing grammar from processor while at the same time making no commitment to the hypothesis that to make such a distinction is wrong. Third, the grammatical analyses that have been put forward are not characterizations of deficits in terms of systematic levels of grammatical representation. Thus in light of the assumptions made here they are not in principle possible grammatical analyses of particular linguistic deficits. Instead, if a grammatical description of the data at hand is possible in terms of arbitrary aspects of some component(s) of the grammar, then that must ipso facto be an adequate analysis of the grammatical function whose impairment is implicated by the behavior. The sentences of an agrammatic aphasic certainly appear to be syntactically and morphologically ill formed on the surface, since certain elements of a sentence that must have a phonetic realization have typically been omitted. But this observation does not imply that a grammatically adequate account will characterize the deficit as semantic, syntactic, or morphological.

The grammar consists of a partially ordered set of autonomous components—the base, a transformational component, a phonology, a word-formation component, and so on. Each component of the grammar has a particular grammatical function and is uniquely characterizable in terms of the formal properties of its rules and the set of substantive elements affected by those rules. For example, the phonological component of a grammar includes a set of context-sensitive rewrite rules that alter the feature specifications of some set of segments in some specific context. Thus we find in the phonology rules such as the following.

1
$$\begin{bmatrix} + \text{ consonantal} \\ - \text{ sonorant} \end{bmatrix} \rightarrow [- \text{ voice}] \quad /X \underline{\quad} \#$$

Rule 1 has the interpretation 1':

Nonsonorant consonants (stops, fricatives, affricates) become voiceless in word final position.

A rule such as 1 would apply to the final consonant of all words in a language. Not all phonological rules, however, have such broad domains of application; some apply only in certain syntactic categories. For example, there are phonological rules like that schematically given in 2.

2
$$A \rightarrow B \quad / \quad X \underline{\quad} Y]_N$$

A rule of the form of 2 would apply only to items of the category noun. Syntactic categories can therefore provide contexts for the application of phonological rules, though phonological rules cannot alter syntactic constituent structure. Conversely, the formally distinct rules of the transformational component of the grammar apply to syntactic categories and their phrasal projections but are blind to (and hence cannot alter) segmental structure.

In one way or another virtually every component of the grammar makes reference to syntactic categories. In terms of the categories the components are distinguished from one another by the conditions proscribing how they may refer to the syntactic categories. In the example just given, categories may be conditioning contexts for phonological rules, but the rules of the phonology do not alter or deform the categorical structure of a sentence from the one generated by the base and transformations. The rules of the word-formation component of the grammar must also refer to categories, as is evident from observations such as that the suffix -ity in English attaches only to adjectives and not, for example, to verbs, to form derived nominals. Thus we can have the pairs of words *obese/obesity*, *serene/serenity*, *sane/sanity* but not *permit/permitity*, *defame/defamity*, *recite/recity*. The second set of words all have derived nominals with some form of the suffix -ation, a suffix that attaches to verbs. We can have *permit/permission*, *defame/defamation*, *recite/recitation*, but we cannot have *obese/obesation*, *serene/serenation*, *sane/sanation*. The contrast in categories and its importance in word formation is striking in homophones. For example, consider the adjective *divine* and the verb *divine*; from the former we get the derived nominal *divinity* and from the latter *divination*, and there is no ambiguity as to which *divine* each derived form comes from. Another distinct class of rules that makes crucial reference to the categories is the set of rules that spell out the grammatical formatives of sentences, for example, the rule that attaches -ing to verbs when they occur in noun phrases as gerunds. The rules for the logical and semantic interpretation of the items in a sentence must also be sensitive to syntactic categories; for example, nouns have semantic functions different from those of verbs.

Within a theory of grammar where there are autonomous components (defined on formal and substantive grounds) and, at the same time, some overlap in the substantive elements that play a role in the operations of the various components, it is not possible to determine from every surface datum where in the grammar that datum is to be properly analyzed. At the grossest level of speaking, independent of analysis within the context of an explicit theory of grammar, it is impossible to tell whether some apparently categorical phenomenon is syntactic, semantic, morphological, or phonological in character, since all the components of the grammar refer to the categories. It is only when such phenomena are analyzed that any feasible hypothesis can be stated.

An informal characterization of agrammatism is that the so-called major lexical categories (N, A, V) are typically retained while other items (so-called function words) are frequently omitted. From such a broad description of the facts alone, it should be clear that the grammatical blame for the deficit cannot be assigned; the appropriate grammatical description of agrammatism is simply not self-evident from the data. The correspondence between what is "lost" in agrammatism and the distinction between major lexical categories and other categories does not in itself fix the impairment at any particular level of grammatical description.

It is by no means a priori necessary that language deficits will impair single, discrete components of the language faculty, even when such deficits arise systematically from relatively discretely specifiable focal lesions in particular areas of the brain. That is, it is perfectly plausible that focal brain damage may cause impairments that must be characterized grammatically or computationally for processing in terms of more than one component of the system. Whether one or many components of the grammatical and processing systems are compromised by some circumscribed set of focal lesions is crucial to understanding how linguistic function is organized in the brain, and the answer will ultimately contribute to our understanding of the biological foundations of language. But it is of no linguistic interest whether one or many components of the system are impaired by such lesions. Thus the correct grammatical analysis of agrammatism might involve semantics, syntax, morphology, and phonology. Without further analysis of the data each of the potential analyses is equally prima facie plausible.

To judge the adequacy of a grammatical analysis of agrammatism, one must consider how well it accounts for the data. For example, one must investigate whether syntactic representations provide sufficient information for the proper partition of the data at hand and whether interesting predictions follow from such an analysis. That is, an adequate grammatical analysis of agrammatism will automatically differentiate the items that typically occur in agrammatism from those that tend not to occur in terms of some level(s) of representation. It will also characterize a range of data that is not at hand. It is in this latter regard that grammatical analyses of language deficits have their greatest interest, since the available data are inevitably impoverished. In fact, any grammatical account of a language deficit will always describe a wide range of data not given at the start, since the range of structures generated by a grammar is always underdetermined by the data.

Let us consider analyses of agrammatism that characterize the deficit as a syntactic one. If it is not possible to distinguish between the major categories and the function words on the basis of some general property of syntactic representations, then such analyses will fail to be empirically adequate. The notion major lexical category (meaning N, A, V) is not a syntactic primitive; thus if the syntactic analysis is to be maintained, it is necessary to find some structural property of sentences that will uniquely distinguish those categories from all others. One obvious candidate is the distinction between the head of a phrase and its specifiers or complements, where items that can function as the heads of phrases are the major lexical categories. Thus, for example, since nouns and verbs can be the heads of phrases (noun phrases and verb phrases, respectively) they would count as major lexical items. While it is possible to distinguish two sets of categories in such terms, that distinction will not be adequate in an analysis of agrammatism since some function words can appear as the heads of phrases. Prepositions, which are generally classed as function words, are the heads of prepositional phrases. Another problem is that some of the elements typically omitted in agrammatism are inflectional affixes on the heads of phrases and not distinguished in the syntax from their heads under the proposed algorithm. Taking the opposite approach, we would have evidence for a syntactic analysis if we could find some systematic property of syntactic structures that characterized the set of function words and the bound morphemes that are typically lost. The problem with this approach should be evident. While certain function words such as the determiners *a* and *the* are dominated by categorial nodes (the determiner node DET), the inflectional affixes are not. Instead they are elements of complex symbols dominated by categorial nodes. Thus in terms of the properties of syntactic representations we have at best an ad hoc partition of the data into items that can appear as heads of phrases, less the category of prepositions, without their inflectional affixes. Such an account is without particular interest; it makes no predictions beyond the range of the available corpus and is consequently consistent with almost any additional data, since it is amenable to ad hoc modification.

Morphological analyses of agrammatism do not appear to hold much more promise than do syntactic ones. The reasons for this are not, however, like the reasons for rejecting syntactic analyses. In that case the argument was that no principled algorithm could be applied at the level of syntax to draw the necessary partition of the data. In the case of morphology this is not so clearly the case. It is

relatively easy to devise algorithms that might give a fair partition
of the data; however, those algorithms cannot be accepted under my
assumptions of the structure of the language faculty because they are
based on rule systems and not on representations. One of the problems facing a syntactic analysis of agrammatism noted already was
that there was no apparent algorithm for distinguishing prepositions
from the major lexical categories on the basis of constituent structure. If we consider the properties of the word-formation component
of the grammar, we note that prepositions are distinct from the major lexical categories; they do not enter into derivation readily as do
the major categories. In English, for example, one apparently does
not find synchronically prepositions productively derived from
nouns. Worked out in detail, this observation might serve as the
basis for a partially morphological characterization of agrammatism.
We might hypothesize that those categories that productively enter
into derivation are typically retained in agrammatism. The fundamental problem with such an approach is that it is not a partition of
the data based on a systematic level of representation; rather, it
would be a transderivational characterization, that is, one based on
the rule structure of a component, and would require consideration
of the set of derivations available in a language. Furthermore, it is
unclear how a lexical account will imply that syntactically assigned
inflectional affixes are typically omitted. Here we encounter another
quite distinct area of the grammar that is concerned with morphology. There are inflectional affixes assigned as features to constituents on the basis of syntactic structure, and there are grammatical
formatives generated in the base as feature complexes (definite and
indefinite articles in the category DET). Both sets of items receive
their phonological specifications by spelling rules which apply in the
mapping of syntactic surface structures onto phonological representations (which I take to be the inputs to the phonological rules). This
class of items is, of course, typically lost in agrammatism. We could
distinguish them from all other items in terms of the spelling rules
for phonological realization; items whose phonological form is specified by spelling rules are typically omitted in agrammatism. As with
the possible lexical means of distinguishing prepositions from the
major categories, we have here an algorithm for making a distinction based on the functioning of a rule system and not on the structure of the representations generated by some rule system. Thus,
while the partition may be possible if we consider both the morphol-

ogy of word formation and the morphology of inflection, such a partition cannot be an adequate grammatical analysis of the data under my assumptions, since it is not based on systematic levels of representation.

The suggestion that agrammatism might grammatically involve a semantic compromise is the most difficult to defend of the a priori plausible analyses. Consider the set of elements frequently omitted in agrammatism: (1) lexical prepositions whose meanings are specified by lexical semantics; (2) grammatical formatives such as the articles *a* and *the* which carry the essentially logical information about definiteness, cardinality, and so on; (3) grammatical formatives that carry structural information, such as the *of* in *the destruction of the city* which marks the syntactic object of a derived nominal. Given (3), one can immediately see that one set of items is not essentially semantic in character; therefore, whatever the feasibility of providing semantic analyses for some aspects of agrammatism, a semantic analysis will clearly not be sufficient for a complete grammatical characterization of the deficit. With both (1) and (2) there might be some hope for a semantic analysis. However, to accept a semantic analysis as the appropriate characterization for the loss of a subset of lexical items is to offer only a promissory note for a theory of lexical semantics that will allow the appropriate partition of the data. While that promissory note may be honored some day, such an analysis is without synchronic explanatory force and is no more enlightening than the stipulation that there is some tendency to omit lexical prepositions. The omission of elements such as articles is the one case left that is reasonably amenable to a semantic analysis. It is not, however, evident that there is a reasonable partition of the data at the level of representations in the logical form that is available. The logically relevant items that tend to be omitted from the language of agrammatics form an arbitrary and semantically unmotivated subset of the items that play a role in the specification of the logical structure of a sentence.

So far I have been concerned only with outlining my reasons for rejecting hypotheses that characterize agrammatism grammatically in terms of the single components of the grammar, syntax, semantics, morphology. However, that deficits should be characterized grammatically in terms of more than one component of the grammar is as a priori plausible as that they should be characterized in terms of single components of the grammar. As for syntax, semantics, and morphology, such a combined analysis does not seem possible. The possible morphological analyses appear to involve rule systems (in particular, the apparently limited derivational productivity of prepositions) rather than representations, so under my assumptions about the structure of the language faculty and possible analyses, it would appear that lexical morphology can play no role even in an analysis of agrammatism which implicates several components of the system in the characterization of the deficit. In terms of the syntax we might be able to get some help for an analysis involving several components, relying on the structural notion that an element may be the head of a phrase. However, in doing this we would be left to account for any tendency to omit lexical prepositions in terms of some unknown theory of lexical semantics, and we would still be without an account for the omission of inflectional affixes. All the combinations of syntactic and semantic characterizations that suggest themselves seem to run into similar problems.

AGRAMMATISM AND PHONOLOGICAL REPRESENTATIONS

The apparent impossibility of accounting for agrammatism in terms of syntax, semantics, or morphology does not necessarily imply that a grammatical account of agrammatism in terms of phonological representations will be readily available. That is, it does not follow from the foregoing discussion that agrammatism is to be grammatically analyzed in terms of phonology. All that we have established so far is that there apparently are not principled descriptions of agrammatism in the domains of syntax, semantics, or morphology. That established, any number of possible analyses remain open possibilities. Under my assumptions about what would constitute an adequate grammatical analysis of agrammatism, an adequate analysis might involve systematic aspects of phonological and semantic or syntactic representations, for example. Or it might turn out that no completely non ad hoc algorithm or set of algorithms can provide the appropriate partition of the data, either under an analysis that refers to the representations of several components of the system or under one based on the representations of only a single component. At worst, at least from my perspective, my initial assumptions may simply be invalid; perhaps the only representational partition of the available data is essentially ad hoc. Such an analysis would be of limited interest, since it would be nothing more than a restatement of the data. If, however, a principled analysis in terms of the representations of either several or one of the components of the system can be made, then the validity of my initial assumptions is supported. If my initial assumptions about the structure of possible grammatical analyses of agrammatism are invalid, then it would be fortuitous if it were at the same time possible to provide a principled representational account for the data. Such a coincidence would seriously undermine any theory not based on representations, since it would be an apparently inexplicable result.

To outline the phonological analysis of agrammatism, one must first say something about the structure of phonological representations and how those representations arise. The output of the syntactic component, the surface structure representation of a sentence, is a labeled bracketing of a string of formatives. The labeled bracketing characterizes the hierarchical constituent structure of the string; the formatives are the terminal symbols of the constituent structure. There are two types of formatives, lexical and grammatical; the former are phonologically specified, whereas the latter are represented in terms of syntactic features. Surface structures may be represented in tree form as in 3a or simply as bracketed strings as in 3b. (This example sentence and 4, 5, and 8 are taken from Chomsky and Halle, 1968.)

3a

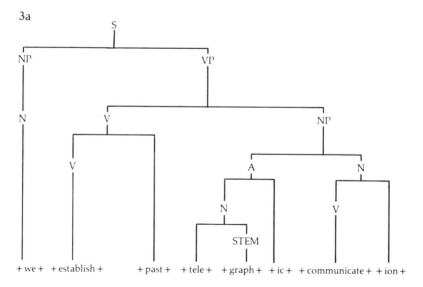

3b

$[_S[_{NP}[_N + we +]_N]_{NP}[_{VP}[_V[_V + establish +]_V + past +]_V[_{NP}[_A[_N + tele +$
$[_{STEM} + graph +]_{STEM}]_N + ic +]_A[_N[_V + communicate +]_V$
$+ ion +]_N]_{NP}]_{VP}]_S$

Necessary to the proper phonological characterization of a string is
the analysis of its elements into a sequence of words. Following the
convention proposed in Chomsky and Halle (1968), as a first approximation of the word structure of a string, we will say that a
word boundary, #, is assigned to the right and left of the lexical
categories N, A, V and to the right and left of all categories
dominating N, A and V, that is, to NP, AP, VP, S. The convention
for word boundary assignment is a grammatical universal. By this
convention, from 3 we get 4.

4

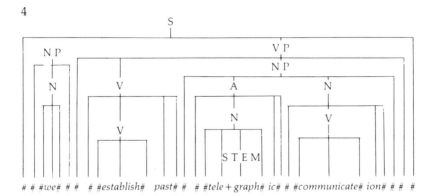

#we# # #   # #establish#   past# #   # #tele + graph# ic# #   #communicate# ion# # #

Continuing to follow Chomsky and Halle, we will say, at least as a
first approximation, that a word is a string of formatives appearing
in the context ## —— ##, where —— contains no ##. This definition
of word is contingent on the particular structure of a sentence. In
sentence 4, the word *tele + graph # ic* is a word by this definition,
but *tele + graph* is not; similarly, *establish* is not a word in *estab-
lish#past*, and *communicate* is not a word in *communication*.

Representations of strings such as that in 4 are not adequate in
every case for the proper application of phonological rules. Consider, for example, sentence 5, where the predicate contains three
noun phrases.

5

This is [$_{NP}$ the cat that caught [$_{NP}$ the rat that stole [$_{NP}$ the cheese]]]

The normal English intonational contour of this sentence clearly does not correspond to its syntactic structure directly; rather, under intonation sentence 5 is realized as if it were a sequence of three sentences: *this is the cat—that caught the rat—that stole the cheese*. Consideration of data such as this has led to the proposal that the mapping from syntactic surface structures onto phonological representations should also include a set of readjustment rules (Chomsky and Halle, 1968). In a case such as 5 the readjustment rules apply to alter the structure of the sentence so that syntactically embedded sentences are restructured as sister constitutents of the matrix S.

6

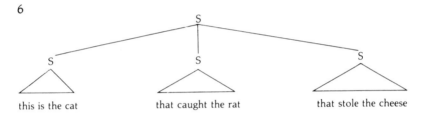

this is the cat   that caught the rat   that stole the cheese

Some functional explanation for readjustment rules such as that just illustrated may be expected to exist. They might arise, for example, as a consequence of performance limitations, a suggestion that seems quite plausible for cases such as this one. Whether this, or some other processing account, proves correct, any such account lies outside the theory of grammar. For discussion of such functional explanations, in general, and of other possible consequences of processing for the theory of grammar, see Chomsky and Lasnik, 1977.

The application of readjustment rules is not invariably so sweeping as in the case of 5 and 6. In some cases readjustment rules affect only a single category in a string. The intonational structure of a sentence is determined on the basis of the syntactic structure of the words (using our first tentative definition of word) in that sentence. That this is so is clearly illustrated by the contrast between 7a and 7b.

7a

Tom has pláns to leave. (Tom is leaving off some plans)

7b

Tom has plans to léave. (Tom is leaving)

Let us assume that Adv (adverb), like N, A, and V, is a lexical
category subject to the boundary assignment convention such that a
word boundary is assigned to the right and left of the category Adv
and to every category dominating Adv. The basis for this assumption is that adverbs can alter the intonational structure of a sentence,
as can nouns, adjectives, and verbs; that the rules of English word
phonology apply to adverbs as they do to the categories N, A, and
V; and so on. That is, the evidence for including the category Adv
along with N, A, V parallels the evidence from those categories.
However, not all English adverbs actually behave like N, A, V; in
particular the intensifying adverbs such as *really, hardly, very, such*
are different. The first two have adverb morphology and the syntactic distribution (move within VPs) of other adverbs (*suddenly,
amazingly*); thus they must be adverbs. However, under normal
sentential intonation these words are relatively unstressed. All words
in a sentence have some stress. What is at stake is relative prominence and the impact of items on the overall melody of a sentence
under neutral intonation. For purposes of focus and emphasis almost
any element, down to particular syllables of words, within a sentence
can be prominently stressed. At issue is not this possibility but rather
what the facts are in the most neutral of cases, that is, in cases having
no special focusing or emphasizing stress. In the neutral case these
adverbs do not affect the overall melody of a sentence. To account
for the peculiarity of these words it is necessary to posit a readjustment rule that effectively erases their associated word boundaries. The need for boundary-changing readjustment rules has been
previously proposed (Chomsky and Halle, 1968).

So far we have noted the following aspects of the mapping from
syntactic surface structures onto phonological representations: (1)
the assignment of word boundaries and (2) the application of readjustment rules. The second aspect involves the rebracketing of
sentences or altering the boundaries assigned by the universal convention. A third component in that mapping is the spelling out of
formatives that have heretofore in the representation been characterized only in terms of syntactic features. By the application of such
rules, the sentence 4 is converted into 8.

8

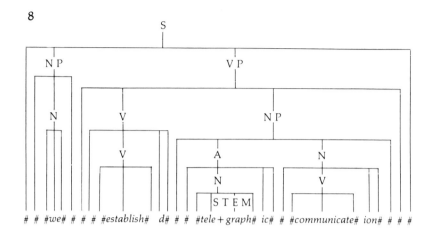

#we# # # # #establish# d# # # #tele+graph# ic# # #communicate# ion# # #

It is only after the application of the universal convention for boundary assignment, the application of all appropriate readjustment rules, and the spelling out of all the formatives of a sentence that a syntactic surface structure has been mapped onto its phonological representation. A phonological representation is then a labeled bracketing of a string of segmentally specified formatives, broken up into a sequence of "words" through the distribution of word boundaries in the string.

The first definition of *word*, a string of segments in the context ## —— ##, where —— contains no ## is only one of the possible and necessary definitions that can be associated with the notion of a word. For example, our adopted definition of word characterizes both *black* and *board* as words in the compound noun [$_N$ # [$_N$ # black # $_N$] [$_N$ # board # $_N$] # $_N$], but it does not characterize the compound itself as a word. That this is so does not necessarily vitiate the previous definition of *word*. It simply reveals that that definition will have to be supplemented in some fashion if it is to be maintained. Clearly there is no reason why any intuitive and conventional notion such as word should have a single systematic grammatical characterization. Instead, to the extent that our intuitions about what is and is not a word represent some grammatically relevant properties of sentences, then those intuitions must be captured in the grammar. There is a systematic set of rules in the phonology that are ordered together and are called the word-level rules; these rules apply to words such as *black* and *board*, which surely are words even in the compound *blackboard*, but not to the whole compound itself. There is therefore an analytic motivation for our first definition of *word*. While that definition corresponds in part to our intuitive notion of what is a word, it does not exhaust that notion. The intuitive concept of words has no more theoretical status in grammar than the intuitive notion of force has status in physics. Just as there is a technical definition of force in physics, so too will word have some technical definition(s) in grammar. To account for the fact that compounds such as *blackboard* are words, we can postulate another definition of words, this one essentially categorial: A word is a string of formatives dominated by a lexical category *modulo* A/A. Under this secondary definition, *blackboard* is a word, but *black* and *board* are not words within that compound. This definition, like the first definition, is a technical definition that does not and need not by itself reflect our intuitions in any complete fashion.

Another case in which the first definition of word does not completely correspond to our intuitions occurred in sentence 4. The string of formatives *tele + graph* in *telegraphic* is not said to be a word even though that sequence of formatives is dominated by the category N, $[_A\#[_N\#\text{tele} + \text{graph}\#_N]\text{lic}\#_A]$. The notion of word required for word-level phonology does not take into consideration the derivational history of words (though the rules of the word-level phonology may make reference to word internal occurrences of #'s). Yet another case in which the word-level definition of words has an intuitively surprising consequence is the definition as words of *the boy, a sandwich*, and *for lunch* in the sentence *the boy ate a sandwich for lunch* but not *boy, sandwich*, or *lunch*. . In terms of the word-level phonology of English, *the boy, a sandwich*, and *for lunch* have the same status and systematic phonological properties as *telegraphic*, ceteris paribus. Such observations, it should be evident, offer strong empirical support for the first definition of word. Just as it was possible to posit a systematic secondary definition of *word* that characterized the compound noun *blackboard* as a word, so too is it possible to posit a systematic definition of word in which *boy, sandwich, lunch*, and *telegraph* will be defined as words in these examples. *A word is a string of formatives in the context # —— #, where —— contains no #.* It is a word so defined that I have previously called a *phonological word* (Kean 1977). This definition of word is independent of the prior definitions; like the prior defini-

tions it is a systematic technical definition. This definition of *word*
should not be confused with the first definition, which defines the domain of word-level phonological rules. While the terminology is less
felicitous than it might be, I will retain the term *phonological word* in
the sense in which I used it previously and use the term *word-level
word* for a properly bracketed string of formatives in the context ##
—— ##, where —— contains no ##.

The definition of a phonological word is made on the basis of
phonological representations of sentences. It is a systematic and
grammatically principled definition. It is on this definition that the
phonological analysis of agrammatism rests. The grammatical analysis, most simply stated, says that the phonological words of a
sentence tend to be retained in agrammatism, all other things being
equal. Of course, there is some variation in the likelihood that
various nonphonological words, which will be termed *clitics*, will
appear in agrammatism; this I take to be a processing factor. It
should be clear that a grammatical account of any deficit cannot account for variability, that variability is a phenomena outside the domain of grammar, using grammar in the restricted technical sense
given in the first section. A grammatical analysis of a deficit can,
under the assumptions made at the outset, only provide a systematic
partition of the data in terms of some level of grammatical representation. Thus of interest here is whether the distinction between
phonological words and the other elements of a sentence provides an
appropriate partition of the data.

The basic bifurcation of the data on the agrammatism involves
the distinction between the major lexical categories and all other
elements in a sentence, such as function words and inflections. This
distinction is made in the phonological analysis through the contrast
between phonological words and clitics. Thus the phonological
analysis makes the appropriate partition of the data, at least at the
grossest level of description. The analysis, however, goes beyond
providing a simple restatement of the basic facts, being based on a
precise property of phonological representations, and it makes particular predictions that go beyond the existing corpus. These specific
details give the analysis its most interesting empirical force and have
caused some people to question the analysis. It is therefore proper to
point out some specific predictions of the analysis.

Let us first consider relatively long derived forms such as *telegraphic*, the class of word-level words containing phonological

words. The phonological account of agrammatism, which states that all other things being equal the phonological words of a sentence will be retained, claims that *telegraph* will be retained in *telegraphic* and that the suffix *-ic* will be lost. It has been suggested to me a number of times that there is no motivation for such a claim, since agrammatic aphasics generally do not use long words in their speech. It seems to me that this is not an argument. The phonological analysis provides for the proper partition of the data for the cases in which the relevant data are known, and in this it achieves a level of descriptive adequacy beyond other analyses that have been suggested. That this analysis goes beyond the corpus at hand is to be expected of any analysis, for the set of structures generated by a grammar is invariably underdetermined by the data. In this case the phonological analysis makes an empirical prediction that *-ic* in a word such as *telegraphic* has the same status in agrammatism as *the* in *the boy*, ceteris paribus. The analysis suggests, then, a further line of research.

A second case in which it might be suggested that the phonological analysis runs into serious difficulties has to do with lexical prepositions. Again the claims of the analysis go beyond the available data. Some lexical prepositions in English are phonological words while others are not. As a rule, monosyllabic prepositions are not phonological words while polysyllabic ones are. It also appears that the greater the semantic specificity of the preposition, the more likely it is to be a phonological word (the notion of semantic specificity is, of course, an intuitive notion with no systematic grammatical status). There are two options for handling this division of the class of prepositions. We might say that the universal convention of boundary assignment applies with the lexical category P as it does with N, A, V, Adv and that there is a readjustment rule that "erases" some of the word boundaries so assigned; that is, prepositions could be treated as adverbs are. Or we might say that the convention for boundary assignment should not be expanded to the class of prepositions and the division of that class into a set of phonological words and a set of clitics should be accounted for on the basis of readjustment rules alone; in that case the readjustment rules would apply to insert #'s when certain prepositions occur. The decision between these two possible approaches is outside the scope of the present discussion and rests on considerations such as how grammars are to be evaluated. All that is relevant to our present purposes is that phonological representations include two classes of lexical prepositions, those that are phonological words and those that are not. The phonological analysis claims that in agrammatism lexical prepositions that are phonological words, such as *beyond*, will be treated in the same way as nouns and that other lexical prepositions will be treated as function words, for example, *in* in the prepositional phrase *in the cellar* (noncontrastively).

A third case in which the analysis goes beyond the data is the case of adverbs, for some adverbs are phonological words while others are not. The issue of adverbs is, of course, superficially confused because many adverbs are derived and thus are word-level words but not phonological words; for example, *badly* is a word-level word containing the phonological word *bad*. To avoid confounding the issues of derivational morphology with the issue of which adverbs are phonological words and which are not, I will restrict my comments to adverbs that are not derived with *-ly*. Goodglass (1973) notes that time adverbs (*yesterday, tomorrow*) are often present in the speech of agrammatic aphasics. These adverbs are phonological words and stand in contrast to the clitic adverbs (non-emphatic/non-contrastive) *such, very*, and so on. Thus the occurrence of the time adverbs that Goodglass observed is consistent with the analysis. The consideration of other sets of adverbs along the phonological word–clitic contrast would obviously be of interest.

No analysis of deficits is of interest if it is restricted to the characterization of particular properties of isolated languages. The phonological analysis of agrammatism is not simply a proposed grammatical account of what is involved in agrammatism for speakers of English. It is an account based on a general property of sentences found in all languages. The phonological analysis makes specific predictions about the partition of retained and frequently omitted items in languages other than English (Kean, 1977). For example, it predicts that in German the distinction between infinitives and neuter nouns should be lost. English is not the only language in which there is a distinction between prepositions that are clitics and prepositions that are phonological words. Thus this distinction represented in the phonology provides the basis for making further specific predictions about agrammatism in other languages as far as the category of prepositions is concerned. An appropriate example of this particular contrast comes from Russian. Morris Halle has informed me that Russian polysyllabic prepositions are generally phonological words, whereas monosyllabic prepositions are clitics. Thus, for example, *prótiv* 'against' is a phonological word whereas *za* 'for' is a clitic. For such cases the predictions of the phonological analysis are clear; the former preposition is classed with the major lexical categories, while the latter is classed with inflections, for example. Of particular interest is the preposition *skvóz'*, 'through' which is phonetically a monosyllabic preposition. Unlike other monosyllabic prepositions it is a phonological word, as is indicated by the stress. But it is not an idiosyncratic exception to the general rule under Halle's analysis of Russian phonology, since at the underlying phonological level *skvóz'*, is a bisyllabic preposition /*skovoz'*/. Russian also has a few prepositions that exhibit peculiar behavior with respect to the general rule. For example, the preposition /*pered"*/ 'before' (in the sense 'in front of') is sometimes realized as a phonological word [p,ér,id] and other times not [p,ir,id]. The claim that is made here for such a word is that when it is realized, it should typically have the phonetic realization of the phonological word and not the clitic form.

The phonological analysis of agrammatism is based on the assumption that grammatical analyses of language deficits must be stated in terms of systematic levels of representation. While it is not logically necessary for a representational analysis of a deficit to be based on a single level of representation, in the case of the phonological analysis of agrammatism only one representational level is implicated. All that is required of a grammatical analysis is that it appropriately partition the available data in terms of some systematic property or properties of representations. One consequence of putting forward any such analysis is that it will be language independent; that is, it will be a universal characterization and not a characterization of the deficit as it occurs in a particular language. The grammatical analysis of agrammatism that I have outlined here appears to provide an appropriate partition of the available data and makes specific predictions that go beyond that corpus. It is a universal characterization, an empirical hypothesis about the partition of words in agrammatism for any language. That is not to say that there is no language-dependent variation in agrammatism; quite the contrary, which items will be phonological words in any language is, quite clearly, subject to variation within certain fixed parameters.

THE DESCRIPTION OF PROCESSING

The phonological analysis of agrammatism is not itself a full linguistic analysis of the deficit, nor was it ever intended to be. Such a description of a deficit can be only one component of an analysis. One
of my initial assumptions was that deficits are to be characterized in
terms of the impairment to some component(s) of the language
faculty and that such a characterization attempts to account for
observed behavior by showing how the impaired component(s) interacting with an otherwise intact linguistic capacity will give rise to
the deficit. The grammatical analysis of agrammatism that I have
just outlined does not claim (or even suggest) that agrammatic
aphasics have lost some aspect of phonological representations.
Rather it claims that the relevant contrast between classes of items
required for any analysis of agrammatism is to be found in phonological representations. To make this claim is to make a claim about
the processor, the claim that in some aspect of normal computation
the processing mechanism relies on the distinction between phonological words and clitics. That is not to suggest that an analysis of
agrammatism in terms of processing mechanisms will in any transparent or obvious sense simply involve locally phonological computations. I assume that levels of grammatical representation are realized in sentence processing. Once a representation has been realized
for processing, then systematic properties of that representation may
be exploited by the processing mechanisms for ends that need not
be directly related to the grammatical functions that gave rise to
the representation. Thus the question raised by the phonological
analysis of agrammatism is how the phonological word–clitic contrast is exploited in sentence processing.

The research reported by Bradley, Garrett, and Zurif (chapter 13,
this volume) is concerned with the role in processing of the phonological word–clitic contrast. In their work with normal subjects
Bradley and Garrett (forthcoming) have shown that in lexical decision tasks there is apparently a systematic difference in the responses
given to phonological words and clitics, in their terminology open-
and closed-class items, respectively. In that work they have demonstrated a role in processing for the distinction. The phonological distinction between the two classes of items is important to their work.
It shows that the experimentally found contrast is a clear representational contrast. Under any view of the language faculty holding that

representations of sentences are generated and that the substantive elements on which the processor operates are systematic elements of levels of representation, data such as those of Bradley and Garrett would lose force were there no representational evidence for the distinction. The phonological distinction between phonological words and clitics offers representational support not only for the lexical access research but also for my initial assumption that levels of grammatical representation are realized in processing, because the processing research is consistent with that assumption. That is, there is a striking convergence between a relatively subtle systematic property of grammatical representations and experimental data on processing. Such a convergence cannot be dismissed as simply a striking coincidence or happy accident. It is just the sort of result that one would expect to find under the initial assumptions.

Consider now the work that Bradley et al. (forthcoming) have done with agrammatic Broca's aphasics. Using the same lexical decision tasks used with normals, they have discovered that the responses to experimental items do not include the normal distinction between phonological words and clitics (or open- and closed-class items). They do not find that the agrammatic aphasics have lost the clitics; rather they have found that the phonological word–clitic contrast is not exploited by agrammatic aphasics as it is by normals. Nor can their data be taken as showing that agrammatic aphasics have lost the ability to systematically distinguish phonological words from clitics in any across-the-board fashion, for the performance, both spontaneous and experimental, of agrammatic aphasics reveals that they make a systematic distinction between the two classes of items. One class tends to be retained and the other class tends to remain unexploited. Therefore we must ask, What is the role of the distinction in processing such that the apparent loss of the contrast between phonological words and clitics in lexical access results in a systematic realization of that contrast?

In answering that question we will begin to develop an analysis of agrammatism that will properly account for observed behavior in terms of the interaction of an impaired component and the intact components of the language faculty. Without an explicit theory of processing, we can only speculate about the impact of the loss of phonological word–clitic contrast in lexical access in terms of the functioning of the processor. However, under the initial assumption that the processor realizes the levels of grammatical representation, we can consider the different functions of these items and say something about the areas in which we would expect problems to arise. For example, since some clitics are inflectional markers of syntactic structures, we would expect agrammatic aphasics to have a syntactic deficit in the sense that they could not properly compute syntactic structures. This notion of a syntactic deficit is not a notion of an impairment to the mechanisms involved in syntactic processing. Since the computational processes must realize syntactic representation, any "prior" loss of information crucial to syntactic processing will impair the proper functioning of the mechanisms of syntactic computation. So, if agrammatic aphasics have lost the normal ability in exploitation of lexical information or accessing routines to distinguish phonological words from clitics, then to the extent that other processing mechanisms crucially rely on that distinction, those processing mechanisms will be impeded in their execution of linguistic computations.

Bradley (1978) has suggested that the reason for the distinction between phonological words and clitics in normal processing is a function of the structure of the syntactic processor. Since clitics as a general class provide a different sort of cue to syntactic structure than do the items of the major lexical classes, Bradley believes that the syntactic processor is abetted relatively early in making the distinction between the two classes. In particular, she has hypothesized that there are special access routines for clitics (closed-class items) and that the parser relies on the clitics to provide the immediate evidential base for determining syntactic structure. If the special access routine for clitics is impaired, then the initial basis for making structural hypotheses is lost. Phonological representations provide a partition of strings into a set of phonological words and clitics; the work that Bradley, Garrett, and Zurif report here hypothesizes one way that the partition is exploited in normal processing and suggests that agrammatism is a consequence of impairment to those routines of exploitation. While the analyses are independent of each other, they are consistent with each other; there is no ground for suggesting that one disproves or undermines the other.

The work discussed so far has addressed the characterization of the impairment that gives rise to agrammatism. An analysis of a deficit must include not only an account ot the actual impairment of the language faculty but also an account of how the impaired component(s) interacting with an otherwise intact language system will give rise to the observed behavior. It is beyond the scope of the present discussion to pursue the issue of interaction of the components of the language faculty in any depth. However, as this must be a major component of any analysis of a deficit, it is worthwhile to briefly consider what such an account might look like.

One area that seems an appropriate starting point for considering aspects of agrammatism that are functions of the operation of intact components of the system is the variation in the likelihood of realization of various clitics. There is, of course, variation in language use among both normal and aphasic individuals. To some extent explanations of that variation may lie far removed from considerations of the structure of the language faculty. Since human linguistic capacity is a complex system that interacts with other complex cognitive systems, cases in performance where there is some degree of interference from nonlinguistic systems (factors such as memory load) are to be expected. Whether one is hungry or irate or tired can reasonably be assumed to affect actual linguistic performance. Among the factors that may lead to variation in speech and comprehension are pragmatic considerations. No doubt pragmatic considerations influence normal speech production, and de Villiers' research on agrammatism points to pragmatic strategies in the speech production of agrammatic aphasics. While much variation in both normal and agrammatic speech may be accounted for by factors outside the domain of the language faculty, surely explanations for some aspects of variation will be grounded on properties of the processor.

Since both normal individuals and people with language deficits exhibit variation in their speech production, for any impaired population the question is whether the variation exhibited is parallel to or different from that of normals. Where the variation is found to be parallel to normal variation we have evidence for the intact operations of some component(s) of the processor, and where it is different from the normal case we have evidence for a true impairment. Since in any language deficit there is an impairment to some component(s) of the language faculty, the realized variation of a population with language deficits will not be transparently like that of normal individuals. What is required therefore is the independent analysis of the corpus from each population over some given domain and then consideration of whether there is congruence in the patterning of that domain in the analyses. Some aspects of the variation in agrammatism seem to reveal a congruence of patterning with normal variation.

The phonological analysis of agrammatism makes a distinction between phonological words and nonphonological words, clitics. From this it does not follow that all clitics are equally likely to be realized or omitted; what follows is that all other things being equal all clitics should have the same likelihood of being realized. But we know quite clearly that all other things are not equal, that the set of clitics contains a variety of types of elements. The only condition under which one might expect complete uniformity of the class of clitics in processing would be if the set of clitics were a uniform class across all the levels of the grammar. The thrust of the phonological analysis of agrammatism is in showing that a disparate class of items—inflections, lexical prepositions—is only a uniform class at the level of phonological representations. Thus an absence of variation in their patterns of realization would be bizarre; one would not expect a class of items so varied at all levels save the phonological to be uniformly treated in processing at all levels.

Garrett's work on the analysis of the spontaneous speech errors of normal individuals provides strong evidence that different classes of clitics are treated differently in sentence production (Garrett, 1975, 1976; also Fromkin, 1971, 1973). While it would be impossible to predict the nature of processing distinctions between different classes of items, that they were to be found was to be expected. In Kean (1977) it was argued that some of the variation in the realization of clitics in the speech of agrammatic aphasics was to be accounted for in terms of normal variation in the processing of different classes of clitics, basing that discussion on the normal speech error research. I will review the arguments that lay behind that analysis to illustrate what is at issue on the local topic of one aspect of variation in the speech of agrammatic aphasics and to provide a model of a deficit analysis that takes into account the otherwise intact components of the system interacting with an impaired component.

In errors of normal speech major class items may exchange, in some instances leaving clitic suffixes behind.

9
McGovern favors *pushing bus*ters

The finding, for example, that there was a hierarchy from clitic suffixes that were invariably stranded to those that were invariably moved along when words exchange would suggest an appropriate parameter for considering variation in the realization of clitics in agrammatism. One does in fact seem to find data which support such a hierarchy of clitic strandability in speech errors. This suggests that computationally some clitics are more closely bound than others to their heads. This raises the question whether the boundedness of a clitic correlates with its likelihood of being realized in the speech of agrammatic aphasics. Congruence would be established if it were found, for example, that the more likely a clitic is to be moved with its head in speech errors (the more bound the clitic is to its head), then the more likely that clitic is to be retained in agrammatism, ceteris paribus. Just such a pattern seems to emerge from analysis of the data. The plural marker, for example, may be moved in an exchange error while the verbal inflection -s is invariably left behind; this parallels the agrammatic data indicating that the plural is more likely to be retained. While the data available for analysis are quite limited, the apparent success of this approach over the available data cannot be discounted. It suggests a new avenue of study that may increase our understanding of which aspects of agrammatism are truly deficits and which aspects are essentially normal.

The linguistic analysis of any deficit, I have assumed, will involve the characterization of the impaired component(s) of the language faculty and an account of how the impaired component(s) interacting with an otherwise intact linguistic capacity give rise to the observed behavior. The language faculty is to be characterized in terms of a grammar and a processor. The grammar is an account of a person's knowledge of the structure of his language, and the processor provides an account of how that knowledge is exploited in use. The grammar generates a series of systematic levels of representation that characterize the well-formed strings of a language. I assume that the levels of grammatical representation are realized by the processor, but I do not assume that the rules of grammar constitute the set of computational mechanisms used by the processor in realizing grammatical representations. I assume that a grammatical analysis of a language deficit is to be made in terms of representations. This position does not exclude forever the possibility that analyses of deficits involve grammatical rules, but it precludes the proposal of such analyses without any explicit theory of the role that rules of grammar play in computation in processing. A grammatical analysis of the deficit having been proposed, it is then necessary to consider how the grammatical partition of the data plays a role in processing. Such considerations make it possible to construct a justifiable hypothesis about the nature of the impairment of the language faculty. Beyond this it is necessary to show how the realized deficit is a function of both the impaired system and the intact components of the language faculty.

In the case of agrammatism we have come a long way in constructing such a full analysis, though much work remains to be done. Agrammatism is alone among the observed aphasic deficits in that there is a start in providing a real linguistic analysis of the deficit. The goal in this paper has been to outline a linguistic analysis of agrammatism, focusing on the role of a grammatical analysis of the deficit. I have argued that suggestions that agrammatism be grammatically analyzed as a syntactic, semantic, or morphological deficit fail to provide an appropriate partition of the data in terms of systematic levels of representation and therefore cannot be maintained under my background assumptions. Consistent with my initial assumptions, and therefore with a grammatical analysis that supports those assumptions, is an analysis that provides a grammatical characterization of the deficit in terms of phonological representations. Having thus provided evidence for the framework of analysis demanded by the assumptions, the next question is how the grammatical partition of the data plays a role in processing such that the observed deficit arises. Bradley, Garrett, and Zurif's paper suggests one way in which the distinction between phonological words and clitics plays a role in processing and proposes a hypothesis about the nature of the impairment of agrammatism based on that role. While that work and the grammatical analysis presented here are independent, together they form a consistent hypothesis that attempts to satisfy my first criterion for a linguistic analysis of a language deficit. The consideration of normal speech errors and variation in the realization of clitics by agrammatics points to one aspect of agrammatic language use that seems deviant but is effectively normal, and it suggests one avenue of research for satisfying the second criterion, which calls for integration of the hypothesized impairment with the nonimpaired components fo the language faculty.

ACKNOWLEDGMENT

Preparation of this work was supported in part by NIMH fellowship 1-F32-MH07189-01.

REFERENCES

Bradley, D. C. 1978. Computational distinctions of vocabulary type. Doctoral dissertation, Massachusetts Institute of Technology.

Bradley, D. C., and Garrett, M. F. 1979. Effects of vocabulary type in word recognition. *Cognition.*

Bradley, D. C., Garrett, M. F., Kean, M.-L., Kolk, H., and Zurif, E. B. 1979. Word recognition in agrammatic aphasia. *Brain and Language.*

Chomsky, N., and Halle, M. 1968. *The sound pattern of English.* New York: Harper and Row.

Chomsky, N., and Lasnik, H. 1977. Filters and control. *Linguistic Inquiry* 8: 425–504.

de Villiers, J. 1974. Quantitative aspects of agrammatism in aphasia. *Cortex* 10: 36–54.

Fromkin, V. 1971. The nonanomolous nature of anomolous utterances. *Language* 47: 27–52.

Fromkin, V. (ed.) 1973. *Speech errors as linguistic evidence.* The Hague: Mouton.

Garrett, M. F. 1975. The analysis of speech production. In *The psychology of learning and motivation: Advances in research and theory*, vol. 9, ed. G. Bower. New York: Academic Press.

–––––. 1976. Syntactic processes in sentence production. In *New approaches to language mechanisms*, ed. E. C. T. Walker and R. Wales. Amsterdam: North-Holland.

Gleason, J. B., Goodglass, H., Green, E., Ackerman, N., and Hyde, M. 1975. The retrieval of syntax in Broca's aphasia. *Brain and Language* 2: 451–471.

Goodenough, C., Zurif, E. B., and Weintraub, E. J. 1977. Aphasics' attention to grammatical morphemes. *Language and Speech* 20: 11–19.

Goodglass, H. 1973. Studies on the grammar of aphasics. In *Psycholinguistics and aphasia*, ed. H. Goodglass and S. Blumstein. Baltimore, Md.: Johns Hopkins University Press.

Goodglass, H., and Berko, J. 1960. Aphasia and inflectional morphology in English. *Journal of Speech and Hearing Research* 3: 257–267.

Goodglass, H., Gleason, J. B., Bernholz, N. A., and Hyde, M. R. 1972. Some linguistic structures in the speech of a Broca's aphasic. *Cortex* 8: 191–212.

Kean, M.-L. 1977. The linguistic interpretation of aphasic syndromes. In *Explorations in the Biology of Language*, ed. E. Walker. Montgomery, Vt.: Bradford Books. The first part of this paper appeared under the same title in *Cognition* 5 (1978): 9–46.

13

Syntactic Deficits in Broca's Aphasia

Dianne C. Bradley,
Merrill F. Garrett,
and Edgar B. Zurif

We begin by sketching some conditions we take to be necessary to any neuropsychological account of language. Minimally we will require a functional description of language; that is one that accounts for language use in comprehension and production by associating particular sentence meanings with acoustic inputs or outputs. The form of description that we will assume is one in which language processes are viewed as the construction of a number of distinct levels of *structural description*; by working hypothesis, these are the levels specified by an adequate formal grammar of the language under analysis. Beyond this, we will evidently require an account of those *information-processing systems* which effect the construction of the computationally relevant levels of structural description. Our assumption is, in short, that the language faculty is decomposable into a complex of subsystems whose interaction yields the observable character of language use.

In the remarks our primary focus will be on evidence for the language-processing subsystem. This bears only indirectly on the formal character of the structures that they yield. To the extent that the computational decomposition of the language processor does correspond precisely to the formal analysis of language into informational subtypes (phonological, syntactic, semantic), the descriptions that are the targets of the processors are specified. The question of such a correspondence is just the feature of the organization of language processors that we wish to address. In particular, we wish to ask whether the available indicants of processing activity—for example, the interaction or lack thereof between semantic and syntactic aspects of sentence structure during language comprehension or production, the existence of a particular aphasic syndrome—suggest the operation of an isolable subcomponent of the language processor devoted to the construction of syntactic representations. Is there a processing subsystem whose activity is independent of the semantic consequences of the representations it builds; that is, is there one whose activity is contingent only on syntactic features of sentence description? We focus on this question simply because we believe that it is most likely to lead to points of connection between a language-processing theory and a neurological theory.

It is self-evident that a specifically neuropsychological account of language must go beyond the issues sketched so far. It requires a determination of the neurological structures that underlie the language processors and a characterization of the relation that holds between language processors and their neurological instantiations. One way to state this requirement is to say that a functional analysis of language must be "structurally adequate" in a neurological sense as well as in linguistic and information-processing senses.

The simplest (but not necessary) manifestation of a correspondence relation between language processors and neurological organization would be an indication that the hypothesized processing subsystems that we have discussed are discretely represented in the brain. By "discretely represented" we do not mean geographically so in any simple sense (though such a circumstance is not impossible). We intend only that discretely represented refer to a neurologically natural separation of function.

In this context the study of aphasia clearly has an important role. The analysis of aphasic syndromes may indicate whether our assumptions provide a viable approach to the discovery of relations between language and the brain. The bare fact is that focal damage to the left cerebral hemisphere does *not* lead to an unstructured, across-the-board reduction in language capacity or proficiency. Rather, it is arguable that lesions in different left-hemisphere locations are quite selective in their effect and that there is considerable consistency in the manner in which such lesions undermine language.

What we will seek to show is that these selective deficits dissociate distinct computational systems in the language process that takes us from sound to meaning.

BROCA'S APHASIA

With this background, we turn to the syndrome that we have examined most extensively, Broca's aphasia. This syndrome is most commonly thought of as resulting from damage to Broca's area, but very possibly it involves a greater cortical area, namely, the territory supplied by the upper division of the left middle cerebral artery. The striking features of this syndrome are the clinically persuasive evidence of a dissociation between production and comprehension processes and the telegrammatic character of the speech produced by such aphasics. Their speech is effortful and fragmentary in the way suggested by the telegrammatic label. The syntactic indicators of structure are for the most part absent; the speaker relies primarily on nouns, although verbs (often nominalized) are also present. In particular, grammatical morphemes (function words and inflectional affixes) are usually omitted. Though we cannot with confidence give a precise formal linguistic or computational description of the preserved and omitted elements, the pattern of production deficit is so consistent that it warrants careful probing to discover whether it does indeed have a coherent linguistic or computational description.

In contrast to their impoverished output, however, these aphasics seem to retain relatively intact comprehension abilities. For the most part they seem to understand the remarks and requests that are addressed to them. Further, the clinical impression is quite strong that they know what they want to say even though they have great difficulty in producing it (Goodglass and Kaplan, 1972; Zurif and Blumstein, 1978).

These circumstances raise a number of possibilities. The first is that the cortical tissue implicated in Broca's aphasia is not important to language; that is, it has little functional commitment to specifically linguistic activity. This notion has been widely disseminated in the form of claims (Locke, Caplan, and Kellar, 1973; Lenneberg 1973; Weigl and Bierwisch, 1970) that the problems of Broca's aphasia have to do primarily with processes involved in the motor implementation of speech and that given such problems the agrammatic character of the speech produced is best understood as an economizing measure. The plausibility of this account draws heavily on the positive evidence of an apparently intact linguistic facility in the domain uncomplicated by motor problems—comprehension. If this sort of account were the correct one, Broca's aphasia would be of little use in evaluating the neurolinguistic issues that we have broached.

There is a second and more interesting possibility, however, even if the clinical picture of spared comprehension and disrupted production were the correct one. That is the possibility that the mechanisms of comprehension and production do not share processing components to any significant extent. From one perspective this seems rather unlikely, for whether we are speaking or listening, the structural facts that distinguish among the sentences of a language must be recovered. But from this it does not follow that the facts are recovered in the same ways. The structural facts of the language may be recruited in different ways for sentence construction on the one hand and sentence comprehension on the other. It is, in short, an empirical question how the processes of language comprehension and production overlap or interact, and in particular, whether they share processing components to a significant extent. Clearly the answer to that question will affect our judgment of the relevance of Broca's aphasia for neurolinguistic theory.

COMPREHENSION IN BROCA'S APHASIA

The first step in evaluating these issues is evidently to examine the comprehension abilities of patients presenting the relevant features of the syndrome. After all, imprecise speaking is a more public event than imprecise comprehension. Thus the clinical impression that one derives may in one way or another be somewhat misleading. That indeed proves to be true. The comprehension of agrammatic speakers *is* disrupted. For example, Caramazza and Zurif (1976) used a picture-matching paradigm to test Broca's aphasics' understanding of center-embedded sentences that varied in the degree to which semantic and pragmatic information could supplant or supplement an analysis of sentence form. They found that the agrammatic speakers could deal successfully with the task just to the extent they could apply a "probable event" strategy. Hence they could understand a sentence like "The apple that the boy is eating is red," where the possible relations among the NPs in the sentence are semantically constrained, but they failed when confronted with sentences like "The girl that the boy is chasing is tall." In this sentence either of the NPs may be assigned agent or patient roles.

This sort of result suggests that when Broca's aphasics cannot use the words of a sentence to infer what would make sense in the world but must instead rely on the syntactically indicated relations among the sentence's elements, they will not comprehend well. Just as they seem to speak primarily in content words so too, one might argue, do they comprehend in terms of direct inferences from the lexical content of sentences, failing to appreciate the grammatical indicants of relations among words.

If these results and their interpretations are correct, then comprehension and production mechanisms are not as readily separable as the initial impression would suggest. They indicate instead a possible separation of semantic and syntactic function that is general to the language faculty. If this line of argument could be sustained, it would have clear interest for a computational and a neurological interpretation of language. However, a number of other issues need consideration before these implications can be pursued.

What are some alternative accounts of the Broca's performance that are nonspecific for language? One suggestion is that there is a loss of general information-processing capacity and that in any perceptually difficult circumstance (for example, semantically unconstrained sentences) performance will suffer. The fact that presence or absence of semantic support for sentence analysis also affects the performance of normal listeners (say, in a noisy environment) lends plausibility to this line of reasoning.

One such deficit of processing ability could be a short-term memory or processing memory loss. It is clear that normal comprehension processes exploit a detailed representation of the input over substrings of several words. The sentences used by Caramazza and Zurif were presented orally and are more than usually complex. If the brain damage associated with Broca's aphasia impairs processing memory and if the specifically syntactic analysis of the sentences is more dependent on such memory than are shortcuts, such as the probable event strategies based on a sampling of the lexical category items, the observed results would follow.

Fortunately, experimental findings of several sorts bear on this issue. Work by Zurif and Caramazza (1976, 1978) and by Gardner, Denes, and Zurif (1975), among others, provides grounds for evaluating Broca's aphasia in circumstances that greatly reduce demands on working memory.

One paradigm in particular seems relevant. In this case a patient is asked to judge how the words of a (written) sentence "go best together." The sentence is always in view, and the patient is required only to point to the words he wants to cluster together. This judgment task depends in large part on an appreciation of the syntactic organization of the sentence (see, for example, the work by Levelt, 1970, using relatedness judgments to elicit intuitions of syntactic structure). What was observed for the agrammatic patients was in sharp contrast to the performance of neurologically intact control subjects. The relatedness judgments of the agrammatic patients, unlike those of the latter group of subjects, did not properly take account of all the elements of the sentence. In particular, the grammatical formatives (elements of the minor grammatical categories as, for example, articles, auxiliaries, adverbial qualifiers) were inappropriately clustered in their initial judgments (for example, an article grouped with a verb); the major contentives were directly joined, thereby violating the integrity of phrasal constituents. In short, the agrammatic subjects behaved as though they had no knowledge of the structural roles played by grammatical morphemes. The corresponding facts for their spontaneously produced speech are, of course, readily apparent.

The same conclusion about the agrammatic population emerges from studies using other paradigms as well. So, for example, in a next-word probe task, minor category items seem adequate to elicit recall of a succeeding noun or verb, but the reverse does not hold true. Given a noun or verb as stimulus, a succeeding grammatical word tends not to be recovered (Caramazza, Gardner, and Zurif, 1979).

Another study makes this same general point, namely, that the comprehension of Broca's aphasics, as well as their production, is agrammatic. This study (Goodenough, Zurif, and Weintraub, 1977) focused on the ability of aphasic patients to use articles appropriately. The paradigm required subjects to point quickly to a single geometric figure from an array of three. The instructions to the patient were either appropriate or inappropriate to the array. Thus, presented with an array consisting of two circles and a square, the subject might be told to "press *the* square one," an appropriate instruction. Alternatively, he might be told to "press the round one," an inappropriate instuction given the presence of two round objects. There were several versions of such commands using shape and color judgments appropriately instructed and inappropriately instructed. For a group of mildly aphasic subjects (likely suffering from posterior lesions) presenting word-finding difficulties but able to speak grammatically, there was a significant increase in latency to press a figure when an inappropriate instruction was given. These longer response times by the anomic aphasics seemed to reflect a response strategy in which they chose an item that shared an un-named feature (color) with an ineligible member of the array. So, for example, faced with an array consisting of a white circle, a black circle, and a black square, they would, when asked to "press *the* black one" (an inappropriate instruction), choose to press the black circle; that is, they pressed the only item that shared the named and unnamed dominant attributes—the black member of the two circles. This result was stable even though the anomic patients could not verbalize their apparent strategy or note the anomalous use of the definite article.

By contrast, a test group of agrammatic Broca's aphasics gave no indication of processing the article. They always chose an eligible member of the group (one with the named attribute), but their response times did not differ for trials on which the article was appropriate and those on which it was inappropriate neither did they show any evidence of a strategy like that of the anomics.

POSSIBLE ACCOUNTS OF BROCA'S APHASIA

On the evidence we have discussed so far, it seems fair to conclude that Broca's aphasia represents more than a problem with the motor implementation of speech. It seems that Broca's aphasics have a comprehension problem as well and, moreover, that their production deficit is interestingly related to this comprehension problem. Both seem to revolve around processes implicating the nonlexical categories—the grammatical morphemes or function words. In comprehension as in production, these elements are poorly controlled. The Broca's aphasic does not seem able to use these elements for phrasal construction, relying instead on inferential strategies to determine the meaning of sentences.

If we accept this characterization, we need to address its interpretation in the linguistic and computational terms outlined in the introduction. We wish to sharpen the issues a bit and bring out the aspects of the problem that we consider most significant. In so doing, we are setting aside any further consideration of the (undoubted) articulatory problems and word-finding problems that Broca's aphasics also suffer from. We will concentrate on the "diagnostic" of their disorder, namely, their incapacity with the nonlexical categories. It is this feature that seems to lend itself to an account in terms of a computational theory of the normal language-processing system. The issue, then, is whether the agrammatism of Broca's aphasia represents the selective impairment of a specific subcomponent or subcomponents of that system.

We wish to consider two possibilities, one briefly, the other at some length. The first account is from a formal linguistic perspective, the second from a computational view, and they are in substantial degree complementary.

Kean (1977) has recently proposed an account of Broca's aphasia that casts it in phonological terms. That account is summarized and extended in chapter 12 of this volume. Our discussion of the problems of Broca's aphasia in syntactic terms reflects a conviction that the obvious features of the agrammatic aphasic's failure are related to the integration of sentence form rather than to sentence meaning. Precisely what the structural and processing antecedents of that failure may be are to be determined, however; and the proper grammatical characterization of the problem may be phonological, even though the most obvious processing manifestation is in terms of syntactically mediated analysis.

The phonological system formally incorporates the major features of the surface syntax of sentences; the representations input to the phonological rule system are fully specified phrasal geometries with phrasal and lexical categories marked. Differences in the phrasal structure such as those dictated by prosodic structure are accomplished by readjustment rules. The result is a syntactic structural representation that is in some real sense keyed to the exigencies of pronunciation. Such a representation is not an unreasonable computational target for an acoustic input processer. Chomsky and Halle's (1968) remarks in the introduction to their work on English phonology are pertinent.

We might expect a language to be so designed that a very superficial analysis into phrases can be performed by a system with limited memory and heavy restrictions on access. To relate this speculation to the discussion of surface structure, it appears that the syntactic component of the grammar generates a surface structure which is converted, by readjustment rules that mark phonological phrases and delete structure, to a still more superficial structure. The latter then enters the phonological component of the grammar. We might speculate, then, that a first stage of perceptual processing involves the recovery of the most superficial structure from the signal using only the restricted short-term memory, and that a second stage provides the analysis into surface structure and the deep structure that underlies it (Chomsky and Halle, 1968, p. 10).

The computational system reflects both the limitations of the processing devices it uses and the computational targets it seeks. Thus that computational target may well be the minimal, interpretively necessary syntactic characterization of the sentence, even though the particular class of elements being exploited is uniformly characterizable only by appeal to the phonology. We explore this matter further in the discussion of computational bases for the relevant vocabulary distinctions.

OPEN- AND CLOSED-CLASS VOCABULARIES

From the standpoint of a device that must assign a phrasal analysis to sentences, the contrasts between content and function words, phonological and nonphonological words, or major and minor grammatical categories all have much the same flavor; they implicate the contrast between sentence form and sentence meaning. Precisely which, if any, of the available formal characterizations is most relevant to a discussion of computational systems is not clear. In talking about the vocabulary contrast from the standpoint of sentence-processing theories, we will refer to the distinction we have discussed under these several labels as that between *open-* and *closed-* class vocabularies. The two (at present, not sharply defined) classes of words seem to have differing roles in sentences, whether from a formal perspective (chapter 12 in this volume) or from a computational perspective. In broad terms, the two classes diverge in terms of what might be called interpretive burden. The closed-class (grammatical morphemes, minor grammatical categories, nonphonological words) includes sentence elements that, by and large, are vehicles of phrasal construction rather than primary agents of reference, as is the case with open-class words (content words, major grammatical categories).

Whether for this reason or for some other, the difference between these classes has a variety of reflections in rather gross features of language performance. The brute facts of agrammatism that suggest the contrast between open- and closed-class vocabularies are mirrored as persuasively in other domains. So, for example, the telegraphic stage of first language acquisition is captured by much the same division of vocabulary. So, too, is there a striking difference in effects of pairing various classes of real words with nonsense words in learning and recall experiments; closed-class elements facilitate learning and recall in different fashion and to a greater degree than do open-class words. Perhaps the most striking illustration of this arises when the nonsense words are arranged with grammatical morphemes to form a "sentence," such as "The Jabberwocky" by Lewis Carroll or strings like "The vapy koobs desaked the citer molently" (which appears in more than one psychological experiment). One has the clear impression that a sentencelike object is being presented, and that impression is reflected in improved recall of such strings when compared with (shorter) strings from which the structural elements have been deleted.

If one states in computational terms what seems to be going on, the matter becomes clearer. The function words or grammatical words support syntactic analysis by permitting the assignment of major category membership (noun, verb, and so on) to the nonsense words. A sentential analysis can thereby be assigned to the string as a whole (Garrett, 1978). It is the availability of this analysis that promotes an enhanced performance.

This view of the difference in computational roles of open- and closed-class vocabulary was explored in a recent series of experiments by Bradley and Garrett (1979). In those experiments they tested the general hypothesis that the different computational roles played by open- and closed-class elements in the assignment of sentence structure will appear as differences in the organization of the word-retrieval mechanisms used for language processing. Their experimental results do, in fact, indicate a strong difference in the retrieval systems for the two vocabularies. Most interesting for our purposes is that when these same experimental paradigms are used for word-recognition tests with agrammatic aphasics, their performances contrast sharply and interestingly with that of normal controls. To make the nature of this difference clear, we will have to summarize the initial results of Bradley and Garrett.

Their research strategy was to contrast open- and closed-class performances on two features of word recognition that are strongly characteristic of open-class recognition: *frequency sensitivity* and *left-to-right scan order*. There are a great many experimental de-

monstrations of long standing that word recognition for open-class
items is positively correlated with frequency of occurrence of a word
form in the language; the more frequently a word occurs, the better
it is recognized when heard under noise, the more accurately reported following tachistoscopic presentation, and the more rapidly
identified as a word in a lexical decision task. It is this last paradigm
that Bradley and Garrett used. Subjects are presented (visually) with
a letter array (CAT or PUDDLE or CUG or PLIGN) and must indicate (by pressing a reaction-time key) their decision that the letter
string is or is not a word in their vocabulary. The higher the frequency of occurrence for a real word, the more rapidly the YES decision is made. Frequency sensitivity, in this and other paradigms,
has been interpreted either as a reflection of variation in the *strength*
of stored representation (Morton, 1970) or as a reflection of the
order in which candidate analyses for the array are considered
(Forster, 1976); in either case frequency sensitivity is taken to reflect
a characteristic feature of the word-recognition mechanism. However, Bradley and Garrett's results, summarized in figure 13.1, indicate that this is true only for the open-class vocabulary; there is no
evidence of frequency organization for the closed class. Hence on

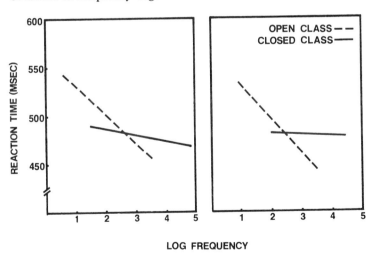

LOG FREQUENCY

13.1
Contrasts in frequency-sensitivity of open- and closed-class recognition.
Linear regressions of item reaction time (in milliseconds) on item frequency
of occurrence (per million, expressed in units logarithm base 10). Data are
for populations of normal speakers (From Bradley and Garrett, 1979)

grounds of frequency as a diagnostic variable, open- and closed-class vocabulary items are contacted in different ways.

A complementary finding arises for tests of interference effects in judgments of nonwords. When subjects are presented in a lexical decision task with an array that is not a word, reaction times are elevated if the initial substring of the array is a real word or stem. So, for example, nonwords like TOASTLE or HOUSELT take significantly longer to reject than nonwords like POASTLE or TOUSELT, which do not have an initial substring that is a real word. This finding holds for *initial* substrings but not for other string positions (nonwords like FLEPOST or MORAG do not differ from nonwords like FLEPUST or MOROG, even though substrings in their final positions correspond to real words). This and a number of other experimental findings are taken as an indication that a left-to-right scan through the sensory array is a basic feature of word recognition. Again, however, this does not seem to hold for closed-class vocabulary. Figure 13.2 shows the results for such a comparison. As with the frequency diagnostic, so with this one: The closed-class vocabulary seems to be contacted in some fashion that eliminates the interference from the partial analyses engendered by a left-to-right pass through the array.

If we take these results to provide a prima facie case for the operation of two distinct recognition routines, one for open-class and one for closed-class vocabularies, we have the beginnings, at least, of a partial computational reconstruction of the contrast appealed to in our discussion of the agrammatic speech of Broca's aphasics. The question that immediately suggests itself is whether this computational difference in the retrieval of the two vocabularies appears for Broca's aphasics. Work by Bradley et al. (1979) indicates that it does not. The same experimental material used by Bradley and Garrett were used for a group of Broca's aphasics and a group of hospitalized normal controls. Figures 13.3 and 13.4 summarize the results for these two populations for the frequency and interference effect cases. Notice that the Broca's aphasics are quite capable of the task. Their error rate is not unusual and their reaction times, though somewhat elevated, are well within the range of the normal controls. The striking difference lies in the close correspondence of performances for open and closed classes by the Broca's aphasics. The same pattern arises for the interference effects; both open and closed classes produce significant interference for the Broca's aphasics. For

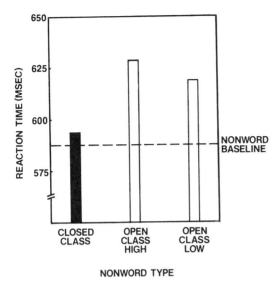

13.2
Nonword interference effects in lexical decision. Mean reaction time (in milliseconds) for nonword decisions as a function of vocabulary class of initial portions. Data are for a population of normal speakers. "High" and "low" categories of open-class interference stimuli refer to their frequency of occurrence in English. (From Bradley and Garrett, 1979)

both types of tests the normal controls show the dissociation of effects for the two vocabularies.

Given these results it would seem that although the Broca's aphasics can successfully recognize the words from both classes, they do not do so in the fashion characteristic of normal language processing. It is, of course, by no means necessary that the poor comprehension and production performances of Broca's aphasics be accountable by the failure of the specialized retrieval system for closed-class vocabulary. However, insofar as the explanation for the existence of the two retrieval types can be connected to the computational processes of assigning syntactic analyses to sentences, it is a plausible candidate for explanation of the failures of Broca's aphasics. (To date, three fluent aphasics, with posterior lesions, presenting word-finding difficulties in the context of grammatical speech have also been tested on the two tasks. Of these three one has performed in an uninterpretable way corresponding neither to Broca's nor normals, while the remaining two show the normal dissociation of the two vocabularies. This increases our confidence that

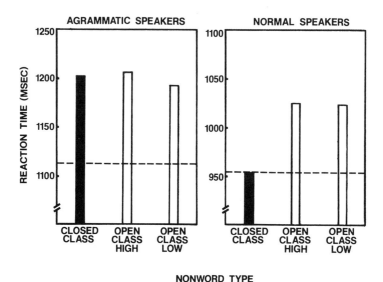

13.3
Nonword interference effects in lexical decision for Broca's aphasics and hospital control patients. (From Bradley and Garrett, 1979)

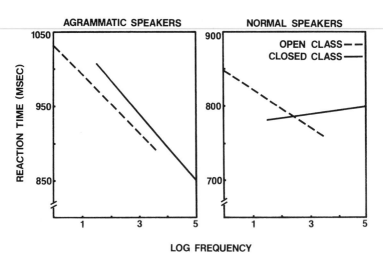

13.4
Frequency effects in lexical decision for Broca's aphasics and hospital control patients. (From Bradley and Garrett, 1979)

the disruption of the closed-class retrieval system is specifically tied to agrammatism and is not the outcome of brain damage in general.)

A final note to be made here concerns the implications of the work with aphasics for our understanding of normal sentence processing. There are two points.

The first is that the results with Broca's aphasics suggest a rather strong connection between the processes that underlie sentence comprehension and those underlying sentence production. Though we cannot say certainly that the same lexical retrieval processes that guide the integration of sentence form when we are speaking also guide our construction of the representations we use when listening, the evidence for the Broca's agrammatic comprehension, coupled with their obviously agrammatic production, strongly suggests something of the sort, given the results of the lexical decision experiments. It is, of course, possible that the tissue damage that yields agrammatic *comprehension* and presumably also accounts for the loss of the characteristic difference between open- and closed-class word recognition is quite unrelated to the production difficulties also attendant upon that tissue loss. If so it is merely coincidence that the nature of the production loss so nearly corresponds in character to the nature of the comprehension deficit. Though possible, this hardly seems the most likely account.

The second point is simply that the character of the agrammatic's successful performance in the lexical decision task for both classes of words tells us that the normal organization of the word system "doubly represents" the closed class. If one rejects the possibility that a new retrieval system, which is organized by frequency in just the same way as the open class, is constructed postictally by the aphasics, the representation of the closed class in the target domain of the frequency organized system must be acknowledged. This conclusion in turn requires us to seek an account of the normal processing that will explain the absence of interference effects in the nonword lexical decision experiments. The attested existence (by the aphasics' performance) of the closed-class items in the target domain for the open-class retrieval mechanism blocks the first obvious account of the difference in interference effects for normals (the "nonexistence" of the closed class for the system that generates the interference) and requires instead an account in which the successful operation of the closed-class retrieval system inhibits the consequences of the open-class access routine. We will not pursue that point further here; we merely note it because it demonstrates that investigation of language disorders is not a one-way street from normal processing models to tests of aphasia. The very consequences of putting our theories of normal language processing to test in the domain of disordered language can lead to advances in our understanding of the normal processes.

CONCLUSION

Our exploration in neurolinguistic theory began with a set of assumptions about the nature of normal language processing and has proceeded, somewhat episodically, through the analysis of a particular disorder, Broca's aphasia. We have argued that the nature of Broca's aphasia, as we evaluated it, is strongly compatible with the componential view of language processing with which we began. In particular, we have tried to show that Broca's aphasia is understandable as a loss of specifically syntactically supported language processes. The character of the processing losses to which we have called attention implicate phonological structure and lexical retrieval mechanisms. Our characterization of Broca's deficit as syntactic depends on the imputation of a syntactic rationale for both the impaired features of phonological structure and the organization of the lexical retrieval mechanisms.

These observations are evidently only a very small part of the elaboration of a plausible neurolinguistic theory. But, the fact that a linguistically justifiable separation of *structural* types also seems to yield an experimentally verifiable account of processing for both normal and disordered language is greatly encouraging. More specifically, to find that a reconstruction of the consequences of brain injury is possible in light of such a functionally defensible decomposition of the language faculty gives concrete evidence for the existence of strong connections between the coherently describable cognitive systems and the organization of the neural systems that subserve them.

ACKNOWLEDGMENTS

This work was supported in part by NIH grant HD 05168 to J. Fodor and M. F. Garrett, and by NIH grant 11408 to Edgar Zurif and Howard Gardner, and by NIH grant 06209 to the Boston University Aphasia Research Center. We wish to thank M.-L. Kean for valuable discussions of the issues raised in this paper.

REFERENCES

Bradley D., and Garrett, M. 1979. Effects of vocabulary type in word recognition. *Cognition.*

Bradley D., Garrett, M., Kean, M.-L., Kolk, H., and Zurif, E. 1979. Word recognition in agrammatic aphasia. *Brain and Language.*

Caramazza, A., Gardner, H., and Zurif, E. B. 1979. Sentence memory in aphasia. *Neuropsychologia,* in press.

Caramazza, A., and Zurif, E. B. 1976. Dissociation of algorithmic and heuristic processes in language comprehension: Evidence from aphasia. *Brain and Language* 3: 572–582.

Chomsky N., and Halle, M. 1968. *The Sound Pattern of English.* New York: Harper and Row.

Forster, K. 1976. Accessing the mental lexicon. In *New approaches to language mechanisms,* ed. R. J. Wales and E. Walker. Amsterdam: North-Holland.

Gardner, H., Denes, G., and Zurif, E. B. 1975. Critical reading at the sentence level in aphasics. *Cortex* 11: 60–72.

Garrett, M. F. 1978. Word and sentence perception. In *Handbook of sensory physiology,* vol 7: *Perception,* ed. R. Held, H. W. Leibowitz, and H. L. Teuber. Berlin: Springer-Verlag.

Goodenough, C., Zurif, E. B., and Weintraub, S. 1977. Aphasics' attention to grammatical morphemes. *Language and Speech* 20: 11–19.

Goodglass, H., and Kaplan, E. 1972. *The assessment of aphasia and related disorders.* Philadelphia: Lea and Febiger.

Kean, M.-L. 1977. The linguistic interpretation of aphasia syndromes: Agrammatism in Broca's aphasia, an example. *Cognition* 5: 9–46.

Lenneberg, E. H. 1973. The neurology of language. *Daedalus* 102: 115–133.

Levelt, W. J. M. 1970. Hierarchical clustering algorithms in the psychology of grammar. In *Advances in psycholinguistics,* ed. G. B. Flores d'Arcais and W. J. M. Levelt. Amsterdam: North-Holland.

Locke, S., Caplan, D., and Kellar, L. 1973. *A study in neurolinguistics.* Springfield, Ill.: Charles C. Thomas.

Morton, J. 1970. A functional model of human memory. In *Models of human memory,* ed. D. A. Norman. New York: Academic Press.

Weigl, E., and Bierwisch, M. 1970. Neuropsychology and linguistics: Topics of common research. *Foundations of Language* 6: 1–30.

Zurif, E. B., and Blumstein, S. 1978. Language and the brain. In *Linguistic theory and psychological reality*, ed. J. Bresnan, M. Halle, and G. A. Miller. Cambridge, Mass: MIT Press.

Zurif, E. B., and Caramazza, A. 1978. Comprehension, memory, and levels of representation: A perspective from aphasia. In *Speech and language in the laboratory, school, and clinic*, ed. J. F. Kavanagh and W. Strange. Cambridge, Mass.: MIT Press.

Zurif, E. B., and Caramazza, A. 1976. Psycholinguistic structures in aphasia: Studies in syntax and semantics. In *Studies in neurolinguistics*, vol. 1, ed. H. Whitaker and H. A. Whitaker. New York: Academic Press.

14

Brain Structure and
Language Production:
A Dynamic View

Jason W. Brown

LANGUAGE, BRAIN, AND THE PROBLEM OF LOCALIZATION

Let us begin with the idea that language is hierarchically structured, that the words I am now speaking have passed through a complex series of levels that form a part of the structure of that utterance, a structure that has to be traversed each moment as an utterance is realized. This process of a more or less instantaneous unfolding of language and cognition over levels is termed microgenesis. An aphasic symptom represents a destructuration within this dynamic hierarchical structure; in other words, the aphasic utterance represents or points to one of the more preliminary levels. Incidentally, it is for this reason that I believe we do not always have to rely on reaction times or other means to explore underlying structure in aphasia, since in certain ways the underlying structure is displayed directly in the aphasic utterance.

Thus, we are dealing with levels in language as revealed in a pathological destructuration; at the same time we know that the brain is built up into a series of layers through evolutionary and maturational growth. These levels in brain organization correspond to levels in language production, so far as these levels can be inferred from their breakdown in aphasia. That is, the microgenesis of language is elaborated over evolutionary and ontogenetic levels in the brain. In such an account the problem of anatomical localization becomes very complicated. There is the building up of brain structure over evolutionary time, its further growth and employment over the life span, and there is the process of cognitive unfolding occurring in a microtemporal frame. Moreover, there is the whole dynamic of the lateralization process, which as we will see repeats in ontogeny the process of neocortical evolution. There is the organization of language into an anterior and posterior sector in relation to motor and perceptual systems, the parallel structural organization of these two zones, the question of age-specificity, and the need to consider ontogenetic factors in the interpretation of brain-language correlation. Educational, sex, and other factors may also bear on this matter, so the problem of aphasia correlation is an extremely complex one. However, I believe that this complexity can be resolved in a genetic account of both brain and language organization.

EVOLUTION AND BRAIN STRUCTURE

The view of the Wernicke and Broca areas as depots in a cortical language circuit has to be discarded. The neocortical language zones and their adjacent perceptual and motor regions are like the tips of an iceberg in brain evolution. To understand the function of these areas, we have to explore the organization of the submerged part of their structure. We know that in the evolution of the forebrain there is a progression from a limbic organization through a series of growth rings to a limbic-derived or transitional cortex. This is represented anteriorly by the cingulate gyrus and posteriorly by the insula and the inferolateral temporal cortex. Generalized ("association") neocortex develops out of this limbic-derived cortex. Sanides (1970) has proposed that the primary motor and sensory cortices develop out of generalized neocortex, that is, that generalized or "association" cortex is older than the primary cortices. This conclusion, which runs counter to a whole tradition of neurological thinking, is one that I reached quite independently a few years ago in a monograph on aphasia and related disorders. If it proves true, a considerable readjustment of our concept of brain organization will be required. In any event, in the mammalian brain an evolutionary sequence can be demonstrated which leads from limbic through limbic-transitional cortex to generalized ("association") cortex to the primary motor and primary sensory cortices.

We may ask how the Broca and Wernicke areas fit into this concept and what is the nature of cerebral dominance. I have proposed that language dominance develops and that this comes about as the Broca and Wernicke regions differentiate within the generalized neocortex of the anterior and posterior brain. These zones would then be interposed as levels in the hierarchial sequence. The development

of these regions would occur as a figural prominence or core differentiation in the course of maturation, a process comparable to the
phylogenetic pattern of core differentiation that characterizes neocortical growth. In other words, the development of the language
zones in maturation seems to occur through the same process as that
which took place in the evolution of the forebrain; it is a continuation into ontogeny of this evolutionary process. These concepts are
summarized in figure 14.1.

The result is a multitiered structure recapitulating an evolutionary
sequence which, as we will see, elaborates levels in language and
cognition.

STRUCTURE OF THE ANTERIOR SPEECH ZONE

Let us look for the moment only at the anterior brain and consider
how the frontal language zone might be constructed. In a young
child, say around age five, damage to the left frontal region characteristically produces a state of mutism. If there is recovery, this

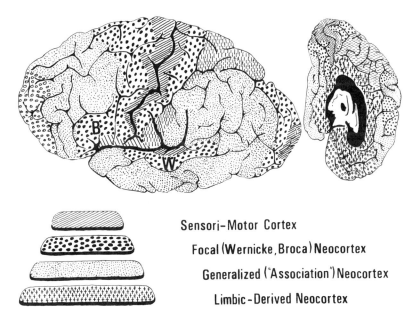

Sensori-Motor Cortex

Focal (Wernicke, Broca) Neocortex

Generalized ("Association") Neocortex

Limbic-Derived Neocortex

14.1
Levels in brain evolution and cognitive microgenesis and corresponding
regions on a standard cytoarchitectonic map

develops into agrammatism. In a somewhat older child, say age ten, a left frontal lesion, probably a more focally situated lesion around Broca's area, may have the same effect, or the lesion may produce a phonemic-articulatory impairment in the context of a nonfluent or semifluent state. There is some evidence that in young children mutism and agrammatism result from more widely distributed lesions, while aphasia in adolescence tends to follow lesions more restricted to the classical language zones. In any event, it is a strong possibility that in young children damage to a wider part of the left frontal region, possibly to either the right or the left frontal lobe, will produce mutism or agrammatism, while a more focal left-sided lesion in older children tends to produce either agrammatism or articulation errors.

Now let us turn to adult aphasia, again only the anterior disorders and only the production aspects. Mutism, agrammatism, and articulatory errors occur in the anterior aphasic and are associated with pathology in different brain regions.

Mutism occurs with a bilateral lesion of the cingulate gyrus. This is limbic-derived cortex. The mutism tends to occur in the context of a global inertia. There is no paralysis but there is little if any spontaneous limb or body movement. Such patients do not even attempt to vocalize, they do not cry out in pain, nor do they gesture. It is difficult to demonstrate any comprehension in such cases. Prolonged mutism may occur with neocortical lesion. It is more common in crossed aphasic dextrals, that is right-handers with an aphasia from a lesion of the right hemisphere, and I believe it may be more common in left-handed aphasics with lesions of either hemisphere.

Agrammatism occurs with a lesion of left generalized neocortex. Although we do not have precise information on this point, studies suggest that agrammatism relates to lesions on the periphery of the classic Broca area, either just anterior or superior to this area or partially destroying it. Since there are no precise limits to Broca's area, it is not possible to state that a lesion surrounds or disconnects this area or that the Broca zone is partially destroyed. In children, in crossed-aphasic dextrals, and probably also in left-handers, agrammatism occurs also with a posterior lesion involving the generalized neocortex of the posterior hemisphere. From the clinical standpoint, one can see transitional disorders between mutism and agrammatism. We do see cases, for example, of mutism with good repetition. At times the repetition is agrammatic, or there may be correct repetition with agrammatic writing. This group of disorders is referred to as transcortical motor aphasia. Similarly, there are patients with agrammatism in spontaneous speech but normal repetition. These agrammatics were explained on the basis of a speech "economy." From here we see a transition to cases of agrammatism in spontaneous speech and repetition, as well as in reading aloud, rote speech, and so on.

One further comment on agrammatism in light of the discussion in Kean's and Bradley, Garret, and Zurif's chapters (chapters 12, 13). I am still unconvinced by the evidence for a specific syntactic deficit in this disorder. In my laboratory, Lucia Kellar (1978) has collected evidence suggesting that the abnormal sorting pattern of the aphasic reflects a heightened sensitivity to stressed elements and a corresponding inattention to unstressed elements. She has tested both posterior and anterior aphasics and found the same abnormal sorting pattern in both groups. Since the deficit in syntactic knowledge shown by the agrammatic is not specific to the production pattern, it seems premature to link this deficit to agrammatism. This leads me to ask whether the prominence of word stress in agrammatic speech might reflect its *lexical* basis in the posterior system, the anterior lesion having disrupted the intonational pattern and its derivation into the temporal programmation of sound sequences. Finally, I want to point out that comparisons of anterior and posterior aphasics should take into consideration the severity of the comprehension impairment, since this may be an important factor. One cannot always assume that the posteriors have the worse comprehension.

Next, the group of phonemic-articulatory disorders is related to a lesion of Broca's area proper. This correlation has been stressed in Continental and Soviet aphasiology, for example in the kinetic aphasia of Luria. From this disorder we proceed into the syndrome of phonetic disintegration with inferior pre-Rolandic lesion.

How can we bring this material together? We have described a sequence in the anterior disorders leading from mutism through agrammatism to phonemic-articulatory errors and to the syndrome of phonetic disintegration. The pathological lesions that produce these disorders involve brain structures in an evolutionary sequence. There is a progression from a lesion of limbic-derived cortex to a lesion of generalized neocortex, to a lesion of focal differentiated cortex and finally to a lesion of the inferior motor strip. Lesions in this progression proceed from a bilateral to a more diffuse left-sided lesion, to a focal left-sided lesion. We know that older evolutionary levels are more bilateral in their organization so that the requirement of a bilateral lesion for the limbic level of disorder should not be surprising.

These pathological disorders are disruptions of levels in normal language production. From this material we can infer (figure 14.2) that the motoric component of language consists of a sequence leading from a stage where the utterance-to-be is embedded in the context of a global motor act, its "motor envelope." It develops from this to an intermediate level, conceivably that of a truncated or attenuated phrase structure, though this may be an artifact of the employment of word stress in production. From this point the utterance develops into a phonological and finally a phonetic form. The progression in the anterior aphasias from mutism to agrammatism to phonological to phonetic impairments represents a disruption at stages in this sequence, and each of these impairments corresponds with a lesion at a sequential state (level) in the evolution and maturation of the forebrain. The sequence of anterior aphasia in children also leads from mutism to agrammatism to phonological

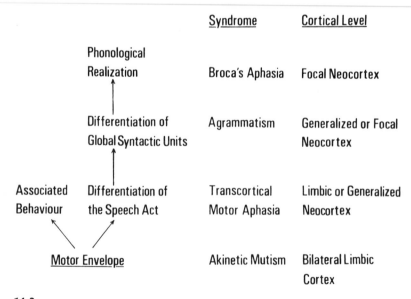

	Syndrome	Cortical Level
Phonological Realization	Broca's Aphasia	Focal Neocortex
Differentiation of Global Syntactic Units	Agrammatism	Generalized or Focal Neocortex
Associated Behaviour Differentiation of the Speech Act	Transcortical Motor Aphasia	Limbic or Generalized Neocortex
Motor Envelope	Akinetic Mutism	Bilateral Limbic Cortex

14.2
Syndromes of the anterior sector with corresponding brain structural level and level of speech act differentiation

defects. This is a maturational sequence that corresponds to levels in speech production as inferred from the adult aphasias. Conceivably in the young child we see the limbic-level speech disorder (mutism) because the child's cognition is essentially based in a limbic mode. Though the utterance of the child develops over all levels in the proposed structure, the child's cognition may reflect a more preliminary stage, and this may have a determining role on the type of aphasia that occurs.

POSTERIOR DISORDERS

Now let us turn to the posterior aphasias. Again we can begin with the age-dependent aspects of these disorders. In young adults a lesion of the left posterior language zone tends to produce a nonfluent or semifluent aphasia characterized by phonological errors. Word-finding difficulty may also occur. In progressively older subjects these symptoms occur in a more fluent context and produce the picture of a "conduction" or phonemic aphasia. This disorder is characterized by phonological errors, substitution, omission, metathesis, and so on, appearing in conversational speech, repetition, reading aloud, and other speech performances. The lesion that produces the syndrome of "conduction" aphasia is in the classic Wernicke area or its continuation more posteriorly as the supramarginal gyrus. There is no evidence that the syndrome is due to pathway interruption; indeed, there is considerable evidence against this idea.

In young adults verbal substitution may also occur. With a unilateral lesion involving the left temporoparietal area, such substitution tends to occur within category boundaries, for example *table* for *chair*. We may see substitution of a more unusual associative type, for example *throne* for *chair*, or asemantic or jargon substitutions, for example *wheelbase* for *chair*, but the lesion in such (younger) cases is ordinarily bilateral involving the inferolateral temporal cortex. This latter type of asemantic error may give rise to semantic jargon. An example of this would be a patient who complained of his poor vision by saying "my wires don't hire right," or another patient who said, "I'm supposed to take everything from the top so that we do four flashes of four volumes before we get down low."

Semantic jargon is similar to the confabulation of (acute) Korsakoff patients, an observation of interest because the latter disorder is also associated with bilateral lesions of limbic structures. Semantic jargon with a left unilateral temporal lesion is more characteristic of the late-life aphasic. Another type of jargon is neologistic jargon. This is also a disorder of the elderly aphasic. It appears to be due to a combined semantic *and* phonological defect. These error types and their syndrome correlations are illustrated in figure 14.3.

The interesting thing about these error types is that there appears to be a correlation between the predominant error form and a lesion of a particular brain-structural level. As I have indicated, the asemantic error results from bilateral lesions of limbic-derived cortex in the young adult. This is true also for the "associative" type of error. Verbal substitution within the correct category, that is, substitution that is semantically close to the target item, is more characteristic of the anomic aphasic and suggests a lesion of the left posterior generalized neocortex. This is true also of the classical anomic who, though not producing semantic errors, fails to access the target noun but gives evidence (through cuing, multiple choice) that an abstract representation of the correct lexical item has been selected. Finally, the phonological disorder, conduction or phonemic aphasia, is associated with a focal lesion of the left Wernicke area or its more posterior extent. Neologistic jargon is also related to a lesion of this region by virtue of its dependence on a constituent phonological deficit. This correspondence of error type to brain-structural level is shown in figure 14.4

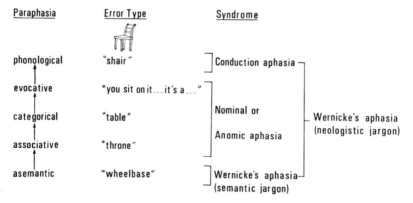

14.3
Aphasic syndromes of the posterior sector correspond to levels in semantic or phonological realization

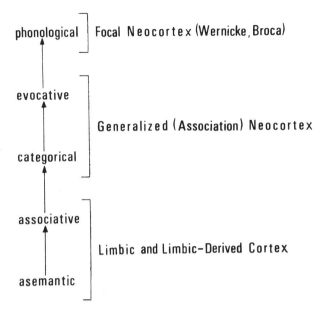

phonological   Focal Neocortex (Wernicke, Broca)

evocative

categorical   Generalized (Association) Neocortex

associative

asemantic   Limbic and Limbic-Derived Cortex

14.4
Levels in language production in the posterior sector and corresponding
levels in brain structure

From this material it is possible to reconstruct a model of the mental lexicon based on its destructuration in posterior aphasia. There
appears to be a series of levels of lexical representation leading from
a level of wide psychological distance from target through a stage
where experiential and affective factors come into play, to a level of
categorical realization. Through this process an abstract representation of the correct lexical item is selected and then realized through a
process of phonological encoding. Levels in the structure correspond
to evolutionary levels in brain organization. The initial (amnestic,
confabulation) stage is related to a limbic representation. Subsequent levels consist of a limbic-derived or transitional cortex, then
generalized or association cortex, and finally focal neocortex which
differentiates out of the preceding stage. Pathological lesions disrupt
these levels. At a limbic level bilateral lesions are required. This proceeds to a more widely distributed but left-sided lesion of posterior
generalized neocortex and then to a more precisely localized left
focal lesion.

    In this model the developing content proceeds through levels in its semantic representation to a phonological phase. This is an emergent system, not a flow process; lesions do not interrupt this flow. The lesion produces a qualitative disruption that points to a level of representation. The symptom refers to that level; it is a fragment of preliminary cognition carried into the endstage utterance. We can see from figure 14.3 how the various error types of the posterior aphasic represent levels in the unfolding of the posterior component.

What then is the function of the Broca and Wernicke areas? In both the anterior and posterior system, these regions mediate phonological realization. If one could remove these areas one would have a right hemisphere. The hemisphere would be agrammatic in production, for example as in the Genie case, due to the attenuated anterior development, and there would be reasonably good lexical-semantic capacity, as in the right hemisphere of splits. The preserved semantic capacity would reflect the adequacy of (already traversed) levels in the posterior development.

Aphasic symptoms do not represent defects of language in isolation. Each of the described error types is accompanied, during that moment when the error occurs, by a specific alteration in cognition, in affect, and in the awareness of the error. We learn from the aphasias that mind is hierarchically organized and that the aphasic utterance taps a level in the hierarchic organization of mind as well as language.

ON THE RELATIONSHIP BETWEEN THE ANTERIOR AND POSTERIOR SYSTEMS

The traditional assumption has been that language is generated posteriorly and is conveyed to the anterior region for articulation. Most of the early and many contemporary neurologists have spent a good deal of time searching for pathways that could mediate this transaction. Initially it was thought that language moved anteriorly over the insula, and conduction aphasia—which had been thought to represent a break in this flow—was attributed to insular lesion. This was the idea of Wernicke and Déjérine but was argued most forcefully by Kurt Goldstein. Then the arcuate fasciculus was implicated, again by Wernicke, and to conform to this change the lesion of conduction aphasia was shifted to the supramarginal gyrus and to the underlying white matter. Geschwind has been especially identified with this view. Subsequently, Penfield argued that the thalamus was responsible for connecting the two language areas, and this initiated the search for thalamic aphasias. Bogen has alluded to a fourth theory, the idea that language somehow percolates over the operculum to Broca's area. Needless to say, there is no evidence to support any of these theories.

In the model that I have presented, contact between levels in the anterior and posterior system is assured through long connecting pathways. However, it is my view that these pathways do not serve to transfer contents from one place to another but rather concern the timing or the phase relationships, between homologous anterior and posterior levels. This would also apply to commissural fibers, which connect limbic-transitional and generalized neocortical levels. In other words, I assume a simultaneous realization or microgenesis over levels in both the anterior and posterior system, the simultaneity of which is guaranteed by these pathways. I do not believe there is an interaction, if by this is meant a conveyance here or there of language content. Moreover, there are short, bidirectional fibers connecting levels within each hierarchical system. Presumably these modulate the (vertical) relationships between levels within each system. This would be the role of short and long pathways in the described model, to see to it that events at homologous levels occur at the same spatiotemporal moment, in other words in the same mind. The actual process of language unfolding, however, would be mediated by a field or wave process moving from one level to another.

DISCUSSION

Caplan

I interpret your theory as the relating of phylogenetic and ontogenetic sequences in brain maturation to structures in adult brain and thence to sequences in the psychodynamics, so to speak, of producing language utterances. There is a distinguished tradition in neurology to do this, including efforts by Jackson, Pick, and others. There are uncertainties and controversies on the anatomical progressions, but what worries me more than that is the psycholinguistic analysis. What evidence do we have that normative production involves the particular analyses that you suggest? In a similar vein, is there any evidence that the particular psycholinguistic analyses you suggest are characteristic products of the brains of species in the phylogenetic sequence defined by the morphology? Last, in the case of ontogeny, I would suggest that there is evidence for a different set of psycholinguistic emergent structures and processes, and I would like to know whether you know of any evidence that children pass through the stages predicted by the ontogenetic aspects of your model.

Brown

This theory is naturally a continuation of the Jacksonian approach, or at least of the idea of levels of representation. Pick tried to extend this approach to deal with the richness of an aphasia corpus unavailable to Jackson, and he stressed also the microtemporal aspects of the system. But like Jackson, he stayed clear of anatomical matters. It is at this point, that of anatomical correlations, that neurologists tend to develop their own aphasia. As I see it, the problem is to resolve the diversity of clinical symptoms with the facts of a real specification, and to do this in a way that is mindful of the complexity of both symptom expression and brain organization.

As to the question of normal and pathological language, it is frankly the reluctance to embrace the evidence of pathology that has insulated the aphasia material from the wider audience that it deserves. Some years ago Janet remarked that memory is better analyzed by pathology than by the psychologists. Today he would have said that language is better analyzed by aphasia than by the linguists. The appeal of the pathological condition is that the structure of a performance is revealed directly in behavior and does not have to be inferred as in the normative studies that you cite. As you indicate, we do see fragments of aphasia in the utterances of normal subjects. Froeschels found this to be prominent in his own transitional speech. In a study that I carried out a few years ago with Arthur Arkin almost the whole inventory of aphasic errors was recovered from the speech of normal sleeptalkers. Obviously, brain injury is not necessary to produce an aphasia. These observations are more consistent with the idea of functional level or state than of components that can be selectively destroyed.

You ask for evidence that levels in microgenesis correspond to stages in the phylogenetic and ontogenetic history of the organism. Certainly, there are points of contact with Piagetian theory. However, the argument from deficits incurred at maturational stages does not directly relate to the order in which capacities are acquired. Indeed, there is considerable evidence against the idea, in its simple form, that pathology unravels the maturational sequence. Yet there is an important insight in the regression hypothesis that can be missed if we throw out the ontogenetic perspective. The regression that occurs in pathology is *micro*structural, not ontogenetic. Pathological symptoms refer to levels in cognition, not stages in cognitive development. The child's cognition clearly unfolds over all levels in this system, the structure maturing as a whole, so that acquisitional stage refers to the system generally and not its level-specific components. In other words, developmental psychology looks at growth of cognition, while neuropsychology looks at levels in cognitive structure.

For this reason one would expect only the most general correspondence between the two fields of study. An example might be the growth of sucking behavior in the infant, where a rhythmic, axial movement organized about the body space at a drive level in cognition, associated with appetitive and hypnic states, proceeds outward to limb movements and increasingly more differentiated, asymmetric, and affect-free digital movements in extrapersonal space. Motility in the adult recapitulates this progression each moment. One can say that this recapitulation forms the structure of the movement. But clearly in development this "structure" is undergoing growth as a whole. Each new performance, and language is no exception, is not grafted to the preceding stage but issues from the entire structure. The same reservations apply to phylogenetic parallels. For example, any correspondence between primate cognition and preliminary cognition in man would be of an extremely abstract nature removed from the actual performances in which this cognition is displayed.

REFERENCES

Brown, J. 1977. *Mind, brain, and consciousness: The neuropsychology of cognition*. New York: Academic Press.

Brown, J. *Language representation in the brain*. In *Neurobiology of social communication in primates: An evolutionary perspective*, ed. H. Steklis and M. Raleigh. New York: Academic Press, forthcoming.

Kellar, L. 1978. Stress and syntax in aphasia. Presentation at Academy of Aphasia, Chicago.

Sanides, F. 1970. Functional architecture of motor and sensory cortices in primates in the light of a new concept of neocortex evolution. In *The primate brain*, ed. C. Noback and W. Montagna. New York: Appleton.

15   Some Comments on the Neurology of Language

Norman Geschwind

My comments are based partially on material that has already been presented in this volume and also touch on some more general issues in the neurology of language. We should be cautious of statements that understanding the neurological foundations of language is a very difficult problem and therefore not likely to be solved in the near future. Such assertions have been made throughout the history of science about all unsolved problems that have apparently resisted solution despite sophisticated attempts. On the other hand, in many cases major advances occur with great speed in fields in which it seemed almost incredible that this would happen. A very striking example is the physiology of dreaming. A quarter of a century ago most scientists and philosophers had considered it impossible to know whether someone was dreaming; now we know that this is easily ascertained even without special equipment. My major reason for making these comments is that some people still believe that one should pay attention only to the phenomena of normal or abnormal language and should not attempt to work on the neurological bases, for the asserted reason that it will be impossible for many years to obtain adequate information concerning these neurological foundations.

What we know about the brain in relation to language is not purely correlational. Let me explain carefully what I mean by this. A purely correlational theory is one that would simply indicate the particular symptoms and signs that occurred with damage to a particular region of the nervous system. Such a description would have no theoretical basis except of the crudest nature. By a noncorrelational theory I mean one that takes into account knowledge from other fields and explains existing facts as well as predicts new data.

There are many examples of such theoretical accomplishments in the literature on aphasia. The first descriptions of the callosal syndromes by Liepmann are striking examples of such theorizing. He described in the early 1900s a patient with a syndrome never previously described, and on the basis of the clinical findings he predicted the lesions that would be present at postmortem. When the patient died several years later and the brain was studied in great detail, Liepmann's predictions were verified. Liepmann's predictions were, in fact, based on an extension of the theory of aphasia advanced by Wernicke under whom Liepmann had worked for several years.

Let me now turn to the question whether language is innate or is the result of experience. The common neurological belief, since the work of Broca over a hundred years ago, is that innate anatomical structures determine the capacity for language in humans. Although nearly all of us share this belief, it should not lead us to overlook environmental effects, in particular those that may be difficult to detect. Oddly enough, one of the main reasons for overlooking an environmental effect may be its universal presence. Let me consider an example from another field of behavior. Newborn goslings follow their mothers. If the gosling is approached by another bird, it will not follow it. Obviously, one would draw the conclusion that the gosling automatically recognizes the mother, perhaps on the basis of some innate representation. Experiments carried out some years ago, however, show that this is not the case. If the newborn gosling is not exposed to its mother immediately after hatching, but to another bird or even to a human, it follows that bird or person at later periods and not its own mother. The apparently universal tendency of goslings to follow the mother was the result of the mother's presence at the time of hatching.

I am not arguing that there may not be innate representations. In fact, there is powerful evidence that this must be the case. Consider, for example, the cat raised in the laboratory who has never seen mice attacked. A classical question is whether such a cat will indeed attack a mouse presented for the first time. It turns out that approximately half of these cats will attack mice, and they attack the mouse in the same manner as the animal who has been raised to observe attacks. He will bite at the nape of the neck, thus cutting the junction between the medulla and the upper spinal cord. If one stimulates the lateral hypothalamus of a cat that will not attack mice, then these cats will also attack.[1] Again, the attack is made in the region of the nape of the neck. If a cat who does not attack mice spontaneously is trained to attack mice, then his biting will occur at random. It seems clear that these data almost require that an innate representation of the nape of the neck be available to the cat.

We thus have certain effects based on innate representations, others based on environmental effects. Let me again stress how difficult it may be to observe environmental effects. Newborn female rats given a single injection of male sex hormone will show many atypical behaviors as adults, including lack of normal female sexual behavior and increased aggressiveness. A recent study pointed out that females who have male litter mates are more likely to be aggressive in adult life than females without such litter mates. The reason for this is that the small amounts of male sex hormone secreted by the male rats in the uterus are adequate to produce a change in the brains of the females.

One of the major problems in assessing our knowledge of the neurological bases of language is that much of the literature ignores the pitfalls in the assessment of neurological factors. It is necessary to know not merely location but whether the lesion is destructive or infiltrating, whether it is sudden or slow in onset, whether it begins in childhood or in adult life. It is thus important to realize that brain lesions involving the speech areas unilaterally in childhood will leave the patient with a permanent impairment that is very mild and indeed even difficult to detect by an unskilled examiner, while the same lesions in an adult will typically produce defects that will be glaringly obvious, even to the most untutored observer.

It is important to consider the reasons why early lesions produce different effects from later lesions, since the reasons have important implications for any theory of the neurological bases of language. One possibility is that language may be laid down not only in the left hemisphere but also in the right hemisphere. The right hemisphere representation might be inhibited in some manner and released only after destruction of the left side. Although this type of mechanism almost certainly takes place, there are other mechanisms. Consider, for example, damage to the speech areas of the left hemisphere that occurs while the fetus is in the uterus. We now know from recent work from Patricia Goldman at the National Institute of Health (personal communication) that early lesions of the cortex in monkeys before birth lead to a reorganization of the structure of the cortex at a distance. Thus the child with a brain lesion dating back to fetal life probably has a brain whose right hemisphere is different from that of the normal adult. Furthermore, even after brain lesions in adult life, we know that nerve terminals may sprout to fill regions of nerve membrane that had previously received nerve endings from a damaged region. Thus even in the adult there is some reorganization of the brain after injury, and we must be cautious about interpreting the functions of spared regions after injury as representing the normal functions of those areas. There is, in fact, a strong suggestion that the fetal brain may be specifically designed for remodeling. The nervous system appears to have a much larger number of nerve cells in fetal life than it does later on. A very large number of nerve cells are lost in late fetal life. Any event that controls which group of nerve cells is lost will obviously lead to a different design for the brain. One should not presume that these reorganizations are always beneficial. Gerald Schneider of the Psychology Department of the Massachusetts Institute of Technology has shown many instances in which such reorganizations are harmful to the animal.[2]

Dennis (chapter 9) was very careful to point out that her subjects were all patients who had undergone hemidecortication as therapy for Sturge-Weber disease, a congenital disorder. Her data clearly show that patients in whom there is a left hemidecortication do not perform as well on certain demanding linguistic tasks as those who have undergone a right hemidecortication. The question was raised whether these were the best cases for demonstrating the linguistic abilities of the two hemispheres. There is, however, no type of material that can be referred to as best. It seems extremely likely that in these cases the result of the brain lesion that was present in the fetus led to a reorganization of the opposite hemisphere so that it was different from the opposite hemisphere of an adult. Indeed, one might argue that the best cases for showing the linguistic capacities of the hemispheres in adults are cases of sudden strokes based on occlusion of blood vessels in adults with previously normal brains. In this circumstance the difference in linguistic capacities between the right and left hemispheres is of course enormous. On the other hand, Dennis's studies make it likely that even under the most favorable circumstances, the right hemisphere never fully attains the capacities of the left. They may also suggest that the innate genetic differences are perhaps small but are magnified by environmental effects, in the course of development.

The difference in the effects of the lesions of the Sturge-Weber syndrome and the lesions of cerebral infarction in the adult are very similar to the differences of congenital disorders and acquired disorders of the corpus callosum. Thus a callosal lesion occurring for the first time in an adult who did not have an early brain lesion or long-standing epilepsy produces a very dramatic syndrome of disconnection of the hemispheres. By contrast agenesis of the corpus callosum, which is a congenital lesion, produces few or no signs of disconnection. The striking feature of the person with agenesis is that his brain shows differences from normal brains in other regions. In particular, the anterior commissure is usually greatly overdeveloped. There is thus another route present for carrying information between the hemispheres.

Brains of different individuals may not have the same organization when there are brain lesions in fetal life. The organization, of course, changes even after lesions later in life. There is, however, another reason for individual differences in brains. One must consider strongly that the genetic endowment of different individuals leads to differences in the organization of the brain in the absence of any damage. It is very curious that individual differences in the brain itself have been so neglected. Thus the classical anatomical textbooks such as Gray's *Anatomy* might spend pages describing individual differences in the femur but have almost nothing on individual differences in brains. It is now quite clear that such individual differences are marked. Some years ago my colleague Walter Levitsky and I described the asymmetry of the upper surface of the temporal lobes in the vicinity of the speech regions. This entire topic of asymmetries has been recently reviewed.[3] A particular area called the planum temporale is larger on the left side than on the right side in about 65 percent of brains, with approximate equality in 24 percent and a larger right side in 11 percent. There is clearly a spectrum of variation. In some brains the left side is very large and the right very small, in others the two sides are roughly equal, and in other cases the left side may be larger than the right side, but only by a small amount. It seems very likely that the brain structures of humans may indeed show enormous numbers of variations, a finding that would not be surprising on the basis of standard evolutionary considerations. This leads to the implication that some of the supposed uniformities of function are probably not present. I have heard it said that the development of language is remarkably uniform in children. I am sure that the investigators are right in arguing that there are major uniformities, but I suspect that there are many variations on this basic pattern, determined by individual differences in organization of the brain.

There is one strong piece of evidence for the existence of such individual differences. Luria pointed out in his study of penetrating brain wounds in the Russian armed services in World War II that left-handers tended to recover from aphasia much better than right-handers.[4] Furthermore, right-handers who had left-handed parents, siblings, or children tended to recover better than pure right-handers without left-handedness in the family. There are now strong data showing that left-handers will develop aphasia after a lesion to *either* hemisphere, while this is not true in right-handers. These data seem to indicate that the left-hander is not the mirror image of the right-hander with respect to the neural representation of language but has a different organization, which is presumably based on a different genetic endowment.

We thus have a whole array of factors that lead to variations in function. First, there are individual differences in brains that may lead to the use of different strategies. Second, there are differences in brains that are the result of reorganization after early brain lesions. Dennis has already shown that the right and left hemispheres of her patients used different strategies in linguistic tasks. Finally, the use of different strategies may depend on certain chance factors in the structure of the language. Let me give an example from the analysis of the alexias. Déjérine first pointed out that patients with alexia without agraphia (who have, of course, great difficulty in reading words) may read numbers easily. Indeed, his patient could barely read even the simplest French word but could read six-digit numbers without difficulty. What clue can we get from this remarkable dissociation? Let us turn to look at Japanese alexics. It has been found that they are more able to read the logographic characters (kanji) than they are the phonetic syllabic system (kana). In other words, they are more likely to be able to understand a symbol that is arbitrarily related to the sound and are less able to understand the strings of symbols that must be deciphered phonetically. The writing of numerals in European languages is clearly equivalent to the writing of logographic symbols in Japanese. A number written in Arabic numerals such as 21 can be understood by speakers of all languages, even though this arbitrary group of symbols has a different sound in each language. Other examples of the behavior of these patients also illustrate this difference. Some of these patients do better at naming objects and pictures of objects than at reading words such as *if*. Furthermore, a word such as *rose* may be misread as *flower*. Hécaen has pointed out that his patients can often read words such as *bank* or *hotel*, names of large public buildings in which the name often appears on the building itself.

I cannot spell out the theory that might account for this in any detail but simply point out that these patients apparently do better when an association is being formed between a visual sign and something that can clearly be pictured. On the other hand, they fail to understand something that must be deciphered phonetically and whose understanding depends very heavily on context. It appears likely that the spared material can be handled by the right hemisphere, which has a different strategy from the left—not an inferior strategy, but a different one.

Even in normal life, individuals may use different strategies to different extents because their brains differ. Such differences will be seen in normals but also in patients with early brain lesions. Thus my colleagues Albert Galaburda and Thomas Kemper have recently studied the serial brain sections of a child with dyslexia. To their surprise they found an anomalous structure of the cortex in part of the left temporal speech region. It is very likely that this anomalous structure (one in which the nerve cells are organized in an unusual pattern) was the result either of a very early lesion (in fetal life) or of an error in the genetic coding of the rules for the formation of this region. This latter explanation is consistent with this patient's familial history of reading difficulty. It is quite likely that this patient had an unusual organization of a region of the brain which led him to use a reading strategy different from that used by most people. In this case one might legitimately argue that the strategy was probably an inferior one.

I have stressed that there may be multiple mechanisms based on differences in brains, differences in experiences, or differences in the language which lead individuals to perform in different ways. I would like to say something about whether language is unitary. Obviously, the answer to this question depends on exactly what one means by unitary. Almost certainly the brain mechanisms for the production or comprehension of language depend on a wide variety of different mechanisms. There may be some type of unity at a different level, but if this is true it must be clearly defined rather than simply asserted as has usually been the case.

As to future directions of research, I cannot predict what the most fruitful lines of attack will be. There are, however, two general categories of scientific problems, the well-designed experiment and the expert observations by talented observers of phenomena brought to them by chance. The second type of approach has been tremendously fruitful. Darwin is a salient example of the superb observer who takes the unexpected finding and uses it to develop new theories and control future observations. There is a tendency today to neglect this type of approach in favor of the large study of preselected groups. We cannot abandon, however, the observation of the unexpected, at least in this field, since a remarkable number of such findings keep coming our way. Let me give you a few examples.

There are patients who develop the so-called Korsakoff syndrome, in which they lose the ability to acquire new knowledge and also lose memories going back for some years, although in general the oldest memories are better preserved. When these patients recover, as they do in some instances, they begin to remember newly presented items, and their retrograde memory deficit shrinks to a very small period, often only the few minutes before the event that caused the syndrome. The phenomenon of shrinking retrograde amnesia was not expected in the psychological literature on memory. Yet it obviously represents the manifestation of some of the major principles of the structure of memory systems.

Let me give you another example. There are groups of patients who do not carry out verbal commands, although they understand the commands and can be shown to be perfectly able to accomplish the required actions in response to another stimulus. The striking feature of many of these patients is that while they fail to carry out actions with the face or the individual limbs, they do very well in carrying out actions that involve the muscles that move the eyes or close the eyelids or involve the muscles of the trunk. Thus some patients who fail to make a fist to command with either hand or to salute or to wave goodbye or to show the use of a hammer carry out with difficulty the sequence "stand up, turn around twice, and then walk," a series of movements that involve the trunk. Even more dramatical is the response of some of these patients to the command to assume the position of a boxer. The patient may leap to his feet in the correct position, leading with the left fist. He has obviously carried out a movement in which the trunk was involved. If he is now asked to punch, however, he will do nothing, this being a command that involves one limb alone.

This remarkable phenomenon occurs in patients with the kinds of syndrome called apraxias[6] but also in patients with severe comprehension deficit. Thus a patient with Wernicke's aphasia may not respond to questions such as "What is your name?" or to questions such as "Is it raining now?" and may not respond to commands for the face or the individual limbs. Yet the same patient may respond dramatically to commands involving the eye movements and the musculature of the trunk. Some years ago I examined a patient who had undergone a complete left hemispherectomy in adult life for the treatment of a brain tumor. In this patient, who had no left hemisphere, I found that the same types of commands were carried out better than any other variety. It is thus clear that the right hemisphere seems to be better at this task. This contradicts the claims that have sometimes been made that the right hemisphere is not able to handle verbs; the right hemisphere seems to be quite competent at verbs as long as they are imperative verbs referring to this special type of movement.

How can we explain this pattern? The preserved movements are not simpler in any sense. They are not acquired earlier, since saluting is surely later than walking. Nor can the variation be due to phonetic or syntactic structure, since one can construct a command in any linguistic form that will either be carried out or not, depending on the types of movement it requires. The relevant factor appears indeed to be the mode of representation of the different types of movements in the brain. Eye movements, for example, have no representation in the classical precentral motor cortex. Movements of the trunk, although represented to a minor extent in this cortex, have multiple, large representations elsewhere. In other words, we have described here a circumstance in which large numbers of patients respond to commands involving certain anatomical systems in the brain but not to commands involving other anatomical systems. This phenomenon would very likely be overlooked or remain unexplained if one started out by considering only developmental, psychological, and linguistic factors. The full explanation of this phenomenon is not clear at this moment. We must be open in the future to similar phenomena that may have important implications for our understanding of the neurological organization of language.

DISCUSSION

Chomsky
What is known about cerebral asymmetries in the great apes?

Geschwind
LeMay and I looked for asymmetries in the brains of monkeys and did not find any. We did find that the great apes show an asymmetry in the Sylvian fissure similar to that in humans. The left Sylvian fissure tends to have a more horizontal course, while the right Sylvian fissure curves upward. In humans this is by far the most common pattern. In left-handers this pattern is still the most common one, but there is a higher percentage of cases without asymmetry of the Sylvian fissure.

Chomsky
What is the function of that area?

Geschwind
This is an asymmetry of a fissure, the indentation between parts of the brain. Obviously the asymmetry of the fissure implies that the brain areas around it must be different in some way. The major classical speech areas lie on the borders of the Sylvian fissure. In the course of primate evolution the Sylvian fissure appears to have shifted from a more vertical to a more horizontal configuration. This evolutionary trend appears to have progressed more on the left side than on the right.

Chomsky
Moving beyond phylogeny, can you say what the functions of the areas around that fissure may be?

Geschwind
In the human the areas around the Sylvian fissure on the left are particularly involved with language functions. It would be tempting to speculate that the regions around the Sylvian fissure in the great apes are subserving some function related to language. I suspect that these areas are asymmetrical because there is some type of dom-

inance, but no one has been able to ask the right question in order to determine what that dominance is.

Chomsky
Can you say anything about the functions of the asymmetries in apes?

Geschwind
Functional asymmetry of the hemispheres—differences in the performance of certain types of activity—are clearly well known in humans. Dewson has suggested that the left temporal lobe of the monkey is superior for certain types of auditory tasks. Denenberg and his co-workers at the University of Connecticut have brought evidence that there is an asymmetry for emotional behavior in the brain of the rat. Some recent work brings evidence that in Japanese monkeys the left hemisphere is better at recognizing species-specific cries. Unfortunately, in none of these species has anatomical asymmetry yet been demonstrated. There is also an asymmetry for bird song, in which the left side of the brain seems to be more important. Nottebohm has found male-female differences in the sizes of areas involved in bird song, but the issue of left-right asymmetry of these areas is still unclear. We do not yet know the function of the anatomical asymmetries in the brains of apes, but I suspect that these are related to functional dominance.

Liberman
Would you comment on the work of Nottebohm? Has he shown a mechanism in birds that is similar to handedness or to cerebral dominance for language?

Geschwind
I have reservations about accepting either analogy, since I am not certain that bird song is a language, at least not in the usual sense of the word.

Liberman
The birds Nottebohm has worked on have two sound-producing mechanisms, and the more important part of the song depends on one of them. It is as if we were looking at human sign language, and all the significant information in signing came from one hand. In that case a lesion involving control of that hand would affect language, not necessarily because of any interference with language in general,

but because of an effect on motor abilities. A hemispheric lesion might then produce a language disturbance, but not because something we might want to call a language faculty was necessarily present in one hemisphere.

Bogen
Are you saying that Nottebohm's birds demonstrate something akin to anarthria rather than amusia?

Geschwind
Humans who use sign language do not use only one hand. Deaf patients who become aphasic in sign language produce errors in signing with both hands. It is therefore not clear that the situation in the bird is analogous to that of the human who signs. I cannot say whether the bird's difficulty is more similar to anarthria than it is to aphasia or amusia.

I think the important question here is the evolutionary one. Why isn't some aspect of cerebral dominance more obvious throughout all the mammals? Was cerebral dominance present in the bird and not present in other mammals, or have we simply missed its presence in other mammals? It is conceivable that cerebral dominance in the bird and human are examples of convergent evolution, similar structures and functions evolving through different routes, but I am not satisfied with that answer.

It would be helpful if we could find intermediate stages. These intermediate stages in the evolution of language may not look at all linguistic. Thus the vertebrate hand eventually became the wing of a bat. In the intermediate stages, the enlarged hand was, I suppose, used for catching insects and not for flying. Thus language might have evolved through systems that were not at all obviously linguistic.

Almost all the theories of the evolution of language, of which there were so many in the nineteenth century, have been theories of the production of language. Obviously the social function of language requires that any mutation allowing humans to produce a signal verbally can be advantageous only if there is a mechanism for understanding that signal in other humans. Here one runs into a problem; the new appearance of a system for producing language would be ineffective, since other humans would not understand it. Conversely, the new evolution of a system for understanding language would not be effective, since there would not be other humans to produce it. This makes me suspect that the forerunners of language were functions whose *social* advantages were secondary but conferred an advantage for survival. I think it possible that the chimpanzee may have dominance for something that is not obviously related to what we now know as language.

The evolutionary trend toward asymmetries and dominance probably goes back a long way in humans. Marjorie LeMay has shown in a study of endocasts that the asymmetry of the Sylvian fissure is found not only in Neanderthal man, who lived 30,000 to 50,000 years ago, but also in Peking man, who lived about 300,000 years ago.

Liberman

Let me pursue the evolutionary question. Given what we know of the behavior of the right hemisphere in human beings with split brains, we might conclude that its capacity for languagelike behavior can be characterized in either of two ways. One is to say that the right hemisphere is capable of at least a little bit of various aspects of language but that it is totally unable to speak. The other is to say that it only appears to be capable of some aspects of language because it succeeds in bringing nonlinguistic strategies to bear and that such strategies are somehow inappropriate for speech. In either case, the right hemisphere is mute; that is, of all language or languagelike processes the motor control of speech is the most clearly lateralized. That being so, we may wish to consider the following account, which is surely not original with me, of the evolution of cerebral asymmetry for language.

Of all the coordinated motor movements that man makes, only those for speech never require different actions on the two sides of the midline in the appropriate musculature. Now if one never needs different movements of muscles on the two sides in speech, then a single motor program would suffice—indeed, two might lead to confusion—and a single program would most properly be located in one hemisphere. Once such a program became lateralized, there would conceivably be selection pressure to bring other language and quasi-language functions into reasonable contiguity with it. Such an assumption does at least accord reasonably well with the fact that lateralization is so complete for the control of speech movements.

Geschwind

That is a very interesting theory. We know that the right hemisphere talks in some cases. It certainly talks in cases with early
damage to the left hemisphere, such as those discussed by Dennis.
The right hemisphere is also capable of speech in cases in which
there is gross destruction of the left hemisphere in adult life. It is my
view that the right hemisphere clearly has some capacity for speech,
although we do not know exactly how great this capacity is. One
can propose many theories as to why the right hemisphere does not
normally participate in speech, although at the present time we do
not have enough evidence to assess exactly what the capacity is.

Like you, I suspect that dominance for language began with the
appearance of *one* aspect of function, although I tend to think it was
receptive function that came first. This speculation, however, would
lead us too far astray at the present moment.

I agree that there is a selection pressure for lateralization. Lateralization has the advantage that space is saved on one side of the brain
for some other function. I think it likely that the development of
another function in the saved space is much more useful to the species than the duplication of a single function on the two sides. It
might appear at first that the duplication of a single function on the
two sides would be beneficial for survival of the animal, since he
would not lose function with a unilateral lesion. On the one hand,
the pressures for survival in the wild are so severe that an animal
with a unilateral cerebral lesion is not likely to survive in any case.
On the other hand, the animal is less likely to be damaged if he has
a greater repertoire of functional abilities.

This leads me to reemphasize my conviction that functional asymmetries are probably found throughout the animal world. We know
there are neural asymmetries even in fish and frogs. We have not
always learned to ask the right questions to find the functions that
are lateralized.

I would also point out that we should not assume that lateralization of function is necessarily equivalent to lateralization of language. It is my speculation that the earliest functions lateralized in
mammals in the course of evolution will not be in language or communication systems. I suspect that they will be found in attentional
systems. By an attentional system I mean a neural organization able
to concentrate on some particular stimulus while at the same time
scanning both the external and internal environment. Such a system

must have a set of rules for determining which stimuli outside the central focus should lead to a shift of the central focus. In general these stimuli will be ones that are important for survival, in particular stimuli that signal possible dangers. I think that it is logical for such a hierarchy of items to be represented unilaterally, and I think there is some evidence apart from human data that these functions are right-hemisphere functions. All this is quite speculative, and I think that only further study of attentional systems can reveal important biological principles related to functional lateralization.

Bogen

Localization of language abilities within the left hemisphere is an important issue in the history of theorizing about language and the brain, with a significant controversy between the "holists" and "topists." My own view is that the notion that a function is wholly localized within one cerebral area and that other areas do not have that function at all is incorrect and that certain extreme topist views of brain function are therefore wrong. On the other hand, the notion that some language function, or any other intellectual function, is represented equally everywhere in the brain or in a hemisphere is also erroneous. I think the correct solution to this problem will require a theory including the concept of gradients. Let me elaborate somewhat on this theme.

First, consider the localization of lesions that impair language to a greater extent than intelligence or other cognitive functions, that is, produce aphasia. Rarely does such a lesion occur in the right hemisphere of a right-hander, although it does occur there with a frequency of about 1 percent. It is even rarer for it to occur in a lesion of the left frontal pole, occipital pole, or temporal pole, but even in these areas the possibility exists; the probability is not zero.

Now consider the types of aphasias and their localization. If we define Wernicke's area as the region in which a lesion produces a comprehension deficit greater than a deficit in general intelligence, we find that this area varies enormously in different reported series and there is virtually no agreement about its full extent, at least within the peri-Sylvian region on the left. The simplistic classifications of aphasia that describe expressive loss from lesions in Broca's area and comprehension loss from lesions in Wernicke's area ignore the great difficulty in delineating these areas, the multiplicity of in-

termediate syndromes, and the changes seen during recovery that
may even turn one syndrome into another with time.

I think that facts like these are best described by a concept of gradient. I conceive of the representation of language within the left
hemisphere as a topographic map, with peaks and contours representing the probabilities that aphasia, or specific types of language
disturbance, will arise if an area is damaged. Each point has a
distinct probability density in this regard. The points with the maximum probability of producing aphasias would be the centers
described in the older literature.

Caplan
It seems to me that this notion is very close to that put forward by
Freud, who thought of a zone in the temporoparietal area on the left
with graded abilities for language. In Freud's thinking, the language
functions of parts of this zone were related to the distance of each
part from the primary receptive koniocortex, those areas nearest
visual cortex most related to reading, those areas nearest auditory
cortex most related to auditory processes, and so forth.

Bromberger
It is unclear to me whether Dr. Bogen believes the graded nature
of the language area is a characteristic of a population or of individuals. If you believe it characterizes each individual's brain, then I
think you must find evidence for that from a source other than
studies on populations, since it is not valid to suppose that each
individual has the same distribution of probabilities as the entire
population. Each individual might have a particular, discrete locus
for language function or for particular language functions, but it
might be in a different place in each brain. Only the population
might show the graded distribution.

Chomsky
If we can make certain assumptions about the homogeneity of brains
with respect to language abilities, the inference from the population
to the individual would be valid. Depending on the nature of these
assumptions, it might be the only valid inference about individuals.

Carey
It seems that different observational techniques, different lesion
types, and so on, have produced quite different notions of localiza-

tion. It seems possible, through theory construction and validation, to discover the right decomposition of function that fits with the anatomy.

Bogen

I agree, at least in part. One problem is to find the correct variables to characterize an aphasic. We have no idea how many such variables there are; there could be three or thirty or three hundred. These would have to be dimensions that varied independently. The next question would be to relate these to the brain, and there I believe a gradient will be involved.

Brown

The idea that we have yet to discover the correct decompositional analysis of language functions is borne out by studies on comprehension deficits. I think several studies on comprehension deficits indicate that there are qualitative differences between the impairments of patients depending on where in the neural net the lesion occurs.

On the other hand, the paper by Hécaen relating the comprehension deficit in Broca's aphasia to the depth of the lesion in the vicinity of Broca's area points to barely explored aspects of the neuroanatomical basis for language. We have been talking as if the only relevant areas of the brain were cortical, yet we know that many deep structures are essential for language, that at least transient aphasias follow lesions in these areas. It is my belief that these views of brain structure, which I call static, are not fruitful and have to be replaced with a dynamic view of brain function.

Geschwind

As I have said earlier, much of the confusion concerning the localization of language processes is the result of widespread disregard of neurological variables. Thus many series mix tumor cases, vascular cases, and trauma cases, as if these etiologies produced similar effects on the brain. Even when the locus of maximal damage is known, the distant effects of such lesions are highly variable and have to be taken into account. I would be very surprised to find a patient with a small focal, frontal pole infarct who suffered from aphasia. If, however, the insult was a penetrating brain missile, it would be less surprising to find aphasia since such a missile might ricochet or hit blood vessels. In addition, there will be an enormous difference between the removal of Broca's area in an adult who has had a brain lesion since the age of two and the removal of the same area in a totally normal person.

A second point is that much of the confusion in the literature has been engendered by the proliferation of different nomenclatures for the symptom complexes of aphasia. While there are many different nomenclatures, there is much less variation in the descriptions of the syndromes and their clinical-pathological correlation. Thus if one reads the actual case descriptions of authors such as Head and Luria, one finds that they are describing (in most cases) classical symptom complexes and localizations. This is overlooked because the change in nomenclature obscures the underlying agreement. This fact also makes it extremely difficult to read the history of aphasia.

The concept of localization thus requires the inclusion of the notion of time course and individual variation in brains. I agree with Jason Brown that it is important to view lesions dynamically, although I am not sure that he and I intend the same sort of view. Let me give an example. Deficits in the carrying out of so-called delayed-response tasks can be seen in monkeys after bilateral lesions of the area around the sulcus principalis, if these lesions are made simultaneously. If there is a delay of a few weeks between the lesions on the two sides, one will find that the animal shows no deficit. We do not yet know why what is apparently the same pattern of lesions when produced serially should produce a different picture from the pattern produced by simultaneous lesions. It is extremely likely that the final pattern of anatomical reorganization is different in the two instances. It is not unlikely that such serial effects are also important in humans, although this has not been well studied.

Chomsky

I think it fair to say that there is a good deal of agreement here with respect to localization of language. Everyone seems to be saying that a very specific picture is emerging, one in which localization plays a large part. The localization picture, however, is a graded one. It may be graded because of intrinsic biological factors; each individual's brain may have graded areas of localization of language functions, as Dr. Bogen claims. On the other hand, it may be graded because of the very definition of aphasia; aphasia is defined as a deficit greater in language than in other intellectual domains, and types of aphasia are defined in relative terms, so the entity may be inherently a matter of relative deficit. When we extrapolate from the graded nature of the definition, we find that relatively small or large lesions in particular areas of the brain have specific probabilities to give rise to particular syndromes, and we can represent this as a topographic map. If we knew more about the kinds of variables Dr. Geschwind described, the nature of the lesion, the time course of events, then variations due to such factors could be excluded, and we would have a map more closely reflecting the contribution of particular brain areas to particular language functions.

NOTES

1. J. P. Flynn, "The Neural Basis of Aggression in Cats," in *Neurophysiology and Emotion*, ed. D. C. Glass, pp. 40–60 (New York: Rockefeller University Press, 1967).

2. The issue of reorganization of the brain is dealt with extensively in the volume *Plasticity and Recovery of Function in the Central Nervous System*, edited by D. G. Stein, J. J. Rosen, and N. Butters (New York: Academic Press, 1974.) The chapter by N. Geschwind, "Late Change in the Nervous System: An Overview," pp. 467–504 in that volume, summarizes many of the data, especially those in humans.

3. A. Galaburda, M. LeMay, T. Kemper, and N. Geschwind, "Right-Left Asymmetries in the Brain," *Science* 199 (1978): 852–856.

4. A. R. Luria, *Traumatic Aphasia* (The Hague: Mouton, 1970).

5. Déjérine's findings as well as other aspects of the alexias are reviewed by D. F. Benson, and N. Geschwind, "The Alexias," in *Handbook of Clinical Neurology*, vol. 4, ed. P. J. Vinken and G. W. Bruyn, pp. 112–140, (Amsterdam: North-Holland, 1969).

6. N. Geschwind, "The Apraxias: Neural Mechanisms of Disorders of Learned Movement," *American Scientist* 63 (1975): 188–195.

List of Contributors

Thomas G. Bever, Department of Psychology, Columbia University, New York

Dianne C. Bradley, Department of Psychology and Center for Cognitive Science, Massachusetts Institute of Technology, Cambridge, Massachusetts

Melinda Broman, Neurological Institute, College of Physicians and Surgeons, Columbia University, New York

Jason W. Brown, Department of Neurology, Columbia University, New York

David Caplan, Department of Linguistics and Computer Science, University of Massachusetts, Amherst, Massachusetts

Susan Carey, Department of Psychology, Massachusetts Institute of Technology, Cambridge, Massachusetts

Noam Chomsky, Department of Linguistics, Massachusetts Institute of Technology, Cambridge, Massachusetts

Martha Bridge Denckla, Department of Neurology, Childrens Hospital Medical Center, Harvard University, Boston, Massachusetts

Maureen Dennis, Department of Psychology, Hospital for Sick Children, University of Toronto, Toronto, Ontario, Canada

Rhea Diamond, Department of Psychology, Massachusetts Institute of Technology, Cambridge, Massachusetts

Merrill F. Garrett, Department of Psychology, Massachusetts Institute of Technology, Cambridge, Massachusetts

Norman Geschwind, Department of Neurology, Beth Israel Hospital, Harvard University, Boston, Massachusetts

Mary-Louise Kean, Program in Cognitive Science, School of Social Sciences, University of California at Irvine, Irvine, California

John C. Marshall, Interfakultaire Werkgroep Taal-en Spraakgedrag, Catholic University, Nijmegen, Netherlands

David Rose, Department of Psychiatry, Childrens Hospital Medical Center, Harvard University, Boston, Massachusetts

Rita G. Rudel, Neurological Institute, College of Physicians and Surgeons, Columbia University, New York

Deborah P. Waber, Department of Psychiatry, Childrens Hospital Medical Center, Boston, Massachusetts

Bryan T. Woods, Department of Neurology, McLean Hospital, Harvard University, Belmont, Massachusetts

Edgar B. Zurif, Department of Neurology, Veterans Administration Hospital, Boston University, Boston, Massachusetts

Name Index

Abernethy, E. M., cit., 9
Akesson, E. J., 109
Altman, J., 31, 32, 36, 38, 39; cit., 31, 32
Amatruda, C. S., cit., 10
Anderson, J., 133
Anderson, J. A., 138n19
Angevine, J. B., cit., 36
Arkin, A., 298
Arnauld, Antoine, 136
Assal, G., cit., 76
Astruc, J., cit., 35

Bahrick, H. P., cit., 61
Bahrick, P. O., cit., 61
Bard, J., 138n26
Barker, R. G., cit., 9
Bartlett, E., cit., 4–5
Basser, L. S., 150
Bayer, S. A., 31; cit., 31, 32
Bayley, N., cit., 9
Beaumont, J., 137n14
Begun, J. S., cit., 179
Bell, G. L., cit., 32
Bell, R. G., cit., 11
Bellugi, U., 115–116
Benton, A. L., 82; cit., 63
Berio, L., 218
Berko, J., cit., 242
Berlucci, G., cit., 63
Berndt, R. S., cit., 155, 171
Bernstein, L., cit., 72
Berry, M., cit., 36
Bertoncini, J., cit., 132
Best, C., 110
Bever, T., 186–230; cit., 113, 163, 199, 200, 217, 226n8, n11
Bierwisch, M., cit., 271
Birkett, P., 225n5
Blaney, R. L., 66
Blumstein, S., cit., 225n6, 271

Boas, F., 9; cit., 9
Bogen, G. M., cit., 109
Bogen, J. E., 136n4, 297, 312, 315–316, 317, 318; cit., 108, 109, 138n16, 225n2, n6
Bonvillian, J. D., 116, 117
Bower, G. H., 66; cit., 74
Bowerman, M., cit., 4–5
Bradley, D. C., 234, 235, 260–261, 262, 266, 269–286, 291; cit., 239, 278, 279, 280
Bradley, J. V., cit., 50
Bradshaw, J. L., 204, 220–221; cit., 63
Bresnan, J., 101
Brindley, G. S., 139n28
Broadbent, D. E., cit., 128
Broadbent, W. B., 126
Broca, P., 186, 187, 216, 233–234, 235–236, 302
Broman, M., 6, 44–58; cit., 46, 81
Bromberger, 316
Brown, J. B., cit., 22
Brown, J. W., 131, 213, 237, 287–300, 318
Brown, R., 115–116; cit., 4–5
Bruner, J. S., 117
Brunner, R. L., 39; cit., 32
Bryden, M. P., 138n16
Bullock, T. H., 125, 136n1
Butters, N., cit., 35

Campain, R., 109
Caplan, D., 97–105, 233–238, 297–298, 316; cit., 130, 271
Caramazza, A., 272–273; cit., 155, 163, 169, 171, 274
Carey, P., 199
Carey, S., 5, 6, 27, 55–56, 60–93, 120, 217, 210, 226n9, 316–317; cit., 4–5, 45, 56, 57, 65, 66, 68, 69, 76, 151, 156, 181, 207

Subject Index